Implementing
Teacher
Competencies

Contributing Authors

ROGER T. CUNNINGHAM
Ohio State University

ODVARD EGIL DYRLI
University of Connecticut

MERYL E. ENGLANDER
Indiana University

DEWAYNE KURPIUS
Indiana University

JAMES R. OKEY
University of Georgia

DORIS A. TROJCAK
University of Missouri-St. Louis

DONALD LEE TROYER
Western Illinois University

Implementing Teacher Competencies

POSITIVE APPROACHES
TO PERSONALIZING EDUCATION

JAMES E. WEIGAND, *editor*

Indiana University

PRENTICE-HALL, INC., *Englewood Cliffs, New Jersey 07632*

Library of Congress Cataloging in Publication Data

Main entry under title:

Implementing teacher competencies.

    Bibliography: p.
    1. Teachers, Rating of. 2. Individualized
instruction. I. Weigand, James E.
LB2838.I46   371.1'44   76-21775
ISBN 0-13-451948-5
ISBN 0-13-451930-2 pbk.

*This book is dedicated to
those teachers who are continually
improving their teaching skills
and behaviors in order to create
more humane learning environments.*

Printed in the United States of America

10 9 8 7 6 5 4 3 2 1

Prentice-Hall International, Inc., *London*
Prentice-Hall of Australia Pty. Limited, *Sydney*
Prentice-Hall of Canada, Ltd., *Toronto*
Prentice-Hall of India Private Limited, *New Delhi*
Prentice-Hall of Japan, Inc., *Tokyo*
Prentice-Hall of Southeast Asia Pte. Ltd., *Singapore*
Whitehall Books Limited, *Wellington, New Zealand*

Contents

Preface

**"STEPS" TO IMPLEMENTING
TEACHING COMPETENCIES**

For years, teacher-educators throughout the country have emphasized that teachers should be told not only what skills they should possess but what materials should be created to help them acquire these skills. As a result of this emphasis I, along with other teacher-educators, prepared *Developing Teacher Competencies*. This book, published by Prentice-Hall in 1971, discussed seven basic skills: preparing performance objectives, question asking, creativity, sequencing instruction, evaluating student progress, assessing intellectual levels, and human interaction. All of these topics were developed into programmed instruction and were field-tested with all levels of preservice and in-service teacher groups. This book has been, and still is, most successful in helping individuals acquire basic teaching skills. However, it does not insure the implementation of these skills. The idea of developing materials that prospective and in-service teachers could study, test in performance situations with students, and then assess was a challenge. This challenge resulted in the publication of *Implementing Teacher Competencies*.

After considerable thought regarding topics, I secured the services of eight experts in their respective fields. I consulted individually with the seven authors and with James Russell of Purdue University who was responsible for the field testing. In these consultations I explained fully the intent of the book and asked each individual to prepare an outline to be used as the basis of discussion at the first group meeting.

At this initial meeting, procedures for the writing, testing, rewriting, and retesting of programs were described. The authors were informed that references could be made to *Developing Teacher Competencies*, but that the new book must stand on its own. Field testing confirmed that this objective was attained. All authors were responsible for writing portions of their chapters and then testing this material with students at their respective institutions. When an author felt satisfied with a chapter, he or she forwarded it to the editor. The field testing of these programs was conducted at all levels of undergraduate instruction as well as with graduate students, and on the basis of this testing each chapter was analyzed thoroughly. As a result of such analysis, flaws in the various chapters were discovered. Discussion with each member of the team followed. Each program was again analyzed, and procedures for correcting all flaws were formulated. Each author then revised his or her chapter. The revised versions were again field-tested, either by the author alone or with different groups of students at Indiana University and Purdue University. Most field testing was with student-teacher populations, but chapters were also tested with preservice and in-service teachers. Upon completion of this field testing, the team felt that the programs were ready for use by both prospective and in-service teachers.

Much thought was given to the linkage of one chapter to the next, and many patterns of sequenced chapters were produced and analyzed. The one used in this book seemed to have the greatest merit. However, each user of the book—whether student or teacher—should feel free to utilize the chapters in any sequence deemed desirable.

Implementing these teacher competencies—assessing intellectual developmental stages, formulating performance objectives, asking qustions, sequencing instruction, utilizing diagnostic evaluation, motivating learners, and developing interpersonal communication—is essential if effective instruction is to materialize. But these seven competencies are not sufficient by themselves. The teacher must realize that implementing these competencies will result in his or her interaction with students and to a large degree will personalize education. The subtitle of this book, "Positive Approaches to Personalizing Education," indicates that when a teacher can implement a competency, positive human interaction will result. This message extends throughout the book, informing the reader that the use of competencies does not make the teacher a robot or a machine but rather a person who is sensitive to and concerned for students. For example, Cunningham states that questioning, "as a form of communication, is one of the most potent means for personalizing interaction." Trojcak says, "A complete person is one who not only thinks but also acts and feels." According to Englander, "The humanistic person-to-person relations ought to be continually practiced as a matter of course independent of the motivational implications." We destroy human interaction, states Dyrli, when "we direct instruction to 'average' students, who really do not exist as such, and the result of mismatched instruction is frustration and anxiety for both students and teachers." Troyer "humanizes" performance objectives when he establishes criteria for measuring a performance objective in terms such as *worth* and *fit* to the learner. Too often, we use evaluation as a means of grading and ranking students. Okey states that "if properly used, *diagnostic* evaluation can be a *positive* force in your classroom." Last but not least, Kurpius informs the reader that what is important is "not only what one *knows* about interpersonal relations, but what the teacher *does* in order to develop and implement a positive interpersonal approach to teaching and learning."

The seven chapters differ in style. No attempt was made to have the seven authors conform to a particular type of program or style of writing. This freedom allowed each author to pursue his or her competency in a unique way. Field testing revealed that students reacted very favorably to the variety of the chapters. It should be noted that major differences exist among the types of competencies explored. Consequently, the sophistication of the various writing styles also differ in order that the utility of each chapter may be maximized. This variety of style was further enhanced by the excellent editorial work of Shirley Stone, production editor for Prentice-Hall, and Bruce Fulton, the copy editor. The authors are indebted to them for their assistance.

The authors are especially grateful to Dr. Russell, who supervised the field testing. Substantial credit for this book must go to him.

We hope these chapters will help the user implement teaching competencies in the classroom. We must point out, however, that in and of themselves the chapters are not sufficient; they merely begin the fuller implementation of competencies. Continual effort and energy are required of the teacher if he or she is to maximize the supplementation of classroom skills. The reward of the effort is tremendous satisfaction with a job well done.

JAMES E. WEIGAND, *editor*

Implementing Intellectual Development Assessments

ODVARD EGIL DYRLI

The University of Connecticut

**"STEPS" TO IMPLEMENTING
TEACHING COMPETENCIES**

To say that the intellectual development of students is fundamental to the entire teaching enterprise is to make no profound statement. To say further that students develop intellectually as well as physically at different rates is similarly obvious. Yet although we often pay lip service to "individualizing" instruction, in reality it is too easy most of the time to teach as if all our students possessed the same intellectual skills and capabilities. That, of course, is clearly untrue.

In the schools of today, it is becoming increasingly important for teachers to truly individualize instruction in order to be as effective as possible. To do so, though, requires the development and implementation of competencies in assessing the intellectual development of individual students.

The Swiss psychologist Jean Piaget discovered that children pass through specific stages of intellectual development and found that children at each level exhibit particular intellectual characteristics. In other words, certain types of thinking skills develop at certain age ranges. If we teachers do not provide for these differences, any instructional sequence will not be as successful as it could be, and individualization will become even more remote.

This chapter is designed to develop such competence through a self-instructional programmed learning format. Piagetian theories and their classroom implications are presented systematically in carefully measured steps that are followed immediately by feedback.

In the course of completing the program, you will prepare a most useful reference chart that identifies the major intellectual characteristics of students at each level. These characteristics are presented in several ways, and you are urged to use the materials described in the text by actually working with children. When the chart is completed, you are given guidance in using that reference to design your own tasks to assess the level of intellectual development at which a given student operates in a particular area, and are provided instruction in conducting diagnostic interview sessions. As a result of these experiences, you will be better prepared to select learning activities appropriate to the intellectual development of your students.

The chapter is designed to be used over a period of many days, and appropriate places to take a break are indicated occasionally in the text. Every effort was made to present the often extremely difficult theories of Jean Piaget in a light and, we hope, refreshing writing style. As some indication of what we mean, you may wish to preview the "Frightening Introduction" to the chapter.

We are definitely pro-teacher and value the opinions of professional teachers highly. In later portions of the text, we advise you to begin tapping these tremendous resources. Appropriately, we have ended the program by identifying some of the most difficult questions that are frequently asked us. When you reach that point, though, you will then have a usable reference chart that will permit you to interject considerable insights into your conversations with colleagues regarding these age-old issues. We recommend strongly that you complete the entire program as written, both "theory" and "practice." Enjoy!

A FRIGHTENING INTRODUCTION

It was a terrible dream! One of those classroom nightmares that happen only to teachers. There I was, walking into a room full of students, my fingers sliding across the perspiration film on my palms. They would see my heart throbbing through my chest. I just knew it. I hummed a few notes softly to myself to make sure that the first words I spoke wouldn't sound like a bird caught in a door hinge. A strange chill ran down my legs as the temperature of my face rose to the danger level. I touched my cheek. It was red hot! My life flashed quickly before me. What would my future be, I wondered, if I suddenly turned and ran from the building, never to return? No, there was no turning back now. I started to teach . . .

I cajoled. I gamboled. I cavorted.

I motivated, agitated, and reiterated.

I laughed, smiled, frowned (and I think I even pleaded). . . . Nothing. Do you know how devoid of response *nothing* is?

Absolute silence.

I squinted my eyes, trying to see through the bright spotlight that had been blinding me in my performance. The students were there all right, but each one was sitting behind a small screen. How old were they? Were they "fast" students? "Slow" students? Boys? Girls? Did they understand English? Were *they* afraid of *me*? I simply had no idea.

A pointless story? Maybe. For the fun of it, though, ask some of your teacher colleagues if they ever have teaching nightmares (while sleeping, I mean). It's probably far more common than you believe. When we become concerned with being the best teachers possible, our worst fears creep into our subconscious and we dream of losing control of our classes, of suddenly not knowing what to say, or even of not being able to find our classrooms. But let's return to our tale.

Fortunately, we *can* tell a lot about how students are responding to our instruction, by becoming adept at "reading" their *nonverbal* as well as their *verbal* communication. We also know how to plan activities in a general way, based upon their ages. But students do sit behind screens intellectually. Although we can easily see that individuals develop physically at different rates, to observe that they also develop mentally at different rates requires some "screening" on our part (sorry).

Too many of the structured activities in our classrooms tend to be directed toward "average" students, who really do not exist as such. The result of such mismatched instruction is frustration and anxiety for both students and teachers. Little wonder, then, that we frequently hear such things as "I don't know why they didn't learn that material; I taught it for a week!" Perhaps it is too obvious, but *without learning there is no teaching;* even more important, learning is an *individual* matter.

All right, but in order to individualize we need to know what the various thinking skills are in *specific* terms, and we need to know when each develops. Furthermore, we need to know how we can utilize this information on intellectual development to better suit the learning capabilities of each student.

If we begin to look for help by scouring the general fields of learning theory, we quickly find ourselves immersed in reports of minute research studies, covered with esoteric terms, lost in conflicting schools of thought, and up to our ears in pigeons, rats, and chimpanzees. Most discouraging. We need instead to consider the *practical in-classroom* applications of a comprehensive theory that accounts for *human* intellectual development throughout life. We don't train students to ring bells, and our payoff shouldn't be corn (though corn is not completely lacking from the repertoires of most of us).

But, gaining a theoretical background is nothing more than isolated mental exercise UNLESS we also develop competencies to implement these findings in the classroom effectively. And who are the real experts when it comes to particular classroom applications? You bet. *We* are— the teachers who know and understand our own students as individual human beings.

FORWARD—AS IN "MARCH!"

(We've Already Heard the "Foreword")

It should be clear that we believe that *all* teachers should be continuing observers of intellectual development and should seek to consciously implement such competence in teaching. Increasing these capabilities, then, is an important priority and is the purpose of this chapter. To be more specific, after completing this program you should be able to:

1. Describe the major thinking characteristics of students at each level of intellectual development.

2. Suggest specific tasks that may be used to determine the level of intellectual development at which a given student operates in a particular area.
3. Conduct diagnostic interview sessions successfully.
4. Better select learning activities appropriate to the intellectual levels of individual students.

Central to the completion of this chapter is the preparation of valuable reference charts that will be useful in gaining a functional understanding of the stages of intellectual development of students, and that will aid in designing tasks well suited to particular levels of development. It is essential that you *use* these completed charts and the suggested tasks when you work with the children. We strongly recommend that you gather the materials described in this chapter and experiment with them in the course of working the program.

In completing the program, it is a good idea to cover each page with a sheet of paper, moving it down until the border separating frames is visible; then, when you complete a frame, move the sheet down to the next border. This process will enable you to concentrate on each frame without inadvertently picking up "cues." OK? Then on to frame 1.

OUT OF THE FRAY, WITH JEAN PIAGET

Introduction to the Stages of Intellectual Development

1. It is our opinion that the most important and pertinent psychologist for teachers to be familiar with is, by far, the Swiss genetic epistemologist (*you* look it up) Jean Piaget. His theories are based upon a lifetime of careful research, are comprehensive, and, of course, are directly related to learning. This position is certainly not ours alone, but it is stated immediately to explain why the many others who have made substantial contributions are slighted in this chapter. The simple fact is that attempting to "cover the waterfront" has no value where developing and implementing specific competencies is the emphasis. There is simply too much to do as it is. The consideration and application of the theories of Jean Piaget is, we believe, the most efficient and purposeful use of our time possible. What do *you* think?

___A. I agree.
___B. I'll take your word for it.
___C. Prove it to me.
___D. Only a fool would hold such a view.

2. Perhaps the *best* response is C, which seems to indicate a healthy skepticism. If you selected one of the other responses, ask yourself if you are approaching this program with enough open-minded criticism. If you made no response because the question was too stupid to acknowledge, beware of the seemingly obvious traps ahead. If, on the other hand, you made no response because you read ahead without using the paper shield, you're not yet ready to profit from this chapter. Make the necessary adjustments and go on to the next frame.

---

3. Jean Piaget discovered that children pass through specific stages of intellectual development, and he found that particular thinking skills develop in certain sequences. Children at any given age, then, operate at different levels of thinking. If we do not make allowances for these intellectual differences in our teaching, we find ourselves back in the spotlight of our nightmare, performing for students who are unable to respond, through no fault of their own. For a teacher, therefore, developing a knowledge of the intellectual capabilities of children at each developmental stage is, in itself, a(n)

___A. Excellent use of time.

___B. Good use of time.

___C. Fair use of time.

___D. Poor use of time.

---

4. If you selected A, you *may* be right; but, too, you may be putting us on. Teachers have so very much to do that available time should be utilized carefully. As we stated earlier, our opinion is that gaining such knowledge as a mental exercise has little real teaching value UNLESS (the capitals, remember?) we learn how to bring these competencies to the classroom. If you are still in the "stupid-question" or "response-skipping" categories, your skepticism is getting the best of you, so tighten up a little more. OK, we won't mention it again.

Before we are ready to try some tasks with children to assess their levels of intellectual development, and before we are ready to try to develop the appropriate materials for doing so, we need to gain some familiarity with the thinking characteristics of students at each level. You will find a detailed treatment of this subject in the chapter entitled "Assessing Intellectual Development Stages of Children" in the self-instructional text, *Developing Teacher Competencies,* ed. James E. Weigand (Englewood Cliffs, N.J.: Prentice-Hall, 1971). Since it is clearly unrealistic for us to assume that each reader has competed that chapter, the next section will

Table 1-1. Stages of Intellectual Development *

Developmental Stage	General Age Range	Characteristics
Sensorimotor	Birth to approximately 18 months	Stage is preverbal
Preoperational	Approximately 18 months to 7 to 8 years	
Concrete Operations	7 to 8 years to 11 to 12 years	
Formal Operations	Beginning at 11 to 12 years and continuing throughout life	

*Chart format adapted from Odvard Egil Dyrli, "The Learning of Science," in Ronald Anderson et al., *Developing Children's Thinking Through Science* (Englewood Cliffs, N.J.: Prentice-Hall, 1970), p. 121.

Figure 1-1. Characteristics of thought in stages of intellectual development

For each of the following items, place a letter in the blank to indicate the developmental stage for which it is a particular characteristic.

S = sensorimotor stage (birth to approximately 18 months of age).

P = preoperational stage (approximately 18 months to 7 to 8 years).

C = stage of concrete operations (7 to 8 years to 11 to 12 years).

F = stage of formal operations (beginning at 11 to 12 years and continuing throughout life).

As an example, S has been placed in the blank of item 1 to indicate that "preverbal" is a characteristic of the sensorimotor stage.

1. __S__ Stage is preverbal.

2. _____ Commonly satisfied with multiple and often contradictory explanations of problems.

3. _____ The ability to think abstractly without having to work directly with physical objects.

4. _____ An object "exists" only when in the perceptual field of the child.

5. _____ The ability to coordinate several variables in thought or action.

6. _____ Logic is bound to the manipulation of objects.

7. _____ The concept of reversibility develops.

8. _____ The tendency to focus or "center" attention on only one variable at a time.

9. _____ Basic physical experience with objects forms the foundation for later intellectual development.

10. _____ Apparent visual contradictions do *not* cause conflict thinking.

Figure 1-1 (cont.)

11.	_____	Most of the concepts of conservation develop (first, conservation of number; then conservation of substance and of length; then, conservation of area; and, finally, conservation of weight).
12.	_____	The ability to combine propositions.
13.	_____	Conservation of volume develops.
14.	_____	Hidden objects are located through random physical movement and without thought.
15.	_____	Elementary logical operations develop, and the child learns to make groupings of classes and relations (for instance, serial ordering).
16.	_____	Bound to *own* perceptions of happenings, to what is thought to be seen.
17.	_____	Learning through simple trial and error rather than through logic.
18.	_____	The ability to make systematic combinations of objects or symbols.
19.	_____	The ability to hypothesize, predict consequences, and consider implications in new situations.
20.	_____	The development of mental symbols and symbolic play.
21.	_____	Behavior and thinking are egocentric.

Note: After each item has been coded, the characteristics should be organized according to developmental stage in Table 1-1. Instructions are given in the program.

serve as a concise summary of the same material. (If you *have* completed that reference, you will probably find the following discussion to be a useful review.)

---

5. In order to systematize our thoughts so that we develop a functional frame of reference for our later activities, we will develop a "master reference chart" such as Table 1-1. (Later, you will probably want to make a similar chart on a larger sheet of paper.) As you can see from Table 1-1, Piaget categorizes mental development into four major periods and identifies particular thinking characteristics for each. When we have completed this first reference chart, we will have made a record of these intellectual attributes in concise terms. The specific characteristics that will be used in organizing the chart are listed in Figure 1-1. Remove these two pages from your book now, and place them nearby. As we briefly consider each stage, code these items according to the instructions in Figure 1-1, when asked to do so. At the end of this section, after all the items have been coded, we will use this information to assemble the master reference chart. In the next frame we will begin the presentation of the sensorimotor stage.

The Sensorimotor Stage
(From Birth to Approximately 18 Months of Age)

6. Although it is true that few teachers work directly with children in this age group, psychologists emphasize the *great* importance of this stage in the later intellectual development of the child. The value of providing the child in this stage with a responsive and stimulating environment, therefore, should not be minimized.

Children in the sensorimotor stage encounter objects through random physical movement, without thought. In fact, particular objects "exist" for the child only when he can see, touch, or perhaps hear them in some way. Scan the list of characteristics in Figure 1-1 and indicate the items illustrative of the sensorimotor stage by writing the letter "S" next to them. Which of the following four statements did you identify as being characteristic of this stage?

__A. Conservation of volume develops.

__B. An object "exists" only when it is in the perceptual field of the child.

__C. Hidden objects are located through random physical movement, without thought.

__D. Basic physical experience with objects forms the foundation for later intellectual development.

---

7. Items B, C, and D. Although we have not yet introduced the concepts of conservation they are of the greatest importance; we will consider them in detail later. Although anyone who has cared for infants might state humorously that they never conserve volume in *any* regard, conservation, as Piaget defined it, has a quite specific meaning, as we shall see.

Are the statements corresponding to items B, C, and D now each coded with "S" in Figure 1-1?

__Yes.
__No.

---

8. If they are *not,* do this before going further.

In the next section we will consider how the intellectual development of children progresses as they leave infancy. In case you wish to take a break as you proceed, we have indicated good places to do so in the course of the program. Therefore, either take a breather now or forge ahead to learn some interesting things about primary-age children.

The Preoperational Stage
(From Approximately 18 Months to 7 to 8 Years)

9. The preoperational stage is the time when mental symbols and symbolic play develop as the child learns to represent things by acting like them. The child also learns to think in this stage, but does not do so through the use of much logic. Given a physical problem to solve, he will characteristically approach it wholly through trial and error. Since he is so bound to his perceptions, to what he *thinks* he sees, the preoperational child lives in an "Alice-in-Wonderland" world where apparent visual contradictions do *not* cause conflict in his thinking. Consider, for example, this interview with a five-year-old child using a now famous demonstration suggested by Piaget.

Teacher: (Shows two full and identical soda pop bottles.) Susan, we each have a bottle of pop. Who has more to drink, you or I?

Susan: We both have the same.

Teacher: How do you know?

Susan: Because both bottles are full.

Teacher: All right, now watch while I empty each bottle into a glass. (Empties Susan's bottle into a tall, narrow glass and empties her own bottle into a short wide glass.) Now then, who has more to drink, you or I?

Susan: Me.

Teacher: How come?

Susan: My pop goes way up to there, and yours goes up to here. (Points with finger.)

In the preceding interview it appears that the preoperational child:

___A. Can focus attention upon the change in liquid height, but cannot simultaneously consider the influence of the difference in glass diameter.

___B. Has difficulty in coordinating several variables at the same time.

___C. Has not developed the concept that the total amount of something remains the same even though its appearance is physically altered (in this case, the something is the amount of soda pop).

---

10. All three are correct. Read the choices again. A was demonstrated in the interview, and B is really a statement of the same idea in general terms.

Consider C carefully. This concept is known as *conservation*. In the interview with Susan, what type of conservation do you believe the teacher was trying to assess?

___A. Conservation of number.

___B. Conservation of substance.

___C. Conservation of weight.

---

11. Perhaps you were able to figure out that this was an example of a problem dealing with conservation of *substance*. In other words, the total amount of soda pop (substance) remained the same even though it looked different when it was poured into a tall, narrow glass. You will find out later why A and C are not correct. Before we go on, though, we would like you to write a simple and *general* definition for a concept of conservation:

---

12. The total amount of something remains the same even though its appearance is altered. Children in the preoperational stage have:

___A. Developed the concepts of conservation.

___B. *Not* developed the concepts of conservation.

---

13. Preoperational children have *not* developed the concepts of conservation. Notice that the plural was used. In addition to the concepts of conservation of substance, number, and weight, you will soon know that the child develops several other concepts of conservation as well.

The preoperational child is also a very egocentric thinker: he has difficulty in seeing anyone else's point of view in thought or feelings. For example, he makes up words like "howassia" and expects everyone else to know what is meant; his talk with peers is best characterized as "collective monologues," as opposed to exchanges of information.

Which of the following characteristics are true, then, of the preoperational child?

___A. He can demonstrate the conservation of weight.

___B. An object "exists" for him only when it is in his perceptual field.

___C. He tends to focus or "center" his attention on only one variable at a time.

___D. He learns by simple trial and error rather than through logic.

___E. He is commonly satisfied with multiple and often contradictory explanations to problems (For instance, an object can be heavy and light, or long and short, at the same time.)

___F. His behavior and thinking are egocentric.

---

14. C, D, E, and F are correct. Preoperational children do not conserve weight (A), and B is a characteristic of the sensorimotor child. Did you really reason out E, or did you select it only because it was long and sounded impressive? Perhaps we threw you a curve, since E has only been implied. Read E again, and remember to look for this characteristic if you work with preoperational children.

Now that you have learned some specific characteristics of preoperational children, what should your next step be?

---

15. If you said "Take a break," you are just slightly ahead of the game. This would be a good time to do so, but the best response is to first code the "P" characteristics in Figure 1-1. You should be able to code seven new items in this manner.

Some very interesting developments take place in the capabilities of children during the next stage of intellectual development. Go on to frame 16 when you are ready.

The Stage of Concrete Operations
(From 7 to 8 Years to 11 to 12 Years)

16. As the name of the stage implies, the child in this age range begins to think logically, but this thought is concrete rather than abstract. In other words, though he can now perform simple operations of logic, the child can do more advanced thinking if he is given physical objects to manipulate than he can if he is expected to do the same problems symbolically.

Take, for example, the operation of *serial ordering,* which begins to develop in the transition to the stage of concrete operations. Serial ordering is the ability to place a collection of objects into some *consecutive* arrangement, such as lining children up according to height, or arranging crayons in a box from darkest to lightest colors. If a child in the stage of concrete operations is asked to arrange a collection of objects into various serial orders, he will be most successful:

___A. In physically arranging and rearranging the objects themselves.

___B. In completing the problem in terms of symbols, using paper and pencil.

___C. By either method, depending on the child.

17. Although he might be successful by either method only if the problem were very simple, the child in the stage of concrete operations would definitely be more successful in working with the objects themselves.

The child in the stage of concrete operations also learns to think in terms of *groups,* such as "warm-blooded animals," "legislators," "symphonies," and "verbs," as he begins to learn the skills of classifying. Among the most significant developments in the stage of concrete operations, however, is the idea that the total amount of something remains the same even though its physical appearance is altered. This idea is known as

18. *Conservation.*

The several concepts of conservation are the key developments in the stage of concrete operations. We will describe each type of conservation in turn, and indicate in column I the age range during which the concept usually develops. You try to match the simple word from column II that identifies the conservation described.

Column I	Column II
___1. The number of items in a group remains the same even though the items are rearranged (6 to 7 years of age).	A. Conservation of length.
___2. The amount of material in some object remains the same even though its shape is altered (7 to 8 years).	B. Conservation of volume.
___3. The total length of a line remains the same no matter how it is displaced (7 to 8 years).	C. Conservation of substance.
___4. The amount of surface covered by plane geometric figures remains the same no matter how the figures are rearranged on the surface (8 to 9 years).	D. Conservation of weight.
___5. The weight of an object remains the same even though its shape is altered (9 to 10 years).	E. Conservation of number.
___6. The amount of liquid displaced by an object remains the same no matter how the shape of the object is changed (14 to 15 years).	F. Conservation of area.

---

19. The preceding frame presented simple definitions for the conservation of number, substance, length, area, weight, and volume, respectively (E, C, A, F, D, B).

The concepts of conservation all develop during the stage of concrete operations:

___True.
___False.

---

20. False. The conservation of *volume* develops at a later stage. (Compare the age range in which this concept develops with those of the other concepts tabulated in frame 18.) All the other concepts of conservation develop during the stage of concrete operations (with the occasional exception of conservation of number).

Since you will soon be translating theory into tasks, for each of the following we would like you to describe some physical task that illustrates the conservation named. When using such examples with children, be sure to use *two* sets of identical materials so that comparisons can be made between the "before" and the "after." We have completed the first item to illustrate what we mean:

A. *Conservation of number:* Using two rows of ten identical buttons each: the number of buttons doesn't change if the buttons in one row are placed in a pile.

(If we were using this task with a young child to assess conservation of number, we would question as we went along, as was done in frame 9.)

Now it's your turn:

B. *Conservation of substance:*

C. *Conservation of length:*

D. *Conservation of area:*

E. *Conservation of weight:*

F. *Conservation of volume:*

---

21. There must be an infinite number of tasks that could be devised. Compare your list with ours to see if you have the right idea.

B. *Conservation of substance:* Using two identical balls of clay: the amount of clay in one doesn't change if it is flattened into a pancakelike shape.

C. *Conservation of length:* Using two identical wires of the same length: the length of one doesn't change even though it is bent into a spiral.

D. *Conservation of area:* Using twenty dominos arranged into two rectangles of ten dominoes each: the amount of table surface covered by one set doesn't change if the ten dominoes are rearranged so that they are far apart.

E. *Conservation of weight:* Using two small and identical sealed bags of potato chips: the weight of one doesn't change even if the chips are pulverized.

F. *Conservation of volume:* Using two identical balls of clay: when they are submerged separately in a glass of water, the water will rise to the same level for each, even if one ball is fashioned into a disc.

Go on to the next frame.

---

22. You may have experienced confusion in distinguishing between conservation of volume and conservation of substance. By conservation of *volume* Piaget means the conservation of liquid displacement specifically (reread example F). Remember again that this operation develops in the *next* stage of intellectual development.

Another important development in the stage of concrete operations is known as *reversibility,* which is the ability of the child to return physical conditions to the state that existed prior to his actions. For example, if he upsets a board balanced with blocks on either end by adding a new block, he is able to see that the same block must be removed in order for the board to become balanced once again.

It is important that you grasp clearly the notion of reversibility, at least in the physical context, before moving on. In fact, the last question usually asked of a child who indicates that he can conserve in a particular task is "How do you know?" The child in concrete operations is able to *demonstrate* reversibility either in action (for instance, by rolling a disc-shaped piece of clay back into a ball) or, where simple problems are concerned, in thought (for example, by stating that the bag of pulverized potato chips in frame 21 maintained its weight since chips were neither added nor removed, the bag having remained sealed). Reread your responses in frame 20, think about how a child might demonstrate reversibility for each, and then continue to frame 23.

---

23. The development of the concepts of conservation is a key characteristic of the stage of concrete operations:

___True.
___False.

---

24. True. Which of the concepts of conservation develops in the *next* stage?

---

25. The conservation of volume (which is, therefore, a good task to use with a student in attempting to assess capacity for "formal" thinking).

At this point we would like you to review the section on the stage of concrete operations and try to identify the appropriate items in Figure 1-1, marking them with the code "C." Then, especially if you haven't taken the earlier breaks, you are probably really ready for some conservation of substance of your own by now. After you have had a coffee or a Coke, move on to frame 26 to find out about the types of intellectual skills that you yourself have developed. Our next consideration is the most advanced stage of intellectual development.

The Stage of Formal Operations
(Beginning at 11 to 12 Years of Age
and Continuing Through Life)

26. The individual in the stage of formal operations learns to manipulate symbols and to deal with ideas verbally without always having to work directly with physical objects. In other words, he becomes able to think in increasingly abstract terms.

The individual in this stage also learns to think about consequences and implications, and can hypothesize results *before* performing some action. By reasoning, he can use his previous experience to predict what might happen in a new set of conditions and can then perform the operations necessary to either prove or disprove his suppositions. How would a child in the stage of concrete operations tend to differ in his approach to the same problems?

---

27. A child in the stage of concrete operations would tend to be bound quite closely to the manipulation of physical materials. He would probably forge ahead quickly to see what might happen rather than first trying to reason out a solution.

How would a child in the stage of concrete operations differ from a child in the stage of formal operations in trying to solve the following problem?

A student has a coin, a shell, a rock, a twig, a dowel, and a paper clip on a tray. What two-item combinations can he select from this collection of objects?

The child in the stage of concrete operations would:

---

28. Once again, the child in the stage of concrete operations would be more successful if he manipulated such a collection of objects than he would if he were expected to do the same problem more abstractly by using symbols.

Also illustrated here is a major development in the stage of formal operations, the establishment of a *combinatorial system* in the logic of the individual. The child in the stage of formal operations becomes able to make *systematic combinations* of objects, symbols, or even ideas. A good example is the problem stated in the last frame. In order for you to confirm that fifteen combinations are possible, it is necessary for you to utilize this systematic combinatorial skill (try it). On the other hand, a child in the stage of concrete operations, in attempting the same problem, could name various two-item combinations but would find it difficult to report *all* the combinations possible.

Go on to the next frame.

---

29. In addition to being able to solve problems that require the use of combinations, another unique development in the stage of formal operations is the ability to coordinate several variables in controlled experiments. By doing so, one can isolate single variables in turn to observe their effects upon some phenomenon. Although this operation has applications in every subject area, a physical problem involving a simple pendulum will illustrate what we mean:

Given some string and two different "weights," experiment to determine which of the following factors affect the rate of movement of a pendulum (*hint*: count the number of swings each time for some specific period of time—say, twenty seconds):

A. The length of the string (long or short).
B. The "weight" of the pendulum (heavy or light).

C. The height of release (high or low).

D. The "push" on the pendulum (strong or weak).

(The characteristics in the parentheses are, of course, relative to each other.)

We suggest that you try this problem yourself to experience the type of thinking described. You can use any two objects that can be tied easily and swung as a pendulum. We do, though, recommend that you let some-one else time the twenty-second period for each test while you count the swings.

Which factors did you find would influence the rate of movement?

---

30. Since you are in the stage of formal operations, you probably had fine success and are already sure of your results. If you experienced difficulty, though, it was likely due to problems of technique rather than logic. If such *was* the case, it would be good to compare notes with a colleague.

The final characteristic that we will consider is the ability of the student in the stage of formal operations to combine propositions (statements). Given any series of factors whose interaction to produce certain results is to be determined, the individual may, for example, reason as follows:

1. "It must be factor A *and* factor B."
2. "It is *either* A *or* B that is responsible."
3. "It is *neither* A *nor* B."
4. "If it is A, then C will be true."

And so forth. Such combining of propositions is useful whether the subject in question is the language arts, the social studies, the sciences, or mathe-matics. The ability to do it, however, does not develop until the stage of formal operations.

Go on to the next frame.

CONSTRUCTING THE MASTER REFERENCE CHART—
CUT AND GLUE AND SOON YOU'RE THROUGH

31. Your introduction to (or review of) the Piagetian stages of intellec-tual development is now complete. Code the remaining items in Figure

1-1 that are characteristic of the stage of formal operations. Reread all your responses and then compare them with the list that appears in the next frame.

---

32. *Note:* If, by chance, you happen to read this frame without first having completed the preceding program, we urge you to read no further until you *have* done so. The maximum value of this program can be gained only if you complete each step in sequence and carefully consider the concepts in the order presented.

On the other hand, if you have completed the program as described, you should check your responses against the following list prior to assembling the reference chart.

1. S	4. S	7. C	10. P	13. F	16. P	19. F
2. P	5. F	8. P	11. C	14. S	17. P	20. P
3. F	6. C	9. S	12. F	15. C	18. F	21. P

Go on to the next frame.

---

33. You are now ready to assemble the master reference chart that will serve as a useful resource for your in-classroom activities. Perhaps you have been asking yourself why we didn't simply give you a ready-made chart initially. The reason originates from the fact that although Piagetian theory is most pertinent for all teachers, understanding Piaget is a difficult undertaking requiring years of study. We have tried, therefore, to select and present the major characteristics of thought of the stages of intellectual development as clearly as possible, through carefully measured steps and with a minimum of terminology. Although our experience has been that too much theory at once is totally overwhelming, considering Piagetian ideas systematically and in several different ways is both manageable and engrossing.

You have two options in assembling your chart: either rewrite the characteristics from Figure 1-1 on Table 1-1 or make a similar chart on a larger sheet of paper as was suggested earlier, cut Figure 1-1 into strips, and then tape or glue each characteristic in its correct position. In either case, be certain that all the items in a given stage are together. If you have a record player nearby, how about some mood music for cutting and pasting?

Go on to the next frame when you are finished.

USING THE CHART—
FIRST TIME THROUGH, AS AN OVERVIEW

34. A reference chart, such as the one we completed in the last section, provides us with good insight into the intellectual development of students. We should now have a much more specific view of the characteristics of thought of children at each level. In theory, therefore, we should be better able to determine proper teaching procedures in general, to adjust procedures for specific students, and to assess the appropriateness of available curriculum materials. We will consider these three topics as we seek to translate theory into practice.

To begin, we would like you to observe the students in your class informally over a period of time, using the chart as a guide. (You determine the length of time required to complete this activity; several days may be necessary.) In the space below, list observations that illustrate the characteristics of thought described for children at that level. For example, observations of four-year-olds might be recorded as follows:

Stage and Age Range: Preoperational - 18 months to 7 to 8 years

Characteristics   *Observations*

1. symbolic play.   1. Jenny made "butterfly" hand shadows

2. bound to *own perceptions*.   2. Jack believed the sun followed him across the sky as he walked.

Try to illustrate as many different characteristics as possible, and then go on to the next frame.

Stage and Age Range: _____

Characteristics   *Observations*

35. Although the preceding activity was not easy, we trust that you are now starting to focus your attention upon the *evidence* that specific skills have been developed in each stage. As some indication of the accuracy of your observations, discuss your notes in frame 34 with a colleague, preferably someone who has either completed this program or is in the process of doing so.

If you were able to complete the activity with a minimum of time and effort, it is likely that you are a teacher of younger children. Our experience has been that it becomes increasingly difficult to make such observations informally as the age of the students advances. Why do you suppose that is true?

36. The major reasons most likely include the following:

1. Evidence of the higher-level characteristics of thought is more difficult to observe.
2. Younger children usually exhibit greater freedom of movement and expression and thereby provide more opportunities for observation.

But (again) a far more disturbing reason for difficulty, regardless of level, may be that:

3. The curriculum in use is *not* appropriate to the thinking capabilities of children at that level and does not provide opportunities for students to demonstrate the skills they are capable of using.

We will present some additional thoughts on this subject as we continue.

37. Since you have observed students at only one level, you will gain a much more comprehensive view if you observe students at the other two levels as well. (We will limit our discussion to the preoperational, concrete operational, and formal operational stages.) If possible, conduct the same type of activity with such students yourself. Otherwise, copy the results obtained by colleagues who worked with students at those levels (again, preferably individuals who have completed or are completing this program).

Stage and Age Range: _____

Characteristics   *Observations*

Stage and Age Range: _____

Characteristics   *Observations*

38. By now you must certainly agree that it is not possible to become an "instant expert" in observing intellectual development, although you are clearly rewarded for the time you invest. You may also be raising some questions regarding the curriculum at a particular level and the opportunities to utilize thinking skills in general. These questions are compounded by the fact that most classes consist of students who are at different levels of intellectual development; even more important, individuals operate at different levels at the same time. In other words, a student who exhibits formal thought in certain subject areas may approach other areas through concrete thinking.

Perhaps, too, you are now asking the "big question" so commonly directed to Piaget: "Why don't we teach students the various thinking operations and accelerate their intellectual development?" At this point, what do you think of this idea?

___A. It's a good idea.

___B. It's not such a good idea.

___C. I need more information.

---

39. Although accelerating intellectual development certainly sounds like a good idea, attempts to do so through teaching operations have been almost uniformly *un*successful. It appears that the operations that we have categorized in our chart *cannot* be taught as such but must rather develop naturally as opportunities for such development are presented. Furthermore, there is evidence that if a child is not given direct experience with objects and materials, for example, it is unlikely that he will develop later operations adequately. And, too, a given child may at first develop more slowly intellectually and then go farther in the long run.

Speaking generally, then, which of the following should be characteristic of all teaching below the high school level?

___A. *All* curriculum areas should be "materials-oriented."

___B. Each child should manipulate materials directly, as opposed to simply watching demonstrations or looking at displays.

___C. The child should draw conclusions himself, as opposed to being told what to conclude by a text or by the teacher.

___D. Emphasis should be placed upon providing opportunities for skill development rather than upon memorization.

___E. Skills should be utilized in as many contexts as possible.

---

40. There wasn't much of a challenge here, but we needed to stop and consider these important points. We believe that *all* the items should be characteristic. We believe, further, that support for this position can be found in your reference chart.

At the high school level, on the other hand, students will be able to deal with problems that require abstract, hypothetical thinking for solution:

___A. Agree.

___B. Disagree.

---

41. Believe it or not, the better choice is "disagree"! Students are theoretically in the stage of formal operations when they reach high school, but that is *not* necessarily so. Particularly if a student lacked concrete opportunities for intellectual development in his early experience, he may still be thinking on a concrete operational level. As a result, the instructional characteristics listed in frame 39 might apply to high school teaching as well. If you are a high school teacher, reread those items and briefly consider the implications of each in your subject area.

So, we're back to the point that intellectual development is an *individual* matter and should be regarded in this way as we seek to present those opportunities for development. In the next section we will gather some data on the levels of thinking of *individuals*.

BACK TO THE FRAY, WITH A CHART (AND SOME CLAY)

42. As we try to get behind the "intellectual screens" of our students, we can often find out a great deal through simple observation of behavior, as we did in the last section. In order to gain more specific information, though, we need to *interview* individuals directly. If we can adequately establish a student's level of thinking, we will then have a better idea of his potential for learning, since he will likely be able to exhibit other intellectual characteristics of that stage as well. Our first undertaking, therefore, is to determine which types assessment tasks are *easily administered, easily observed,* and *significant* in identifying thinking as being preoperational, concrete operational, or formal operational.

Many of the characteristics of the stages suggest tasks that might be used in assessing intellectual development. You may wish to do some experimenting of your own in this regard. For purposes of our illustrative interviews, though, which of the following characteristics will best meet the three task criteria stated above? (Refer to your chart.)

__A. Egocentric behavior.

__B. The concepts of conservation.

__C. Acceptance of visual contradictions.

__D. Trial-and-error thinking.

43. We believe that B is the most appropriate response. Although suitable tasks that focus upon the other items might well be developed, they would tend to be more open to ambiguous interpretation. Furthermore, there are times when thinking at all three levels is characterized by items A, C, and D.

In addition to meeting the three criteria stated in frame 42, by referring to your chart you may also be able to state another major reason why the concepts of conservation are so useful to consider:

---

44. The six concepts of conservation develop at different times and span two or three of the stages. Although the specific age at which each will develop varies with the individual, the *sequence* of development is always fixed. We can therefore utilize such tasks to focus quite closely upon the development of thinking. Now you know why we devoted so much time to the concepts of conservation earlier.

Go on to the next frame.

---

45. This may very well be the first time you have ever gathered data to either support or dispute a theory. It is an exciting prospect. We will be using Table 1-2 to record our findings, so look this chart over briefly before you start.

In conducting the interview sessions you will need some carefully defined conservation tasks, such as the ones suggested in frames 20 and 21. We recommend that you make a list of the ones you decide to try on a separate sheet of paper prior to the first session. The reason we mentioned clay in the title of this section is that clay is easy to obtain and can be used conveniently to illustrate several of the concepts. Using clay, therefore, may simplify your initial search for materials.

To begin the interview, sit down with one student and present him with *two* sets of identical materials (see frame 20). Ask him if the two sets are equivalent, and do not continue until this fact has been established to *his* satisfaction in some way (for example, by lining up both sets, or by measuring each). Then transform one set as you have planned and use a questioning approach to determine if the student can conserve in that particular task (for instance, "Do I now have more, or do you have more, or do we both have the same?"). Be careful, though, not to cue or lead the interview. After the student has stated his conclusion, question him further to find out the reasons for his choice. If he is able to support his contention through reversibility of thought or action, make a note that he was able to conserve successfully, before moving on to the next concept.

When the session is completed, summarize the data in Table 1-2: Find the appropriate line for the age of the student and designate a name code in the first column, such as "S = Stephen." Then, for each conservation

Table 1-2. Data Sheet for Conservation Interview Session

Codes for Names	Age in Years	CONCEPTS OF CONSERVATION											
		Number		Substance		Length		Area		Weight		Volume	
		+	−	+	−	+	−	+	−	+	−	+	−
	4-5												
	5-6												
	6-7												
	7-8												
	8-9												
	9-10												
	10-11												
	11-12												
	12-13												
	13-14												
	14-15												
	15-16												
	16-17												
	17-18												

place the code in either the "+" column or the "−" column to indicate whether the student was able or was not able to conserve in that particular task.

If possible, try conservation interview sessions with several students of the same age and also with students of different ages. When you have completed this field research, compare your observations in Table 1-2 with the theoretical development of the concepts of conservation in frame 18. Finally, try to conclude which level of intellectual development best characterizes each student you worked with. Which categories of thinkers did you identify?

___A. Preoperational.

___B. Concrete operational.

___C. Formal operational.

---

46. If you are a high school teacher, it is possible that you found that a number of your students were not able to conserve volume, and maybe not weight either. Perhaps, too, you felt ill at ease trying to assess formal thinking on the basis of only one formal task (and rightly so). Why would doing so *not* be a good idea?

---

47. A particular task might not have been well formulated, or the interviewer may not have communicated properly with the student. It is advisable, therefore, to try several related tasks and various questioning techniques.

In order to gain some additional information for identifying formal thinking, you may wish to try the coordination-of-variables problem from frame 29, or you may wish to try to devise some problems in your own subject area. These might include problems to determine the ability to make systematic combinations, the ability to combine propositions (see frame 30), or the ability to think abstractly. In the next frame we will introduce a new problem that requires the use of formal thinking for solution. You may wish to use this problem in an interview session. It is particularly interesting to observe the operation of the solution strategies that it elicits.

---

48. The "Formal Challenge": The problem in Figure 1-3 and the accompanying materials in Figure 1-2 focus upon the use of logic in classi-

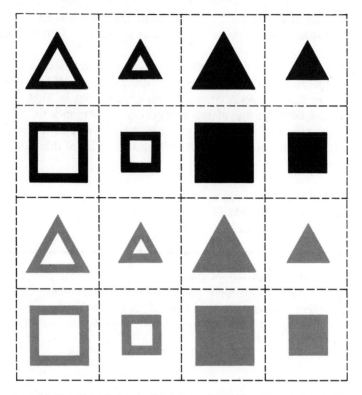

Figure 1-2. Materials for the "Formal Challenge." Make a similar set and cut out to form a deck of sixteen cards

fication systems.[1] Although there are a *number* of solutions, you and your students will be challenged indeed. Try it.

---

49. You should now be able to demonstrate that you have completed the first three objectives of this program successfully. We trust that your work with students has been both enjoyable and inspiring. If, though, you would now like to observe someone else conducting interview sessions and working with Piagetian theories in the classroom, you would do well to view several of the films listed on page 35. They may be bought from the producer, Davidson Films, 3701 Buchanan Street, San Francisco, Calif., 94123, or rented from local audio-visual centers. Additional information can be obtained from Davidson Films.

[1] The "Formal Challenge" appeared originally in Odvard Egil Dyrli, "Follow a Different Drummer." Reprinted by special permission from LEARNING, *The Magazine for Creative Teaching,* December 1972. © 1972 by Education Today Company, Inc., 530 University Avenue, Palo Alto, Calif.

The 16 cards in your deck are different in four ways:

1. Shape: *triangles or squares*

2. Size: *large or small*

3. Color: *black or gray*

4. Amount   *filled or open*
   of shading:

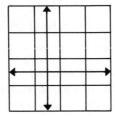

Arrange all 16 cards in a square so that there are *two* of everything in *each* column and in *each* row.

This row, for example,

has two triangles and two squares,
    two large and two small,
    two black and two gray
    two filled and two open.

Figure 1-3.   The "Formal Challenge"

Conservation (28 minutes)
Classification (17 minutes)
Formal Thought (32 minutes)
The Growth of Intelligence in the Preschool Years (30 minutes)
Jean Piaget, Memory and Intelligence (45 minutes)

Go on to the next frame.

50. This is a good time to ask a very basic question: Which of the following is the least justifiable reason for learning to implement assessments of student intellectual development?

___A. To teach the characteristics of thought and to accelerate intellectual development.

___B. To understand why certain thinking operations are so difficult for specific individuals.

___C. To provide experiences for the child that will encourage intellectual development.

___D. To evaluate the appropriateness of curriculum materials for individual students.

___E. To gain a more positive view of the thinking potential of each student.

---

51. A is least appropriate. Research indicates that the thinking operations cannot be taught as such. In fact, in an interview published in 1973 ("Piaget Takes a Teacher's Look," *Learning, The Magazine for Creative Teaching,* October 1973, pp. 22–27), Piaget stated that the marketing of curriculum kits for the expressed purpose of "accelerating" the development of operations is simply "idiotic." He also denounced the substitution of photographs and films for contact with actual objects, and the use of materials with narrowly limited possibilities. Since the article mentioned above contains so many unique insights of value to teachers, we strongly recommend that you secure a copy and read it in its entirety.

The tasks, then, are *diagnostic* rather than "instructional." They provide us with direct information regarding the levels of thought of individuals, and this information can subsequently be used in a variety of ways, as indicated by items B through E in the preceding frame. Reread those responses and then go on.

---

52. The final objective of this chapter is concerned with the selection of learning activities appropriate for individual students. It is likely that you have already developed some strong opinions of your own on this subject. We trust that after having completed most of this program, you are now better able to look critically at the materials available in your area of curriculum interest. We hope too that you will carefully reexamine the teaching procedures in your own classroom.

Curriculum developers have given us plenty of "answers" in a shotgun-barrage approach to our teaching needs. What has been lacking, though, is enough *questions*. When we encounter programs that are wholly textbook-centered for primary school children, programs that require abstract thinking at the intermediate level, and programs that involve a minimal use of logic in the high school curriculum, we need to raise some fundamental objections. But before we examine questions of appropriateness in specific contexts, it is advisable that we first consider a particular caution illustrated by the following question: If you were suddenly confronted with having to take an examination in an area in which you didn't have the slightest idea what was going on (did this ever *really* happen to you?), what do you suppose you would do to cope with the situation?

---

53. You may have responded with "Get help," "Study more," and so forth, but in most cases you would probably start immediately to *memorize*. (We're assuming, of course, that completing the examination successfully is a desirable outcome.) You might not have a single clue about the meaning behind what you were storing for later recall, but you could try to stuff as much as possible into some categories in your brain in order to get by.

When the curriculum in our classrooms is inappropriate, our students too can learn to cope by memorizing, and, often, this thin veneer presents us with the illusion that our students are learning. It is therefore easy to be misled by apparent verbal facility (or, for that matter, by the *lack* of it). Remember to look past this memory veneer when you seek to evaluate the success of particular materials and curriculum programs. In the next frame we will raise some really knotty questions in this regard.

---

54. Listed below are several questions of the type we need to ask continually. They are knotty problems indeed, and considerable controversy can be engendered by each. We would like you to refer to your reference chart, consider these questions in light of your experiences in working this program, and then discuss your point of view with colleagues. The nature of these concerns is such that it is not possible to come to any decisions that will be accepted by all—as you will soon find out.

A. Can we justify the introduction of abstract concepts and hypothetical situations (for instance, the solar system, or children in other countries) at the primary school level?

B. Since reading requires the use of abstract symbols, is reading really an appropriate focus of early education?

C. When should the various mathematical concepts and skills—numerals, the use of a ruler, the computation of area, the concepts of weight, and so forth—be introduced?

D. Is there a gap between the curriculum materials you are using and the reasoning abilities of your students? What specific evidence can you cite to support your position?

E. Are symbolic games and activities in the elementary school important in the development of thinking as well as being important in the emotional life of the child? What thoughts and observations have led to your conclusions?

F. Does your research indicate that students in grades 7, 8, and 9 *must* interact with concrete objects in order to learn most efficiently?

G. Should high school teachers consciously seek to "wean" students from concrete to abstract thinking?

H. How should the learning environments compare and contrast at primary, intermediate, junior high, and high school levels?

I. Which curriculum materials at each level are clearly *in*appropriate?

J. Does each student have an optimum speed of intellectual development? How does your belief support or dispute the "normal" curriculum?

A REASSURING ENDING

55. At the beginning of this program we stated that *teachers* are the experts in practical classroom application of educational theory. We really believe this. The importance of a strong theoretical background is undeniable and has, of course, been a major emphasis in this chapter. But although learning theorists can share the benefit of their thinking, it is the function of the professionals in education to implement these ideas in the classroom in practical ways. And, again, "they" are "us"! Your opinions in the last frame, therefore, should be valued highly.

Many times in the course of this program we have suggested that you compare notes and discuss your thoughts with colleagues. Those were not idle suggestions. As professional teachers, we need to establish continuing conversations regarding the fundamental issues we have raised here. *Every* teacher is a research worker, trying to develop and implement new and improved competencies. As a result, we have fantastic resources close at hand in the form of our teaching colleagues. There is no need whatsoever to feel alone on the stage of our nightmare, since experts abound. If you haven't been part of such a "teaching conversation" lately, why don't *you* initiate the dialogue? The questions in frame 54 are good places to begin.

This is it. If you have come this far with us, we are indeed honored to have shared your company. We wish you teaching success and teaching joy! Act Two is under *your* control.

On Motivation

MERYL E. ENGLANDER

Indiana University

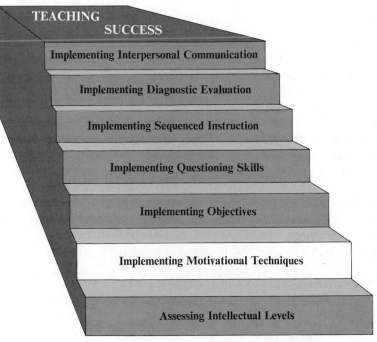

**"STEPS" TO IMPLEMENTING
TEACHING COMPETENCIES**

Do you hope to motivate your pupils as you have been motivated by most of your teachers?

Threats of low grades

Promises of college choice for high grades

Withdrawal of affection for nonconformity

Ridicule and punishment

Demand for conformity to social mores

Grades, Grades, Grades, Grades, Grades, Grades

If you answered in the affirmative, read no further because this material is antagonistic to your objectives.

If you answered in the negative and are wondering what to do next, read on . . .

Motivation is like the weather: everyone talks about it; no one does anything about it. Pupils explain their failures with such statements as "The teacher didn't motivate me," and we teachers respond that "so-and-so is just too lazy to learn." Unfortunately, the experts have not been too helpful. Much is made of such concepts as intrinsic motivation, but after you define it and cheer it there isn't much you can do with it.

This chapter identifies a variety of specific functional ways for you to encourage pupils to get on task. The chapter is divided into two parts. Method I offers a process for motivating individuals. It does not call for us to adapt our course content to fit the interests of pupils. However, we can use these interests as indicators of underlying needs and thereby identify the kinds of activities that would be attractive to the individual. Everyone has needs that can be utilized for school learning, but in order to take advantage of them a teacher must undertake three steps:

1. Observe, categorize, and interpret pupil behavior.
2. Infer the underlying needs being expressed through that behavior.
3. Arrange activities that incorporate those needs.

Method II directs our attention to means for stimulating group or class participation. Such techniques as "grabems," mood creations, contracts, and peer teaching will enable us to make "being involved" worthwhile for all or most of our pupils.

Whereas the material of Method I is unified and can best be understood and applied by reading and doing the exercises in sequence, the principles of Method II are discrete and the reader may find it most useful to be guided by his appetite, as whetted by the "HELP!!! Directives."

The reader will be asked to compare and share with others the reactions and creations in various exercises. Therefore, for optimum value readers are encouraged to meet periodically with others to exchange views regarding ways of motivating pupils. In addition, several of the exercises in Method II suggest that you develop materials and test them on pupils. For those of you who are not actively teaching, we recommend that you find, through religious organizations, youth groups, or other social agencies, a group of children whom you can observe and work with. Fellow students can also be used as subjects.

Some readers may be disappointed by the absence in this chapter of Maslow's need hierarchy. (See Chapter 7 for a presentation of this hierarchy.) We agree with Maslow that motivation by deprivation is degrading and contrary to educational objectives. We agree with the philosophy and mechanisms that enable pupils to feel safe, esteemed, self-respecting, and loved. The notion that as pupils find their needs satisfied they will seek additional stimulation, understandings, and relationships is consistent with the processes of Method I. However, the hierarchy itself does not offer clues as to what the teacher ought to do. The intent of this chapter is to develop skills that are habilitating. None are based upon deprivation, threat, or coercion. As a matter of course, humanistic person-to-person relations ought to be practiced continually, independent of motivational implications.

Caution! The purpose of this chapter is to engender skill in identifying pupil needs and the means for involving pupils in the learning task. Developing this skill takes practice in a variety of slightly different situations. It takes time, reflection; you will not be able simply to read and recall. To repeat: if we are to become skilled we will have to practice.

Help!!!! Directives

Ordinarily, an author anticipates that readers will proceed through the material in the order in which it is presented. However, we recognize that you may have some particular immediate concerns for which you are seeking help.

Let's Make Them Wanna—Not Hafta

The importance of motivation for learning and living is not in question. Our concern is to develop processes whereby teachers can induce pupils to become involved in learning activities that the teacher deems important. Second, the teacher wishes to develop in the pupils a system of motives that will enable the pupils to be creative, productive, independent, and emotionally stable. The question is this: How can a teacher achieve these two broad objectives?

Human beings do not have a natural aversion to learning, creativity, productivity, or emotional stability. On the contrary, if the individual is free to do so and if the conditions are appropriate, the opportunity to participate will be welcomed. Furthermore, learning, creativity, productivity, independence, and emotional stability are not only compatible but also interdependent.

It may help us to better grasp our task if we visualize motivation in terms of three conditions. Visually, it could look like an Idaho potato divided into three sections (see Figure 2-1).

Condition A is *on task*. Condition C is *off task*. The difference between A and C is motivation. The status of the pupils just prior to beginning a successful lesson is condition C, a holding position that includes all types of behavior except doing what is required to achieve the teacher's objective. Condition B represents the rewards of having successfully completed the task. Unfortunately, some students rarely reach condition B and only sometimes attain condition A.

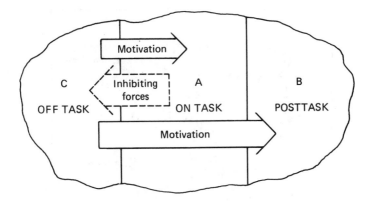

Figure 2-1.　Motivation in terms of three conditions

Pupils know that being involved in learning tasks is appropriate for school, but for a variety of reasons—competing motives, procrastination, fear, boredom, indifference, hostility, and so on—they often remain passive, preoccupied, or resistive. In other words learning may be inhibited by a set of forces, because to be on task requires that:

1. Pupils must give up the ongoing tasks in which they are involved and for which they may be highly motivated.
2. Pupils must focus attention on learning cues, thereby ignoring competing stimuli.
3. By the definition of learning, pupils must change some beliefs and natural ways of performing.

So just to be on task takes effort. No doubt, the inhibiting force is greater for some than others. A counterforce, which we call motivation, is needed to help the pupil become engrossed in the task and to work successfully through it to the posttask, condition B.

Motivation may be achieved by any of three general strategies. First, the pupil in condition C, off task, may be made to feel very uncomfortable by means of threats, physical attack, guilt, and other coercive means and thereby driven out of condition C into the on-task condition. Though various animal studies, common school practice, and traditional realists support such methods as a viable alternative, we will forthwith exclude this strategy since its consequences are often de-habilitating and counter to educational purposes. Our experience is that such adverse conditions, rather than encouraging learning, often drive pupils either physically or psychologically right out of school. Even when coercion succeeds in getting the pupils on task, they are so perceptually constricted, fearful, and hostile that learning,

Figure 2-2.   Strategy 1: Motivation by coercion

trust, and personal development are severely restricted. The stick is out of place in education.

Second, condition A, on task, can be made so attractive that pupils will overcome the inhibiting forces. This strategy is the most natural and in all respects the most desired one. It is the strategy that offers us the joys of many nonwork situations. Let's see if we can naturally integrate this joy into the work and learning segments of pupils' lives. Happiness is satisfying one's needs, controlling destiny, meeting and overcoming challenges, being secure, achieving, and feeling competent. Condition A can be the horn of happiness for everyone.

Third, make condition B, rewards of toil payable after the task is successfully completed, so attractive that the pupils will undergo whatever undesirable experiences are inherent in condition A. Many folks find this extrinsic motivation undesirable, but it is reasonable, probably encompasses minimal harm, and is consistent with the real world. After all, even the most ardent idealist among us would probably not teach were we not paid, and most of us feel that it is only just that we be paid for achievement rather than for simply being. Various techniques will enable us to organize lessons so that pupil participation will pay off for everyone. The carrot may have a place in education.

Go for Condition A—Where the Action Is

Give the teacher an A grade when the pupils are happy and joyfully on task. We are going to learn three ways to earn our A. In Method I, the

Figure 2-3.   Strategy 2: Motivation by compatibility

Figure 2-4.   Strategy 3: Motivation by promise

teacher picks up the cue from the individual pupil who is to be motivated. This method is primarily applicable to individual pupils or to clusters of pupils who have the same needs, not to the entire class. So, Method I is most applicable to the reluctant learners who don't readily respond to the general program. For our immediate purposes, we are going to consider reluctant learners in two categories. First are those who find activities other than classroom learning as the means to satisfy their dominant needs. They are the youngsters whom we tend to label as "lazy" or "don't care" when we observe them in class, but whose behavior betrays the label when they are observed in other situations—the playground or athletic field, working on a car or model airplane, walking home with friends or attending a party. They are not lazy; they simply do not expend their energy on school work. The "individual keys" of Method I suggest means of unlocking the energies of such pupils for use in learning tasks.

Whereas Method I focuses attention on pupil behavior as cues for motivation, Method II focuses on materials, atmosphere, and teacher behavior as general stimulants. It assumes that everyone can be "turned on" by the right conditions because of a set of natural inclinations in all of us that just awaits arousal. Admittedly, some reluctant youngsters don't seem to get much joy out of anything. They are beaten. The inhibiting force for this group is a bigger barrier than extra effort or competing motives. This force includes conflict and fears and, therefore, the teacher must be more gentle, genuine, empathetic, and supportive with such pupils. Specific processes to these ends will be considered within Method II in the section "Eliminate the Negative."

METHOD I: INDIVIDUAL KEYS

Every child is motivated for some goal. The teacher must find that goal and graft a motive for academic mastery on it. (Kagan, 1971, p. 78)

Method I is designed to help us identify the factors that encourage individual pupils to approach some activities and avoid others.

The objectives are to:

1. Pinpoint the types of behaviors that suggest that a pupil is attracted to or repulsed by a given activity.
2. Infer from the observed behavior the underlying personal needs that make the activity attractive or repugnant.
3. Describe activities or conditions appropriate for the inferred needs that would be satisfying and thereby encourage approach behavior from that individual.

We will achieve these objectives by analyzing a number of situations.

There are certain activities that each of us values and enjoys. Identify one of yours and indicate four ways in which someone watching you could tell that you really enjoy that activity.

1. Name of activity:
2. Observable behavior that shows you enjoy it:

   a.

   b.

   c.

   d.

There are also activities that you dislike. Identify one of them and indicate four ways in which someone watching you could tell that you do not enjoy that activity.

1. Name of activity:
2. Observable behavior that shows you dislike it:

   a.

   b.

   c.

   d.

You have just listed possible approach and avoidance *behaviors* toward an activity. Being able to identify the behaviors that indicate an individual's attraction or repugnance to an activity is a first step toward motivating that individual.

Let's find out more about ourselves and our behavior. Listed below are ten different activities. Indicate for each whether you find it (a) satisfying and enjoyable (approach behavior), (b) repugnant and distressing (avoidance behavior), (c) irrelevant (neutral), or (d) both enjoyable and repugnant (ambivalence).

_____ 1. Listening to a lecture on chemical bonding.
_____ 2. Looking at a nude foldout.

————————— 3. Riding in an elevator with a group who have been drinking.

————————— 4. Riding a motorcycle.

————————— 5. Telling an off-color joke or story at a party.

————————— 6. Being chosen to run for homecoming queen (king).

————————— 7. Being in a room with strangers.

————————— 8. Running into an old friend whom you haven't seen for ten years.

————————— 9. Sitting next to a U.S. senator at a banquet.

————————— 10. Being asked to help someone who is hurt or in trouble.

Compare your responses with those of others in your class. It is likely that even though most of us are very much alike, we do differ in what we find enjoyable or repugnant. That is because we have different needs, or perhaps different ways of satisfying the same need. Our unique pattern of needs is one of the things that make us individuals.

It is reasonable to assume that people, if given the opportunity, will engage in activities that are enjoyable and satisfying to them. If that is true, then we should be able, conversely, to deduce what is satisfying by noting what people do. That is, there should be a connection between what people value, enjoy, or prefer and their behavior. Observable behavior is our best clue as to how to motivate an individual.

Let us see if we can infer the basis of enjoyment for four individuals by observing their respective behavior in a given episode.

It is 3:30, and most of the students and teachers have departed. However, behind the school we see several young men coming out of the locker room and heading toward the football field. They are in twos and threes, and because they are wearing football uniforms we assume they are *interested* in football. But are they? Let's observe their respective behavior more critically.

1. Number 19 goes from one little group of players to the next, chatting, laughing, and shoving. He plays football hardly at all and pays little attention to the coach. The coach often repeats instructions to him. Number 19 prefers talking and joking with the other players to running plays.

2. Number 11, on the other hand, stands apart from all of the other players. Unlike number 19, he absorbs every word the coach says. After each play, he returns to the coach's side. He is highly respectful of the coach's opinions. He often asks the coach for advice or suggestions.

3. Number 49 likes to tackle and run hard. On a long touchdown play he pursues the runner many yards after the others have quit chasing

him. If he misses a tackle, he becomes mad at himself, stamps his foot on the ground, and shakes his head sideways.

4. Before every play, number 78 glances toward the sideline where the cheerleaders (mostly female) are practicing. He plays his best to impress them. Whenever he is involved in a play, he returns via the side of the field where the cheerleaders are. Once, he stopped to ask one of the girls if she had seen the pass he had just caught.

Are these boys interested in football? Well, they are putting forth much energy and time to be on the football field. However, perhaps football is only the vehicle through which they satisfy underlying needs.

Let's pursue this thought. First, differentiate between behavior that is observable in the descriptions given above from behavior that is inferred (unobservable). Cross out all of the behavior that is inferred for each of the players. After you finish, check Box A to see if you agree with the list of observable behaviors given there. If your answer agrees with that in Box A, you have already achieved an important part of objective 1 of Method I, pinpointing observable behavior; please continue. If you disagree with Box A, discuss your differences with another student.

Box A Feedback

1. Number 19 goes from one little group of players to the next, chatting, laughing, and shoving. ~~He plays football hardly at all and pays little attention to the coach.~~ The coach often repeats instructions to him. ~~Number 19 prefers talking and joking with the other players to running plays.~~

2. Number 11, on the other hand, stands apart from all of the other players. ~~Unlike number 19, he absorbs every word the coach says.~~ After each play, he returns to the coach's side. ~~He is highly respectful of the coach's opinions.~~ He often asks the coach for advice or suggestions.

3. Number 49 ~~likes to tackle and run hard.~~ On a long touchdown play he pursues the runner many yards after the others have quit chasing him. If he misses a tackle, he ~~becomes mad at himself,~~ stamps his foot on the ground, and shakes his head sideways.

4. Before every play, number 78 glances toward the sideline where the cheerleaders (mostly female) are practicing. ~~He plays his best to impress them.~~ Whenever he is involved in a play, he retruns via the side of the field where the cheerleaders are. Once, he stopped to ask one of the girls if she had seen the pass he had just caught.

Note: We can observe number 19 chatting, laughing, and shoving. We can only infer that he prefers this activity, but it is a fair guess, one that we will utilize, keeping in mind that we are guessing. You may feel that the second sentence in our account of number 19 describes observable behavior. Our decision is marginal, but we decided that we cannot observe a person "not do something." We can only observe him do something else.

Our next task is to learn to use these observable behaviors to infer the underlying source of enjoyment (that is, the psychological needs of each of the players). Box B will help us identify these needs.

Box B

The following list is an arbitrary selection from a group of twenty needs originally identified by Murray (1938). Physiological needs are omitted.

Inferred needs	Typical observable behavior indicators
Achievement (competence)	Seeks and reacts positively to competitive situations. Responds positively to suggestions and criticisms relative to tasks. Takes on challenging and difficult tasks, but only if possible to score (ideal is 50-50 chance). Puts forth much effort. Sets high goals.
Activity (play)	Excessive energy: runs, jumps, skips. Manipulates objects: takes things apart only to rebuild them. Playful: gay, laughing, joking.
Affiliation (acceptance or belonging)	Draws near and stays with others. Demonstrates good will, cooperativeness, and love. Readily greets, joins, touches others. Readily gives information, exchanges stories and sentiments.
Autonomy (independence)	Defies authority, convention, rules, and definite routines. Shuns direction and guidance. Demands free speech and other freedoms. Avoids responsibility. Works for long periods alone.
Deference (antithesis of dominance)	Conforms to wishes of those in superior positions. Moves toward, watches, listens, and applauds superiors. Eulogizes, acclaims others, expresses gratitude to them. Asks advice and direction from superiors.
Dominance (power)	Argues own viewpoint with zest. Organizes, guides, regulates, dictates, judges, attacks, and punishes others. Controls others by suggestion, seduction, persuasion, or command.
Exhibition	Talks a good deal: tall stories, anecdotes, and jokes. Wears unusual clothes, clowns, uses dramatic poses, expressive gestures, and overemphatic speech.
Nurture	Offers aid, comfort, and affection to the young, the distressed, and the sorrowing.

Inferred needs	Typical observable behavior indicators
	Indignant when weak or young are mal-treated.
Sexuality	Works and plays with one other, excludes third parties. May spend an inordinate amount of time in fantasy. Flirts, holds hands, embraces others, moves toward body contact.
Understanding	Asks and answers questions, reads, inspects, and explores. Speculates, formulates, analyzes, generalizes. Emphasizes logic, reason, preciseness. Debates with others.

With the observable behaviors in mind, let's see if you can use the information in Box B to infer the underlying source of enjoyment (need satisfaction) for each of the football players.[1]

Player 19:

Player 11:

Player 49:

Player 78:

If you agree that player 19 is striving to satisfy affiliation needs, player 11 has needs to defer to authority, player 49 has high achievement needs, and player 78 achieves satisfaction from exhibitionism, then we have something going here. We have pinpointed behavior and used it to *tentatively* identify underlying individual needs. Remember that these needs belong to the individual and that they may be motivators not only on the football field but in the classroom as well. Identify activities other than athletics that you think might attract each of these boys, assuming that our inferences above are correct. That is, how could a teacher use the information we now have to make coursework attractive to (that is, to induce approach behavior from) each of the boys?

---

[1] It is probably true that the needs of most individuals function in combinations. That is, a given behavior is an attempt to satisfy two or three needs simultaneously. For the sake of our learning, however, try to select a single predominant need.

| | *Needs* | *Possible Attractive* *Classroom Activities* |

Player 19:

Player 11:

Player 49:

Player 78:

Ostensibly, then, these activities represent goals that are attractive to the respective individuals. Knowing this, we could use such activities to encourage these pupils to become involved in learning. For example, the exhibitionist might work very hard to develop something that he knows he can show off. He will find satisfaction in the activity, and the teacher will have involved him in learning.

Let us now look at some comments made by a group of fifth graders to see if we can infer the underlying individual needs from what they said. Refer back to Box B, and then write the respective pupil needs in the blank spaces.

The following are responses made by a group of fifth graders who were asked this question: What do you think of school?

1. _____ "There is too much work and I do not like all of the teachers in the school, and school lasts too long, and the noon hour is not long enough, and you can't do nothing because there is nothing to do it with."

2. _____ "I like school because I don't like to sit around home all day. I like to be with my friends. I don't care about the work at all but I don't mind it. I would rather do the work than sit around home all day with nothing to do and no one to talk to."

3. _____ "I like school sometimes, but there are other things I like more than school. I like school when the teachers are not crabby and mean, and I like teachers to help me out on things if I am stuck on a problem or other thing. Some of the books don't tell about certain things you want to know about."

4. _____ "School is the best part of your life, and, too, when I grow up I will be able to say I had an education. I enjoy some of my subjects and some I don't. It will help me when I get older and want to get a job. Going to school is much more fun than going to the show or staying at home. I am very glad to have a school like Dillon to go to."

5._____"The work is too hard! When we have parties they are like baby parties. Some of the teachers give us too much work to do (especially one). We do not have enough recreation. Oh, I know a recreation hall is being built but that doesn't do us much good now —does it?

(I ABSOLUTELY DO NOT LIKE IT!)

PS. You should have another bus too because it is too crowded and most of our lunches get squashed before we get to school."

6._____"Hell no—and I'll tell you why. For one thing the teachers—ther nuts because when you are working and talking of course you will be sitting there so fine and then all of a sudden—Wack wright in the goddam face—but if we had a rackreashen hall we would be much happier then we are. So have time for basketball, football, and all diffierent things like that. Thast why I don't like this goddam school, damit!"

While doing this exercise, one student noted, "Hey, some of these don't fit." Remember, we did not include all of the motives, and everything that people say or do is not an obvious expression of a need. For your information, the needs identified by other readers for the respective pupils are as follows: (1) (?), (2) affiliation, (3) understanding, (4) deference, (5) autonomy, and (6) autonomy/activity. Of course, these were not unanimous selections. In item 6, one reader recommended "an understanding teacher."

Sometimes we can supplement our observations of natural events to identify a person's needs by such activities as the following.

Just for fun, let's see how imaginative you can be. Write an eight-line story, the title of which is:

A Boy and a Violin

When you have finished, turn to Box C.

In order to obtain a different perspective we asked Todd, a ten-year-old who obviously loved sports, why he enjoyed them so much. We had to probe behind his initial general responses, "Because it is fun" and "I just like to do it." Soon we had these explanations:

1. "Other guys play."
2. "It's fun when the score is close, it's exciting."
3. "It feels good when you are winning or when you hit the ball."
4. "It's fun when you play with guys who are good."
5. "You are doing action."

Is it reasonable to say that sports are fun for Todd because they offer an opportunity to satisfy these needs of his: affiliation (1 and 4), achievement (2 and 3), and activity (5)?

Box C

"A Boy and a Violin" is a type of projective test useful for determining a person's needs. Analyze your story with respect to the needs listed in Box B and to what the boy did, felt, or said. Did your boy achieve greatness, yearn to be with friends, or illustrate some need other than achievement and affiliation? Whatever you had him do, it is a *suggestion* of your needs. Of course, we would want more than one example before drawing conclusions. This is a simple method that you could use to induce behavior that would in turn help you identify the underlying motives of your pupils.

With these needs in mind, list some academically-oriented activities that Todd might find enjoyable.

	Need	*Academic Activities*
A	Affiliation	
B	Achievement	
C	Activity	

Discuss your list with another student. If you identified some activities that would attract Todd, you have just suggested some means for turning Todd on to school. Todd's teachers have been less successful despite threats of low grades, promises of future glory, or punishment for misbehavior. Todd hates school.

Take a few minutes and reflect on some activity that offers you much enjoyment and satisfaction. Or, if you prefer, interview someone who was deeply involved in the school paper, athletics, cheerleading, or church and club activities, etc., while in high school.

What made these activities attractive?

1.

2.

3.

Needs being fulfilled

1.

2.

3.

Suggested comparable academic activities that could be attractive

1.

2.

3.

What conclusions can we now state?

1. Some activities are attractive to us; we approach them. Other activities leave us cold, and we tend to exhibit avoidance behavior. In either case the behavior is observable and its qualities are discernible.
2. If we observe an individual, we are able to pinpoint certain aspects of his behavior as approach or avoidance.
3. We can use this pinpointed behavior to *tentatively infer* underlying needs.
4. We can use this information to organize the learning activities so that they will be satisfying and enjoyable.

It appears that we have already achieved our objectives, as listed on page 46. Hallelujah!!! Before we try a test case, however, let's look at two more situations.

The teacher passed back a test in which Johnny received a high grade—

unusual for him. In returning Johnny's paper, the teacher called attention to the grade. Johnny had no expressive reaction on his face and simply put the paper aside and continued his ongoing activity. This would suggest to the teacher that Johnny was not motivated by achievement. At another time, however, it was noted that Johnny was ecstatic when his team project was awarded a blue ribbon at the science fair. The hypothesis regarding Johnny had to be revised. He is rewarded by achievement, in group activities. The goal of individual achievement through high grades seemed not to reward his need for achievement, whereas the group achievement did. Johnny apparently has a high need for achievement that is stimulated by group—not individual—challenges. The teacher, of course, will need to test this hypothesis further, but we have here a good clue as to how to motivate Johnny.

Johnny's behavior raises two issues. First, Johnny, like Todd, has more than one need, and the desired activity will be more attractive if it satisfies these needs in tandem. Second, a given activity may seem attractive because it has elements that appear compatible with an inferred need. In fact, however, it may be repulsive because it is antagonistic to another, more powerful need. Todd and Johnny seemingly have high needs for achievement, and we might therefore suspect that competition for grades would be attractive to them. However, in striving for good grades, if only a few are available in class, pupils risk friendships and thereby threaten their need for affiliation since they are by necessity earning good grades at the expense of their friends. Some teachers acknowledge this conflict and sponsor team competition rather than individual competition. More on this in Method II, in the section entitled "Power to the Pupils."

A more subtle expression of needs:

Kevin is a quiet, clean, unobtrusive-appearing boy. He never volunteers, and he seems to approach any situation only halfheartedly. In most classes there are three or four youngsters like Kevin, who are so anonymous that a year or two later many of their classmates can't recall their names.

No one selected Kevin on a sociogram in which pupils chose two others in the class to be their partners for (1) planning a party, and (2) developing a project. He chose three other pupils, however, including Bill Jones for both (1) and (2). Bill is the most popular boy in class. During recess Kevin mostly watches the other children play. Before class he sits quietly in his seat seemingly watching closely the activities of various small cliques of pupils. He smiles faintly when something funny happens within these groups. Kevin's test results suggest that he is slightly above average intellectually, but his academic achievement is low. He is awkward and timid when playing games, though he appears healthy and there is no record of his being physically impaired.

What are Kevin's needs?
What kinds of tasks and situations would offer Kevin satisfaction and involvement in learning activities?

Did you say that Kevin had an *affiliation* need? If so, we agree. However, we can't say this on the basis of his doing things with others; rather, it must be inferred from more subtle, almost hidden behaviors. In fact, people sometimes act contrary to their needs. They may want very badly to participate, but if asked they refuse almost violently. We don't want to make too much of such apparent incompatible behaviors, but we ought to remind ourselves that things are not always the way they appear. We must be very tentative when making inferences about a pupil's needs, and we must continually check and recheck the inferences we do make.

Kevin's case is important to consider for a second reason. Kevin appears to be in conflict. His affiliation need causes approach behavior at the same time an apparent *fear of failure* causes avoidance behavior. Fear of failure might be thought of as a negative motive in that it immobilizes and dissipates what would otherwise be needs available for involving pupils. Thus, it is among the inhibiting forces shown in the potato in Figure 2-1.

Earlier, we noted that avoidance behavior is common, and we listed certain activities that were repugnant to us. Some avoidance behavior is due to boredom, or lack of stimulation, but some is due to fear of failure. We have discussed the process of grafting an existing motive onto activities so that pupils will become involved, thereby making potentially boring situations sources of satisfaction. In Method II we will develop several alternative ways to stimulate involvement. Fear of failure is considered in particular in the section, "Eliminate the Negative."

If what we have learned thus far is of any value, it ought to enable us now to set up some learning activities that our pupils will enjoy for their own sake. Let's try two experiments.

Experiment I. Engage some of your pupils in conversation, either individually or in small groups, and ask them to identify what they like to do in or out of school—any place, with any one. Accept whatever they say, but probe them for why they like to approach certain activities. You might facilitate your inquiry by encouraging them to fantasize a bit—for example, "If we had no regulations in school and you could do anything you wish, what would you do?" Remember, the activity isn't as important as the underlying need. The need is the key to knowing what makes the activity attractive.

Are you able to identify for each one, two, or three needs as described in Box B on page 50? Use as clues the nature of the activities they mention, their expressed fears, what they do, their goals, and what they related as having happened to them. Record as step 1 in Box D the names of the pupils, their respective preferred activities, and their inferred needs.

After you have completed step 1, list as step 2 an activity for each pupil that utilizes the identified need and that allows you the opportunity to focus on some academic learning. Perhaps something that heretofore hasn't been too stimulating will be a good test. Note that the activity will probably not be the same as that mentioned by the pupils. Pajama parties, making dinner with Mommy, or cruising around town in a convertible are not easily arranged in reading or English. Think of an activity compatible with your subject and with the real limitations of your school, but one that might satisfy the needs identified in step 1.

Finally, try the respective activities with pupils 1, 2, and 3. Note the consequences. What did you see, feel, and hear? Ask the pupils how they liked the activity. Record the pupil reaction as step 3 in box D.

Experiment II.   Select three different pupils and repeat steps 1, 2, and 3, but this time us your observation skills. Be aware of your pupils in their free time. What are they chatting about, or planning for after school or for the upcoming weekend? What do they find repugnant or attractive in other classes? What do they do when they are not directed to do something? List your findings and creations for pupils 4, 5, and 6 under the heading "Experiment II" in Box D.

Let's take a mashed potato sandwich break before going on to Method II, where we will consider various methods for arousing latent pupil motivation in the entire class.

METHOD II

A Spontaneous Happening

It was 8:29 A.M., and in one minute the school bell would ring, announcing that the school was to begin. More than that, the bell signals the moment after which any arrivals to the classroom are to be marked tardy, a mark that is noted in a record to be sent home at report card time, a mark put on one's permanent record to be noted by every teacher having that pupil in the future, a mark to be noted by the high school administrator when making recommendations for college, establishing employment interviews after the pupil completes high school, or perhaps encouraging him not to complete high school.

Mrs. Jones, a mother who was on safety patrol, knew the importance

Box D: Recording Space for Experiments I and II

Pupil's Name	Step 1 Preferred Activities	Inferred Needs	Step 2 Learning Activity	Step 3 Pupil Reaction
Experiment I.				
1.				
2.				
3.				
Experiment II.				
4.				
5.				
6.				

of that mark, and as she saw Toby Smith, a third grader, ambling to school a hundred feet from the corner she shouted a warning and waved Toby to hurry. Toby had been told of the importance of the mark and ordinarily would have sprinted to make the bell.

Today, however, Toby stumbled into something. It was a sunny October morning, and there along the walk were huge piles of fallen leaves. Toby heard the warning shouts, but gleefully jumped into the leaves and became engrossed in the sensation of walking waist deep in leaves. The mark on the record and the satisfaction of obeying Mrs. Jones were happily traded for a few minutes of the sensation of plowing through the mountains of leaves.

Toby has the same needs to be deferent—to obey adults and do the right thing, as others do—but also, there was a need for unique experiences, a curiosity to feel uncommon sensations, which from 8:29 to 8:46 this day were very strong.

What to do with the Tobys? The schools are full of them—youngsters doing all sorts of things just for the sensation of it, ignoring the demands of the teachers to become involved in the daily learning activities. We teachers wail, "Most of the pupils aren't interested in learning; look at them—they do everything but study."

Can we learn from Toby's behavior? Is it fair to say that tumbling through the leaves is an indicator of stubbornness, laziness, and indifference, or in Toby's case was it a spontaneous, unplanned, positive reaction to stimuli? The resistance of the leaves triggered in Toby an almost overwhelming desire to experience more—to feel the softness, the resistance, the response of the leaves as they are kicked and thrown into the air. Ordinarily, Toby would have pushed on to be in school by 8:30, but the sight of the leaves aroused a desire to experiment, to experience. We could have expected that Toby would soon tire of bouncing through the leaves. Within an hour it would have become boring, and Toby would have sought other activities. Also, it is not difficult for any of us to understand Toby's behavior because each of us experiences the same elation from time to time in various activities. It is as if within each of us, waiting to be ignited, are certain latent common needs to experience.

Unlike the situations in Method I, where we found that needs exist uniquely within individuals, we are sensing here that the stimulation resides within the activity. Most of us enjoy eating an ice cream cone, hearing a well-told story, or romping in the snow for the sheer joy of it. We need not be hungry, competing for a grade, or with someone. We may not yearn for it as we do friendship, but given the stimulation we respond vigorously.

Let's see if we can dig up some clues as to what that stimulation is. Search out your own experience and describe below three conditions or situations that seem to arouse and involve people regardless of their individual needs. I'll take a look at the educational psychology literature and note what I find on the following pages. You put yours here. Don't look ahead to mine until you have noted at least three. We'll compare notes along the way.

Would you believe the educational psychology literature offers several interesting notions? I will share them, one at a time. These are discrete ideas, not unrelated, but for our purposes we ought to consider each of them independently. From each we should be able to develop a variety of tactics for getting and keeping pupils on task.

Will the Real Teacher Please Stand Up

In *The Process of Schooling* (1970), J. M. Stephens describes a set of urges, or "spontaneous tendencies," that he feels are common to most people. The first cluster includes the playful manipulative tendencies that lead many of us to deliberately expend time and energy on activities that have little immediate payoff or acclaim from others. The second group, the spontaneous communicative tendencies, include the following: to tell what we know, to applaud and commend some performances while disapproving and correcting others, to supply an answer that eludes someone else, and to moralize about others' behavior. Stephens concludes:

These forces, let loose within the existing school, would, in and of themselves, induce a substantial measure of educational attainment even in the absence of rational, deliberate decisions, in the absence, indeed, of any intent to teach. (1970, p. 58)

Is Stephens correct?

Well, many people certainly develop and put forth much energy in hobbies that do not seem to have any external payoff. As examples of the manipulative tendencies, people collect everything from autographs to valentines, draw, doodle, sculpt, bird-watch, and build sand castles on the beach.

In terms of the communicative tendencies, some human beings do a lot of talking. It is difficult to keep from telling a juicy secret, congratulating someone who has just done well on a difficult task, or chastizing another for a goof. If you have ever stood behind someone playing bridge, solving a puzzle, or playing solitaire, you can sympathize with the kibitzer.

So Stephens has a point. How does this relate to motivating kids to learn? Curiously, he uses this phenomenon to explain why *we* teach school the way we do: the teachers' and society's spontaneous tendencies perpetuate teacher-dominated schooling. Let's throw in a couple of observations. If Stephens is right, then what he says ought to be equally true for many if not most of our pupils. That is, everyone in school is a potential teacher in terms of the spontaneous tendency to communicate. Second, teaching is a great learning experience for the simple reason that when we teach, we are attentive, active, and searching for explanations and relationships. Most teachers find that they learned more subject matter in their first semester or two of teaching than they did in the many college courses they took. "But," some of you doubting Thomases are thinking, "How can pupils who don't know teach pupils who don't know?" Good question, but it is an empirical question, and, fortunately, the results of several studies of peer teaching show that under such circumstances both pupil-learner (tutee) and pupil-teacher (tutor) improve achievement. For instance, in situations in which poor readers are given the task of helping other poor readers learn to read, we find that everyone improves in reading ability.

Conclusion: By arranging peer teaching, we can capitalize on the spontaneous schooling tendency to motivate pupils to learn—really learn. Furthermore, pupils will receive the individual attention that is so important, and other pupils will not be ignored in the process.

Let's take a moment to reflect on the topics or skills from your own subject matter that pupils could peer-teach. In the following space identify some topics and the pupils who you feel could work together as tutor and tutee. Schedule a time period for them to work together. You will need to experiment a bit to find the right combinations. For those of you who are not currently teaching, try a match-up with some of your fellow students. Give it a try—start today.

Topic or skill	Pupils involved		Time
	Tutor	Tutee	

How can we enlarge our tutor-tutee population if a knowledge base
is necessary? A careful selection of topics to fit particular pupils' knowledge is one way; getting the pupils to develop a special expertise in order
to become a pupil tutor is another. How? Peek ahead to the next section.

Don't Fight Them; Deal with Them

Intrinsic motivation should be the goal of teachers, since it results in students
themselves wishing to learn in order to achieve objectives. . . . Marks,
prizes, degrees and the like are motives outside of the individual and only of
transient interest. When teachers rely on these (as we all must do!) they
should attempt to have students transfer this external temporary drive to an
internal, lasting motive. (Travers, 1970, p. 210)

This quotation exemplifies the message from the advocates of intrinsic
motivation. The ideal is beautiful, but most often the advocates tell us what
we ought to do, not how to do it. The other sections of this chapter focus
attention on arranging conditions so that the learning activities are themselves made attractive. In contrast, we are going to consider now a method
of arranging conditions so that pupils are encouraged to work at certain
activities (what we want them to do) as the means to achieve other conditions (what they want).

We often find ourselves at odds with our pupils. We are frustrated
because they are disruptive, passive, or distracted. But most of their behavior isn't really bad, or even unreasonable; it is simply incompatible with
the learning activities. Lloyd Homme offers a simple, reasonable, positive,
and, most important, successful plan for achieving the idealized intent of

intrinsic motivation: "Arrange the conditions so that the child gets to do something he wants to do following something you want him to do" (1970, p. vii).

Recall the potato in Figure 2-1. Condition A represents a task or activity that seems necessary if the pupils are to achieve the objectives. They begin off task, condition C, and for any of a variety of reasons are repelled by the task. You may recall that B represents the posttask condition. Contingency contracting is a process whereby the teacher agrees to pay those pupils who have successfully gotten on task and achieved the objective, by allowing them to do something they like to do. Like any other contract, contingency contracting is an open arrangement—no small point. A pupil agrees to master desired prescribed objectives in exchange for some explicit desired activity, reward, or opportunity that he values.

Before we begin, we ought to note that contracting isn't just a clever way to get pupils to do a nasty task.

1. It is consistent with the real world in which most adults function.
2. It communicates to pupils that performing pays off and that *they* control whether or not they will be paid.
3. It leads to independence; pupils learn to design their own contingency contracts.
4. Classrooms become productive, happy places where the emphasis is on the positive.
5. Communication becomes explicit through the agreements, thus reducing misunderstandings and confusion about assignments.
6. It facilitates individualization because pupils can be working simultaneously on their respective contracts.
7. It is not an all-or-none tactic. The procedures offer flexibility: any part of your teaching-learning process can be uniquely contingency-contracted while other activities are motivated by other means.

Homme (1970) offers us an excellent prescription for contingency contracting. The following procedures are adaptations of his recommendations.

1. Begin by discussing contracts with pupils, the reasons for them, and the pupil's rights therein. Pupils of any age can understand a contract. The purpose is not bargaining, but acknowledging that it is more comfortable to work at explicit, well-defined tasks that offer closure and a sense of accomplishment with specific reinforcement.

2. Describe as explicitly as possible the task to be performed. Remember, the procedure will be new to many of your pupils. (See Chapter 3

for suggestions regarding the specification of objectives in performance terms.) At first, short, easily managed tasks are desirable and, especially in the beginning, a number of small contracts is preferred. Better to say; "If you do four mathematics problems you can play dominoes for three minutes" than to say, "If you work all week we will have a party Friday afternoon." Tasks must be something the pupil can perform. Remember, in the beginning the pupil is learning primarily that if he works and performs, he receives a payoff.

3. Identify the payoff. It must be something desired by your pupils. The payoff should take up a small amount of time, three to ten minutes. It should be something that can be administered easily and quickly. Delayed, extended payoffs are sometimes valued by pupils, but they lose their power as reinforcers. At the very least, use tokens, which may be accumulated for a large payoff. Just as it helps to specify objectives in planning a unit, it is wise to identify possible payoffs in advance. Payoffs may be entertainment, freedom, or an academic activity that pupils value more than the required work. We should not ignore, for example, the fact that, on the average, adolescent girls spend 35 percent of their free time reading. Other possible payoffs include puzzles, mathematics games, quiet time, and opportunities to write and present plays to the class, to put on a demonstration, or to miss a test. We have a start. With the help of your pupils, list ten events that would be attractive payoffs.

1.

2.

3.

4.

5.

6.

7.

8.

9.

10.

One more point: place may be as important as activity in determining the payoff. If possible, designate a place in your room for payoff, and don't use this space for any other activity.

4. Set the terms of the contract. Note the differences between these two contracts:

    a. Do your work, and then we will have some fun.

    b. Conjugate the four verbs on page 123, and then you can work on your pun puzzles for ten minutes.

Contract *b* is superior because it tells what and how much performance is expected of the pupil and what and how much the pupil can expect as a payoff.

Consider these three contracts:

    c. Every pupil who writes a twelve-page paper comparing the styles of Robert Frost and Ezra Pound on three criteria will be able to meet the football coach in person.

    d. Every pupil who demonstrates mastery of the subject matter by passing the final examination with a score of 80 or better will receive a free ticket to the spring rock concert.

    e. Every pupil who spells all ten words on this list correctly in Friday's class will receive one dollar from me.

Note that both sides of the agreement must be of relatively equal weight. Contract *c* seems to be heavy on the requirement side whereas *e* is exorbitant in payoff, at least for my pocketbook. To be worthy, a contract must be consistent from one task to the next and from one pupil to the next. It follows that if two pupils are working on the same objective, the payoffs ought to be equivalent. Is that the case in your class now? Reflect on this question because in most classrooms we pay off differentially, in small but explicit ways.

The contract must be positive. Example *f* is *not* a contract.

    f. If you don't stop talking to your neighbors and complete the arithmetic assignment, I'm going to move your seat.

However, *g* is:

    g. When you answer the questions after Chapter 9, you may go to the payoff center and chat with your friends for seven minutes.

Note that in *g* the payoff offered a pleasure.

The payoff comes after performance. There is no payoff in either of the following:

  h. I'll let you chat for a few more minutes, and then we will do the last page of the assignment.
  i. We just have forty-five minutes to complete the experiment, better get going.

Reward performance, not obedience. Which of the following demands are better?

  j. If your papers meet the criteria on the board, then . . .
  k. If you sit still and don't talk to your neighbor, . . .
  l. If you are good boys and girls, you may . . .
  m. If your papers are neat and have no misspelled words, then . . .

Example *j* is clear and performance-oriented, but *l* is clearly a mandate for obedience. The other two are a bit more fuzzy: *m* qualifies as performance, and *k* would be obedience except for the rare occasion when sitting still and attending to the teacher are the prime objective. We need to heed Homme's warning: "Reward for accomplishment leads to independence. Reward for obedience leads only to continued dependence on the person to whom the child learns to be obedient." (1970, p. 19)

The payoff should be immediate, here and now. Note the difference between *n* and *o*.

  n. If you identify four ways to differentiate the materials on the table, you can specify the activity for some Friday afternoon.
  o. If you can show how these rocks can be made into homogeneous piles in three different ways, then you can challenge me to an arm wrestle.

Yes, there are several differences, but the point is that *o* pays off immediately rather than at some unspecified time in the future.

From what we have said thus far, it is apparent that you may have several contracts in effect simultaneously. Different pupils may have different contracts. You may have a contract with one pupil, a group, or the whole class.

5. Monitor the contract to make certain that performance has occurred and that the payoff follows immediately. Don't compromise by giving partial payoffs for jobs half done. If you are tempted to do this, your task was inappropriate—either too difficult or too long. In establishing the contract and monitoring it make sure that the payoff condition is not obtainable

outside of the conditions of the contract. It is important that all parties feel that no one is welching on the specified terms.

Homme emphasizes that the goal of contingency contracting is independence: to encourage each pupil to set up and administer his own contract. He presents a five-stage paradigm in which we can encourage pupils to move from dependence to independence. In stage 1 the teacher has full control of the contract's two conditions: pupil task to be performed and payoff. In each of the next three stages, responsibility for stating the respective conditions is shared and gradually taken over by the pupil. In the final stage, the pupil himself establishes the conditions of the contract, whereby he rewards himself for performing rather than procrastinating. See Box E for details.

The task for you remains to determine contracts for several objectives for several or all of your pupils. It is now just a matter of writing the con-

Box E: Stages Toward Self-Contracting

Stage 1	Stage 2	Stage 2b
Teacher identified contingencies, which pupil accepts	Teacher identifies task Joint control of payoff	Jointly establish task Teacher identifies pay
T : I propose if you . . . then you can . . .	T : If you . . .	We agree; the task is . . .
P : OK, I accept, I will . . then I can . . .	We agree the payoff will be . . .	T : Then you can . . .

Stage 3a	Stage 3b	Stage 3c
Jointly determine task Jointly select payoff	Jointly determine task Pupil selects payoff	Pupil determines task Jointly identify payoff
We agree for . . .	We agree . . .	P : I will . . .
We agree the payoff will be . . .	Then I can . . .	We agree the payoff will be . . .

Stage 4a	Stage 4b	Stage 5
Pupil proposes task Jointly agree on payoff	Jointly determine task Pupil establishes payoff	Pupil establishes own contingencies
P : I will . . .	We agree if . . .	P : First I will . . .
For which we agree . . .	T : Then I will	P : Then I will . . .

tract, since from Chapter 3 you will be able to specify the performance desired and in Method I we identified some of the payoffs that you feel will be valued by your pupils. Write several contracts below, and share them with colleagues or others in your class. After that, give it a go with your pupils.

Power to the Pupils

James Coleman (1961) reports a condition that is not very surprising. Boys are more interested in athletic prowess than academic achievement, and girls are more interested in being datable and being in the right social clique than in being academic achievers. It would be easy to shrug this off with the explanation that professional athletes are paid six-figure salaries and glamour girls receive all the acclaim. It is obvious from our salaries that society values athletics and show business more than knowledge. This is probably an erroneous explanation for pupil preferences. More important, it does not solve our motivational problems.

Coleman urges us to consider ways to capitalize, not cop out, on his findings. He reminds us that the adolescent society has power:

Peers can offer as rewards popularity, respect, praise, acceptance by the crowd, awe, support, and aid.

Peers can punish through isolation, ridicule, exclusion from the crowd, disdain, discouragement, and disrespect.

Competition in the classroom is most often between the pupil and the teacher: pupils strive to obtain good grades with minimal effort, while the teacher tries to maximize the effort required for such grades.

Athletes represent the school or some group, and the victories are thereby shared, whereas classroom scholarship is for self and probably at the expense of others.

Teachers often demand attention, obedience, quiet, and studiousness, which encourages irresponsibility, since pupils have no authority to make decisions or take action on their own.

In a given class, the same exercises are often prescribed for everyone. Little opportunity is offered for individual preference or specialization within the system.

The teacher's role as judge of the winners overshadows the teacher's roles as resource, helper, and supporter.

The subjectivity and dependence on the teacher's judgment of success breeds conformity, alienation, and subservience.

Classroom learning tends to have a floor (arbitrary minimal levels of achievement for survival) and a ceiling (do only what is required).

We stand challenged. Many of the just-noted conditions can be changed by us. Some of them can be turned around and utilized to our advantage rather than in opposition to us. However, we need to be imaginative and to share our ideas if we are to succeed.

Name three innovations you could inaugurate in your classroom to take advantage of the adolescent society.

1.

2.

3.

Here are some suggestions for comparison.

1. Competition need not be interpersonal; it can be intergroup.
2. Pupils want recognition, so let's publicize their achievements and tasks

with letters to parents, articles in the paper, letters to the editor, and such pupil initiated promotional schemes as displays and fairs.

3. Use as goals of learning the ability to overcome natural obstacles or solve problems, rather than the earning of good grades. The daily newspaper, popular magazines, TV news, all describe conditions, situations, or dilemmas that can be used in focusing on various areas of subject matter.

4. Set up games in which objective scores, not the teacher's judgments of what is right, decide the winners. Have preestablished criteria or use tasks which have firm rules.

5. Differentiate learning from testing. You be the teacher—resource, aid, and supporter—and let someone or something else declare winners. Athletes and their coaches are on the same team, which may explain why they most often have good relationships.

Let's look at an innovation that worked.

An insightful first-year teacher, Laura Rasmussen, was given the task of teaching Greek mythology to a class of ninth graders. She was told by a fellow teacher that the selected textbook was a good one because it had thirty-six chapters, each with specific study guides that could be assigned as homework. Furthermore, the teacher's guide included a very good set of questions that could be used for testing. In other words, the publishers had furnished all that was needed for sound, straightforward teaching.

Recalling her own ninth-grade "straightforward" study of Greek mythology, Laura realized that she had to find an alternative. What to do? First, she stacked the books on one side of the room so that they were available but unobtrusive. Since adolescents are very concerned with and interested in the human body, she obtained two films that paid particular attention to Greek-statue nudes. Finally, to accommodate the urges of the students to express their feelings in poetry, four-letter words, and drawings, she draped a strip of butcher paper around two walls of the classroom for graffiti. Laura showed the films and invited her pupils to draw any images that came to mind on the butcher paper. There were only two stipulations: whatever they wrote or drew had to be consistent with Greek mythology, and there were no territorial rights, so anyone could contribute to any part of the drawings. Among other activities, the pupils wrote and performed plays depicting the roles of the gods.

Even though Laura did not assign the text chapters or use the study guides, she administered an examination at the conclusion of the unit and found that the pupils had no difficulty passing it. By the end of the unit the class had created a beautiful mural depicting the power and relationships of various gods respectively to Greek history, ancient life style, and current beliefs. More important, the pupils spontaneously included Greek mythology in their jokes, conversations, and explanations of other aspects of literature.

As an organizer, a teacher often notes on the chalkboard the topic of the day. In Figure 2-5, is *A* or *B* more apt to attract and hold attention?

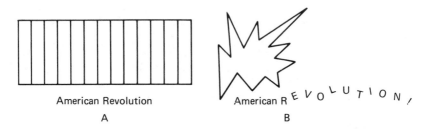

American Revolution
A

American REVOLUTION
B

Figure 2-5

The word "tantalize" is exciting. Do you ever use words like "tantalize," "exotic," "fantastic," or "ecstasy," to create occasionally a Times-Square-at-midnight atmosphere in class?

In producing a play—whether comedy or tragedy—legitimate theater, movies, and television all utilize controlled lighting, music, special settings, and so forth, to establish a mood. Where else but in English classes is one expected to grasp solely from the printed word the emotions underlying the content of poetry or other literature? Where else? In the social studies department, the science labs, and the mathematics rooms—that's where!

I know of an elementary school with a second-grade room. What a second-grade room! It is the only schoolroom that makes me wish I were a pupil again. It has three levels. It has an old easy chair, multi-colored carpet squares, which were picked up as remnants, spotlights, and a rheostat to dim the lights. Movable dividers are used to isolate various parts of the room. A wonderful warm place in which to know, to learn, to relate, to be. Impossible for you? Talk to your principal. Invest some effort in the room where you spend more of your time than in any other single place, except possibly your bedroom. Consider the fact that you and your pupils spend well over a thousand hours there each year. Visit the local merchants, including Goodwill, and you will find that they have a little of everything, including goodwill. We don't have to be interior decorators to know that schools are pretty drab places.

Let's jot down some ideas here to make classrooms more receptive. How about starting off with alternatives to the straight rows of chairs.

Your Ideas:

Grabems

Gaining and directing pupil attention are critical teacher responsibilities. What to do when pupils doze off, continue off-task chatter, reclean their desks for the third time that day, or read *MAD* magazine behind a stack of books? Not only is punishment offensive but it has little effect. Besides, such pupil behavior is not bad; in other circumstances than the classroom, it may be understandable and even desirable. Let's now consider several ways of counteracting boredom and indifference by means of grabems.

Grabem 1

Sex in school? We certainly see it in advertising, and there must be a reason why. The little ad shown below was placed in the personals column of the *Indianapolis Star*. Read the amazing and amusing results.

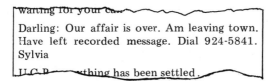

By noon of the first day, over 3,000 calls had been recorded on three telephone lines. Because the calls were jamming other lines—people dialed over and over and over again, hoping to catch a dial tone in between the busy signals—the phone company had to disconnect the telephones. One business firm complained to the phone company that they had received at least seventy-five wrong-number calls asking for Sylvia. The *Star* received hundreds of calls from people unable to get through but wanting to know about the ad. For its own protection the *Star* ran a feature story of explanation in its next issue.

Oh, you don't care about these amazing results from one ad, but you want to know what Sylvia said. If such is the case then you are on task, or at least ripe for a contingency contract. As it happens, the silly typesetter misplaced the message and it is buried somewhere in the next ten pages. Read on, and you too will know.

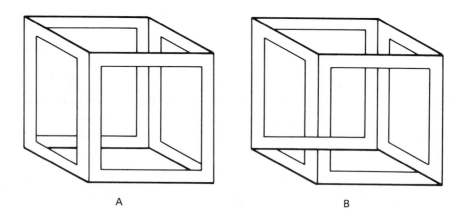

A   B

Figure 2-6

Grabem 2

In Figure 2–6, *A* and *B* have certain similarities but some differences. Briefly note your reaction to each.

Your response to A:

Your response to B:

Did you attend to A or B more closely in terms of details and time on task?

Can you suggest ways in which your reaction to the above figures or to the sex and Sylvia episode might help us get pupils on task?

Berlyne (1960) summarized a number of studies on arousing attention. He identified a number of variables that lead to arousal and more intense attention. Before considering some of Berlyne's variables, we ought to note that there is an optimum level of arousal for each. If too little of the particular variable exists, the result is boredom and loss of interest. On the other hand, if the variable is extreme, it causes panic and such tunneled attention that the observer is not able to profit from the experience. (See Figure 2–7.)

**Figure 2-7.   Hypothetical curve of the relation between produc-
tive attention and strength of arousal variable**

Attention is directed toward material when the material is characterized by one or more of the following:

1. *Incongruity*. This occurs when incompatibility exists between the stimuli and the knowledge or expectations of the observer. Cube B above is an example, as would be a two-headed calf. It is the case of the familiar made strange. The stimuli must be familiar enough to arouse expectations,

which serve as the basis of conflict with the strange elements of the stimuli.

2. *Novelty*. This is felt when one undergoes stimuli never before experienced. Animals placed in a strange environment, whether they are hungry, thirsty, sexually aroused, or satiated, will sniff about and explore the locale with some thoroughness before searching out the resources that will satisfy their biological need. At the very least, this suggests that we ought to change our routines, teaching strategies, and ways of introducing material and units.

3. *Irregularity*. Arrangements of heterogeneous materials, irregular shapes, and skewed pictures all attract more attention than does the symmetrical, well-organized, homogeneous presentation. This phenomenon could be called stimulus variation. We all know that an audience reacts differently to a dynamic speaker than to a lecturer who speaks in a monotone, grasps the lectern, and is as immobile as a mummy. To gain pupil attention, it would help to break up patterns of sound, light intensity, seating arrangements, and so forth. Surprise the class occasionally.

4. *Complexity*. More complex designs with more content and more details seem to be more attractive than simplified versions. The danger here is the potential of overwhelming the pupil. Nevertheless, in our intent to make material understandable, we perhaps oversimplify it to the point of boredom. Perhaps the optimum level of complexity is just beyond that with which the individual is familiar.

Let's take a few minutes to jot down for discussion some specific ways you could arouse and direct the attention of your pupils. Man abhors boredom—a nonstimulating environment.

Grabem 3

Anyone who has searched for a child's book within the last ten years has come across numerous books by Dr. Seuss: *Whoville Where the Whos Live, The Cat in the Hat,* and *The Grinch Who Stole Christmas* are examples. He is one of the most prolific and popular authors of children's books today. Why? His books are different and unreal, they are written in a peculiar script, and they contain ridiculous story lines. But, they are popular. Well! we say, that is for children. True, but since most older youngsters have turned off school, perhaps we ought to occasionally take a page from Dr. Seuss.

Relatively few teachers enjoy statistics. Here is a variation advocated by Howard Wainer (1972). Give it a try.

The Kandy Kolored Korrelation Koefficient

Up and up and down and down and around and through . . . they followed!!!! ALMOST. Almost? Yest almost!!!!!! As one went up the other followed, everywhere one went the other followed. As one led, the other was there also. ALMOST. But why? What held them together???? Why almost? How much is almost??????? The wise old statman leaned over chewing on his pencil and snickered, "They're Korrelated!"

KORRELATED?

KORRELATED!

WOW!!!

STANDBACK

LOOK

. . . . what else? "When one goes up the other pretty much follows. That's Korrelated."

HUH?

"Yeah, just a crossproduct summation normalized."

WHAT!

"It's easy."

Easy????

"Yeah . . . . Easy!"

Did he say EASY?

"Sure, easy. It's just the slope of the best fitting straight line between two normalized variables."

NO JOKE?

"That statman sure is weird . . . . he thinks I know what he's saying."

RAP ON STATMAN

Wainer doesn't advocate that whole texts, courses, or even days be this way, but he does challenge us to consider styles other than "See Dick, see Dick run" as an occasional alternative for presenting knowledge. Let's have some fun. Put on your creative hat and write a two-paragraph grabem 3 to introduce a story, topic, or assignment that will bring a smile to the face of your most reticent pupil and an echo of WOW! throughout the class. If the Wainer style is too far out, try writing a dialogue. After all, Socrates didn't do too badly with that style.

Share your creation with others in class or your colleagues. They will not only help you sharpen your grabem but will undoubtedly contribute to your collection.

Grabem 4

Examine the two card hands in Figure 2–8. Can you spot at least eleven differences?

Did you skip the task above without a try, without a second look? If yes, don't bother with the rest of this idea. If you did examine the cards— if you took the time and effort 'to differentiate one hand from the other— then perhaps we have a grabem. This. is not an idle game. The isolation and discrimination of details and properties are critical learning variables. Many children's reading problems stem from an inability to differentiate *b,* from *d, was* from *saw,* or the sounds of *dub* and *sub.* Likewise, kids disappoint us in physics, history, and English because they fail to differentiate the critical properties of concepts.

Let's set up some warm-up games tailored after the card game above to alert pupils to critical differences in the concepts of your respective subject. Is it worthwhile? You did take time to find those differences between the two hands, didn't you? Grabbing them is the first condition of

Figure 2-8.

teaching them! I'm still trying to find that eleventh difference. How did you make out?

Design one game, share it with three other individuals, and you might end up with five grabems that can be used at various times to warm up the class, ease a tense moment, or bring that kid who sulks in the back of the room an inch closer to the rest of the class.

Game Description

Read this sentence:

> FINISHED FILES ARE THE RE-
> SULT OF YEARS OF SCIENTIFIC
> STUDY COMBINED WITH THE EX-
> PERIENCE OF YEARS.

Now count aloud the Fs in that square. Count them only once; do not go back and count them again.

There are six Fs in the sentence. One of average intelligence finds three of them. If you spotted four, you're above average. If you got five, you can turn your nose up at almost anybody. If you found six, you're a genius. There is positively no catch.

Before going on, I owe you an answer. Remember Sylvia? Those 3,000 callers who were able to get through to 924-5841 heard a breathy-voiced young woman implore them not to give her up. Beseechingly, she recalled "those delicious, lazy mornings over coffee" and "the nights . . . when you could touch me whenever you felt the need." She concluded, "You know who this is, don't you? Why, silly boy. I thought you knew. I'm your cigarette. And remember, you *need,* me!" Upon which a man's voice warned, "Yes, you do need your cigarette. That is, if you want to risk cancer, heart disease, or emphysema. The Little Red Door, your United Fund cancer agency, urges you to break up this affair now, before it's too late!"

Was it a sleazy trick for the Little Red Door to use Sylvia this way? Perhaps so, but a lot of people heard the message, talked about it, laughed to and at themselves, and perhaps reflected about smoking, in a new light. Ouch! Isn't that what motivation is all about?

Holdem and Helpem

Men climb mountains, allegedly just because the mountain is there. Does the same hold true for seeking knowledge?

It is readily apparent that much of the behavior of young children is knowledge seeking. The number of legitimate questions that a three- or five-year-old asks would put a scientist to shame. "Why doesn't the sky fall down?" "What holds your skin on?" and "How do worms breathe?" are just samples of the seemingly unending series of whys, hows, and whats. Every mother has had the harrowing experience of hearing or seeing her two-year-old reestablish the law of gravity by sliding a vase, dish, or lamp off the table—repeatedly. The young child gains increasing mastery of his world by this process of active exploration: manipulating objects, creating change and noting consequence, and asking questions. This need to find out seems to disappear in what is sometimes called the fourth-grade slump— or does it?

Critics of education claim that we stupefy our pupils with boring, unstimulating chores. We have to admit that some schooling is drab, repetitive, unchallenging, and unimaginative. Even though this may occasionally be the case, alternative hypotheses are apparent:

1. The need to know is already superficially satisfied. By the age of ten, children have pretty well satisfied themselves with respect to the obvious concrete questions about their physical environment.
2. Inhibiting forces accumulate. Children may fear exploration because they have been punished repeatedly for inquiry, attempts to find out and know. Failure is devastating.
3. Competing needs become more dominant. For example, society places great pressure on children at about the age of ten to shape up socially. Motor skills are emphasized, girls are feminized, getting along with others is stressed, and so forth.

We have already learned, in Method I, how to capitalize on the competing-needs hypothesis (hypothesis 3). The inhibiting-forces hypothesis (hypothesis 2) is real and deserves further study. We will consider the means for dealing with that in the next section.

So, can we do anything with the satiation hypothesis (hypothesis 1)? I'm glad you asked. At worst, the need to know is latent—waiting to be aroused. We have much evidence that man abhors boredom and blandness and is a natural seeker. Any organism placed in a strange environment will explore. A monkey will work harder to see what is on the other side of a screen than he will for food—if what is on the other side of the screen keeps changing. The antidote to the first hypothesis as well as to our critics is to create strangeness within the familiar environment.

Berlyne (1965) has offered a five-stage model for designing a pattern for knowledge seeking.

Stage I. An *environmental paradox* of some sort is established. This is a creation by the teacher with a built-in incongruity. Some examples may help:

In a science class: Everyone knows that an unsupported object or fluid will fall toward the earth. Remember, we learned that as a toddler with mommy's best vase as a prop, with devastating results. It would therefore be a paradox if we were to fill a glass with water, lay a flexible screen or piece of paper over the top, tip it upside-down and have neither the cover nor the water fall out.

A paradox in history: If someone were to refer to Honest Abe, most of us would think of Abraham Lincoln. The teacher writes the following two statements on the board—both of which were made by Abraham Lincoln.

Statement A

Let us discard all this quibbling about this man and the other man, this race, and that race and the other race being inferior, and therefore they must be placed in an inferior position. Let us discard all these things, and unite as one people throughout this land, until we shall once more stand up declaring that all men are created equal.

Statement B

I will say, then, that I am not, nor ever have been, in favor of bringing about in any way the social and political equality of the white and black races: that I am not, nor ever have been, in favor of making voters or jurors of negroes, nor of qualifying them to hold office, nor to intermarry with white people. . . .

And inasmuch as they cannot so live, while they do remain together there must be the position of superior and inferior, and I as much as any other man am in favor of having the superior position assigned to the white race.

Stage II.   Reaction occurs within the pupil. It is called *conceptual conflict*. It follows an observed paradox naturally and surely.

"How come the water doesn't leak or spill out?"
"Was Abraham Lincoln dishonest, an opportunist who took advantage of limited communication and traded on audience bias?"

Stage III.   Knowledge-seeking behavior is aroused by the conceptual conflict. Pupils ask questions and gather information by setting up their own experiments and by reading and discussing alternative explanations.

Stage IV.   The *conflict is resolved* when one of the competing sides of the paradox "wins" by reason or evidence. Possibly a new, previously unconsidered alternative is advanced to explain the phenomenon, or the knowledge seeker sometimes finds that the paradox was not real, that more evidence reconciles the apparent incongruity. Given the total context, audience, and general circumstances totally consistent, honest men may make two different statements such as those attributed to Lincoln.

Stage V.   The *consequence* is new knowledge, increased intellectual potency, and confidence. Knowledge appropriated through search and discovery is different from that handed down from another person. It is the knowledge of fine differences, of more sharply defined useful concepts and principles. More important, the pupil learns that knowledge is something that he can generate, that problems are solvable, and that he has the ability to inquire, to experiment, and to find answers.

Berlyne (1965) has also reported an interesting twist from research conducted in Russia. The Russian researcher Marazova found that both interest and content mastery were optimal when a child hero with whom the pupil could identify was locked in a struggle or faced a dilemma. The pupil, along with the hero, actively searches for explanations and answers to resolve the issue. Most American school-age children read the comics— many of which are not funny. Comics are adventure serials, and, like the soap operas, they contain contrived dilemmas in which the heroes and heroines are repeatedly trapped in struggles. Marazova also found that Russian pupils prefer books that raise questions and stimulate efforts to think out answers from limited information.

Theresa T. Brown, a very enterprising student teacher, developed the following episode of "Arithmetic Man" for one of her pupils who had steadfastly resisted any involvement in mathematics. The pupil not only completed the program correctly, but the next day asked for work on additional capers. Ms. Brown has generously agreed to share this episode of The Adventure of Arithmetic Man with you.

85

87

PUT YOUR ANSWERS HERE, ________!
ANSWERS
CLUE #1 ________
CLUE #2 ________
ADD THESE ANSWERS AND SUBTRACT 1008 FROM THAT TO FIND OUT WHO THE FIEND IS!
WHO IS THE FIEND?
WORK SPACE
WORK SPACE
THANKS, ________! WITH THE ANSWER YOU HAVE GIVEN ME, I CAN STOP THE FIEND AND KEEP RECESS AND VACATION SAFE!
THE END

Let's put on our thinking caps and conjure up a paradox to confront our pupils with tomorrow.

Conjuring Space

Eliminate the Negative

The second hypothesis for explaining the alleged eroding of curiosity is that inhibiting forces accumulate (see page 81). Children may fear exploration because they have been punished repeatedly for inquiry—attempts to find out and know. Failure is devastating.

Whereas boredom and competing motives are enabling, in that the teacher has ample opportunity to immediately reset the stage to take advantage of the potent needs, fear of failure is disabling. Unlike competing needs, it is not a source of pleasure. On the contrary, it makes the individual feel miserable. It is insatiable—it just doesn't disappear. Furthermore, as a counterforce to natural motives it keeps one not only off task but also immobilized. It inhibits joy, creativity, and productivity.

Fear of failure is rather common. Few of us are gladdened by the thought of an approaching test. Most of us, however, are not continually concerned about failing—failing a test, not being promoted, making mistakes for which others will laugh at us or otherwise ridicule us, or offending group mores. On the other hand, many bright, imaginative college students seldom contribute or test their ideas in class discussions because of the forbidding possibility of being the fool. Their potential is drained by self-protectiveness in their need to avoid trouble, embarrassment, punishment, or disapproval. Kevin (See page 56) is a good case in point. Recall that Kevin has above-average potential but that he is an apparent nonparticipant in life. He is socially isolated; he mostly watches the other children play and relate; he never volunteers. He is a bystander. Contrast his behavior with that of the creative learner who tends to exhibit the following characteristics: "always asking questions . . . attracted to the mysterious . . . playful . . . likes to toy with ideas . . . offbeat ideas . . . emotionally sensitive . . . a faultfinder . . . spirited in disagreement . . . courageous . . . takes risks . . ." (Laggemann, 1963, p. 123). The fearful ones are conformist, conservative, and passive. A frightened child is neither as perceptive nor as flexible as he must be to learn.

The symptoms of fear of failure are exhibited in voice, gesture, facial expressions, and bodily positions. The coping strategies are to be timid and to avoid trouble and disapproval. Pupils who are thus characterized by avoidance behavior are pessimistic about their ability to perform. They set levels of aspiration and expectancies below their actual performance. If given a choice of tasks, they tend to select very simple ones where success is certain or very difficult ones where failure would be "understood," thereby avoiding moderately difficult tasks, in which the probability of success is open and dependent upon persistence. Thus, we see the fear-of-failure motive to be a near antithesis of the need for achievement.

Perhaps we have described the fear-of-failure symptom sufficiently to enable us to identify those pupils in our classes who are so encumbered. After you make your list, discuss the behavior of the youngsters with your colleagues. We need to pinpoint the telltale behavior before we can create the conditions for inducing risk-taking, reflective, creative learning.

Pupil(s)	Fright symptoms	Defensive behavior

Now that we have identified one or two pupils who seem to be inhibited by the fear of failure, and now that we have broadened our concept of the behavior of such pupils, the task for us remains to put together a strategy for inducing approach behavior and, more important, an enhanced self-concept.

Expectancy seems to be the critical factor in differentiating pupils who have a need to achieve from pupils who focus their energies on a need to avoid failure. This self-expectancy of a pupil is derived from two sources:

1. The communicated expectations that significant others have for him; that is, his perception of their judgment of his competency to perform.
2. The history of success experienced by the individual; that is, the degree to which he has achieved his aspirations.

The significant others for most pupils are parents and teachers. Let's start with ourselves. If we harbor any judgments about another person, it is quite likely that in many subtle ways we communicate our feelings to that person. Making judgments about others is not only natural but necessary for effective teaching. We must know our pupils in order to arrange appropriate learning environments. Method I is a case in point: we use such information about the pupil to create appropriate conditions so that he may learn. This is different from using such information to decide that the pupil will probably fail, and not profit by our teaching. The former leads us to communicate to a pupil, "I am getting to know you and with this knowledge we are going to help you succeed," whereas the latter possibly leads us to reflect an expectancy of failure. We reflect our expectancies in very subtle ways—by the way we ask questions, reprimand, reinforce, frown, smile, and so forth.

Let's see if we can identify any pupils whom we may be favoring or disfavoring. Assume that your class is a bit overcrowded and that some adjustments are to be made. Which two pupils would you *least* like to lose? _____ and _____. Which two pupils would you most readily give up? _____ and _____. If a mother were to drop in unexpectedly to check on the progress of her child, which two pupils would you be least prepared to discuss spontaneously? _____ and _____. You may wish to have a colleague observe your class and join you in answering the following questions? Do you treat any of these pupils differently than you do others? Might such differential treatment be reflected in the approach or avoidance behavior of the respective pupils toward class? Brophy and Good (1974) report a series of studies that show that teacher attitudes, as reflected in answers to questions like those above, have an extensive effect on teacher-pupil interaction. It may be useful for you to reflect a bit about the pupil characteristics from which you derived your attitudes.

Reflecting Space

How about trying a little experiment?

Hypothesis.   If a teacher sends home positive, explicit comments regarding a pupil's behavior and schoolwork the pupil's parents will communicate a higher level of respect for the pupil's capabilities, which in turn will increase the approach behavior (or reduce the avoidance behavior) of the pupil.

Procedure.   Take every opportunity to communicate to parents whatever the pupil does well. For some pupils this will take some real searching! Telephone, send notes home, put items in the school paper, and write positive comments on papers, tests, and anything else that the pupil might take home. See if you can really dream up ways of telling Mom and Dad that they may have a winner—in some way. Be honest, be specific. It is better to say, "John's handwriting is neat and clear" than to say, "John submitted a nice paper today."

Results.   Whereas the input is the communication that goes home to the parents, the results will be in terms of an increase in observable approach behavior and a decrease in observable avoidance behavior. Establish a base line by selecting a sample of pupils and systematically recording for two days the frequency of their approach and avoidance behavior. You may refer back to pages 47–48. After carrying out the procedures for a month, record the behaviors of the selected pupils for another two days. At the same time, record pre- and post-observations for a second group of pupils for which no unusual home communications have been initiated. Compare your results.

	Frequency of Preexperimental behavior		*Frequency of* Postexperimental behavior	
	Approach	*Avoidance*	*Approach*	*Avoidance*
Experimental group				
Control group				

Let's now consider the second and more potent means for raising pupils' self-expectancy. Expectancy of success is built upon success. Incorporated in this expectancy is also the feeling of power to control one's destiny. Before considering a general strategy for developing an expectancy of "I can do" through success, let's note that failure-avoidance individuals seem to thrive in an affiliative, supportive atmosphere, in tests in which they can elaborate upon their answers and thereby receive positive reinforcement. Several positive remarks are needed to offset the degenerating impact of one negative comment. Finally, failure-avoidance pupils seems to perform best in highly structured situations, such as those with programmed instruction.

James Block (1971) prescribes an approach called mastery learning, which assures success on appropriately difficult material for 95 percent of the pupils. This approach has a firm theoretical foundation and is confirmed by a number of empirically based studies. Mastery learning accepts the following assumptions:

1. Success is measured in terms of standards set by the individual, the teacher, the parents, or peers.
2. The pupil is likely to approach subsequent tasks with a bit more enthusiasm and confidence if he senses evidence that he performed well in preceding tasks.
3. The pupil's perception of his adequacy to perform in a given subject area is cumulative, and becomes more consistent and stable with continued success.
4. Individuals differ in their aptitudes for particular kinds of learning. Such differences, if plotted, resemble a normal distribution curve.
5. If pupils who differ in aptitude are given identical *instruction* and identical *learning time,* their level of achievement will resemble a normal distribution curve.
6. Aptitude is the length of time it takes the learner to attain mastery of a given learning task. Given sufficient time, nearly all pupils can master the prescribed curriculum.
7. If instruction and length of time for study were adapted to the style and needs of each pupil, then every pupil would reach an optimal level of achievement.

To summarize the mastery learning postulates: Traditional education functions with common instruction and equal time allotments for all pupils, who differ in learning aptitude, with the result that achievement is distributed normally. Mastery learning teachers vary instruction and time allowed to fit pupil differences, thereby enabling nearly all of the pupils to learn the subject to a high level. Whereas traditional teaching inevitably leaves some pupils either bored or failing, mastery learning teaching [1] enables everyone to succeed.

If we were able to function this way, not only would we achieve our academic objectives but our pupils would feel successful, thus eliminating

---

[1] The quality of instruction is a rather complex phenomenon, one that embodies the matching of explanations, practice sessions, reinforcement schedules, language, and so forth, with pupil needs. This chapter is too limited to detail such procedures, but many of them are covered elsewhere in this book or in other teacher-education materials.

the negative. The strategies outlined below were adapted from Block's (1971) summary of the status of mastery learning.

1. Expected levels of performance are established, and the standards by which they will be judged are communicated to the pupils. (*Note:* this is similar to some aspects of contingency contracting. See page 69.)

2. The course of study is broken into well-defined segments. For example, a segment or unit may cover a specific operation in mathematics, or the properties that differentiate one concept from another, or the application of given principles to problems. (Chapter 5 of this book, on sequencing, will be of help here.)

3. For each of the described units, a brief diagnostic-progress test is constructed to determine if the pupils have or have not mastered the unit. The test ought to include subparts that will pinpoint the specific tasks within the unit that will need special attention if they have not been mastered. Chapter 6 of the present text will enable you to complete this strategy. The tests are for information only and should not be officially graded. We are simply trying to pinpoint particular learning difficulties, or areas that need additional attention.

4. Preferably, each unit has a very specific prescription of alternative instructional materials and processes that pupils can resort to in order to overcome the identified weaknesses or otherwise master the objectives. Possible alternatives are small-group discussion, tutorial assistance, alternative texts, programmed materials, and selected audio-visual materials.

Perhaps the primary value of mastery learning is the communication that you expect each pupil to perform to a given standard, that the standard is well defined, and that you will assist each pupil in very specific ways to reach that standard. Note that mastery learning is not a matter of making content easy by lowering standards so that every pupil can pass. It is a matter of making standards explicit so that pupils know what is expected of them in terms of performance, working with pupils in a variety of ways to help them reach standards, and affording them all the time they need to achieve the standard. Worth a try?

BIBLIOGRAPHY

BERLYNE, D. E. *Conflict, Arousal and Curiosity*. New York: McGraw-Hill, 1960.
———. *Structure and Thinking*. New York: John Wiley, 1965.
BLOCK, J. H. *Mastery Learning: Theory and Practice*. New York: Holt, Rinehart and Winston, 1971.
BROPHY, J. and T. GOOD. *Teacher-Student Relationships: Causes and Consequences*. New York: Holt, Rinehart and Winston, 1974.

96   On Motivation

COLEMAN, J. *The Adolescent Society.* New York: Free Press, 1961.

HOMME, L. *How To Use Contingency Contracting in the Classroom.* Champaign, Ill.: Research Press, 1970.

KAGAN, J. *Understanding Children's Behavior, Motives, and Thought.* New York: Harcourt Brace Jovanovich, 1971.

LAGGEMANN, J. K. "How We Discourage Creative Children," *Redbook,* March 1963, pp. 44, 123–125.

MURRAY, H. A. *Explorations in Personality.* Cambridge, Mass.: Harvard University Press, 1938.

STEPHENS, J. M. *The Process of Schooling.* New York: Holt, Rinehart and Winston, 1967.

TRAVERS, J. F. *Fundamentals of Educational Psychology.* Scranton, Penn.: International Textbook, 1970.

WAINER, H. "On Style in College Textbooks," *Educational Researcher,* Fall 1972.

3

Performance Objectives: Formulation and Implementation

DONALD LEE TROYER

Western Illinois University

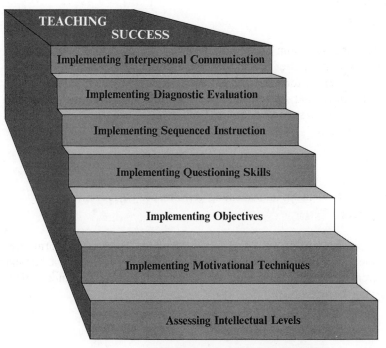

TEACHING
SUCCESS

Implementing Interpersonal Communication

Implementing Diagnostic Evaluation

Implementing Sequenced Instruction

Implementing Questioning Skills

Implementing Objectives

Implementing Motivational Techniques

Assessing Intellectual Levels

**"STEPS" TO IMPLEMENTING
TEACHING COMPETENCIES**

Everyone who starts to read this chapter can be classified into one of two groups: those who have to and those who want to. In either case, no doubt most of you prefer to glean the major ideas from the chapter and get on to something else. For that reason we will organize the chapter in such a way that you need only study the parts with which you are not familiar.

This chapter deals with implementing performance objectives. However, common sense tells us that before we deal with implementing performance objectives, we must have some knowledge of performance objectives. Hence, the chapter is divided into two sections. Section I deals with developing performance objectives. Section II deals with implementing performance objectives. You may wish to complete this chapter in one or more sittings.

In Section I you will find:

1. Objectives.
2. A pretest.
3. Instructions.
4. A posttest.

If you meet the minimum acceptable level on the pretest, skip to Section II. If not, you had better work through Section I to brush up on your ability to develop performance objectives.

Once you have met the objectives of Section I, by passing either the pretest or the posttest, move on to Section II. Here the format is the same as in Section I—that is, there are four parts:

1. Objectives.
2. A pretest.
3. Some instructions on implementing performance objectives.
4. A posttest.

First, try the pretest. If you meet the acceptable level of performance, go do something exciting: see a good movie, play tennis, or eat a banana split. Better still, start developing and implementing performance objectives for your classroom.

SECTION I:
FORMULATING PERFORMANCE OBJECTIVES [1]

Objectives

1. After completing this chapter [1], and without the aid of reference materials, you should be able to list the three components of a performance objective. Acceptable performance would be naming the situation, the behavioral term, and the acceptance-level statement.

2. Given several objectives that are stated in performance and nonperformance terms, you should be able to identify the performance objective. Acceptable level of performance would be identifying 80 percent of the performance objectives.

3. Given a performance objective, you should be able to identify the situation, the behavioral term, and the acceptable level of performance required. The acceptable level of performance would be correctly identifying the three components of the objective 90 percent of the time.

4. Given an objective stated in nonperformance terms, you should be able to rewrite that objective in performance terms. Acceptable level of performance would be writing an objective that contains all three components of a performance objective.

5. Given the opportunity to select any topic you wished, you should be able to write a performance objective for that topic. Acceptance level of performance would be an objective that contains all three components of the performance objective.

Pretest

The purpose of the measure that you are about to take is to determine if you have already mastered the objectives. After writing answers to the questions, check your answers by comparing them with the ones given on page 101.

Pretest Questions

1. Apart from the rationale, list the three components of a performance objective.

---

[1] Section 1 is a summary of the author's chapter, "Formulating Performance Objectives," in *Developing Teacher Competencies,* ed. James E. Weigand (Englewood Cliffs, N.J.: Prentice-Hall, 1971). Refer to this book for a more complete treatment of formulating performance objectives.

A.

B.

C.

2. Examine the following statements. Are they acceptable performance objectives?

yes   no

__ __A. After completing the mapping unit, the student should have an understanding of mapping.

__ __B. After completing the unit on division in which the divisor has a value between 10 and 100 and the quotient may have a remainder, the student, given a work sheet of similar division problems, should be able to calculate the correct answer to 80 percent of the problems.

__ __C. After completing the unit on rocks, the student should be able to demonstrate on a test an understanding of rocks.

__ __D. Given five shapes (cone, cylinder, cube, pyramid, sphere), the student should be able to name all five.

__ __E. After completing the swimming class, the student should be able to demonstrate a knowledge of the crawl, backstroke, and side stroke.

3. Examine the following objective. Identify the portion of the objective that constitutes (A) the situation, (B) the behavioral term, and (C) the acceptance-level statement.

Given a short story, paper, and pencil, the student should be able to identify the major theme the author was presenting. The theme will be considered identified when the major idea presented by the author is expressed in one or two complete sentences.

A. Situation:

B. Behavioral Term:

C. Acceptance Level Statement:

4. Change the following nonperformance objective so that it is a performance objective.

The student should demonstrate a knowledge of the use of comma, semi-colon, and colon.

5. Write a performance objective on any topic.

Pretest Answers

1. A. The situation.
   B. The behavioral term.
   C. The acceptance-level statement.
   (Answers similar to A, B, and C are acceptable.)
2. A. No.
   B. Yes.
   C. No.
   D. Yes.
   E. No.
3. A. The situation is "Given a short story, paper, and pencil."
   B. The behavioral term is "identify."
   C. The acceptance-level statement is the second sentence.
4. Several possibilities exist. Any statement that develops a situation, changes "demonstrate a knowledge of" to some behavioral term that does just that, and adds an acceptance-level statement to indicate how well the student must perform is a satisfactory performance objective. If you did this, give yourself credit for answering the question correctly. Some sample answers are given below.

A. The student, after completing the programmed instruction booklet on how to punctuate correctly with the comma, semicolon, and colon, should be able to punctuate correctly fifteen of twenty sentences that require these three marks of punctuation.

B. Given an examination consisting of twenty sentences, the student should be able to punctuate each with the comma, semicolon, and colon. Acceptable level of performance is correctly punctuating fifteen of the twenty sentences.

C. After completing the unit on the usage of the comma, semicolon, and colon, the student should be able to punctuate correctly fifteen of twenty sentences given him during an examination.

5. Any objective is satisfactory if it contains all three elements of a performance objective. It should be stated so that it is not ambiguous to another person of comparable background and/or a student for whom the objective was prepared.

How well did you do? If you answered all five of the questions correctly you did an excellent job. I see no need for you to read further unless you are curious. Skip to Section II (p 116). If you were accurate on four of the five items, you probably know what you are doing, but a little review will not hurt you. A score of three or less means you should read through the next unit of Section I, which describes how to develop performance objectives.

How To Develop a Performance Objective

What is a performance objective? It is a statement that:

1. Clearly gives the conditions under which the student will be evaluated (the situation).
2. Designates the behavior the student must demonstrate (the behavioral term).
3. Indicates the minimum level at which the student must perform in order to be rated acceptable (the acceptance-level statement).

Instruction needs stated objectives. It does not matter whether the instruction takes place in a formal classroom setting or an informal one, nor does it matter if the instructional level is preschool or postgraduate. What is important is that all concerned (curriculum developers, teachers, and learners) know where they are going.

If we analyze instructional procedure to determine its components, we find something like this: First, it is necessary to decide on the objectives; that is, what do we want the students to accomplish while studying this instructional unit? It follows that we must determine which materials and teaching strategies are needed to best meet the established goals. Furthermore, we must decide the minimum level of performance expected from the students as we assess their performance.

Most teachers do have their objectives in mind prior to selecting their materials and designating the teaching strategy to be followed. Some even consider the type of evaluation to be given, prior to teaching the unit. However, many teachers fail to express these objectives in writing so that both they and their students will be clear as to the type of terminal performance wanted and the level of performance that is acceptable to satisfy the established objective. Here is where performance objectives can play their most important role.

Probably the best way to clarify your thinking and to develop a greater understanding of just what constitutes performance objectives is to formulate some of them. The remainder of this unit is made up of separate parts called frames. Read each frame carefully, and when you are satisfied that you understand the ideas expressed in the frame, answer the questions(s) for that frame. Immediately following each frame are the answer(s) and an explanation of the answer(s). *Use a separate piece of paper to cover the answer(s)* as you work through each frame. Always confirm your answers before going to the next frame.

---

1. The first step in any instructional procedure is to decide which traits you want your students to possess at the end of your instruction. Another way of saying that is:

___A. Behaviorally stated objectives should be written prior to initiating instruction. (Refer to answer A only.)

___B. Goals or objectives that are broadly stated are adequate for planning lessons. (Refer to answer B only.)

Answer

A. If you marked item A, you are correct; good for you! Proceed to frame 2.

B. Since you marked item B, let's take another look. Remember that we must decide exactly where we want to go before we can select the best way to get there. For a teacher this means selecting the traits he wants his students to be able to exhibit upon completion of the instruction.

2. Broadly stated goals may be helpful in giving an overview of what you desire to "get across," but such statements are so general that they are of little value in selecting the instructional strategies for the course. More specific objectives are needed.

In order to be specific when writing your objectives, you must be sure the statements possess three components: the situation, the behavioral term, and the acceptance-level statement. The situation is that part of the behavioral objective that makes clear the conditions your student will be placed under during the time you ask him to perform the behavior being assessed. You must be sure the statement is written so that another competent person can establish like testing conditions from the information provided.

Some individuals prefer to describe in their objectives the type of instruction the student has undergone. This is fine but does not release the writer from the obligation to specifically state the testing conditions.

Select from the three components of an objective the one that was defined as covering the conditions under which the evaluation measure is administered to the student. Mark your selection.

___A. The situation.

___B. The behavioral term.

___C. The acceptance-level statement.

Answer

You should have marked item A, the *situation*. Depending upon personal preference and upon the particular type of performance objective being written, the situation *may* refer to those experiences, materials, and so forth, that the student was exposed to during his instruction. It *must* include the materials and/or the environment to which the student is exposed during the evaluation process. Some objectives describe both the type of instruction undergone and the type of circumstances in which the student is placed during testing.

---

3. In order for the teacher to determine how well a student has done, he must select a performance that is measurable, some capability that indicates the degree of the student's achievement. Since the teacher is unable to look into the student's mind, he must examine behavior—the actions or the product of the actions of the student being tested.

Check the component of a performance objective that designates the type of action required of the student.

___A. The situation.
___B. The behavioral term.
___C. The acceptance-level statement.

Answer

The *behavioral term* (B)—that word or phrase that expresses the type of task required of the student. This word or phrase denotes some action or performance the student must exhibit. Hence, the behavioral term is the basis upon which the teacher can measure how well the student can accomplish the designated task.

---

4. The level of performance required of any group of students is unique to that group. For example, the quality of work expected from a seventh grader in woodworking would not necessarily be the same as that required of a high school senior in a similar class. The degree of performance required within a given grade level or even within a given classroom may vary with the potential of the students involved. Therefore, it is important that the instructor specify the minimum level of performance that is acceptable in such a way that both he and his students will know when it is reached.

Check the component of a performance objective that establishes the minimal level of performance.

___A. The situation.
___B. The behavioral term.
___C. The acceptance-level statement.

Answer

The *acceptance-level statement* (C). Once the pupil meets this level of performance, he has satisfactorily achieved the objective. If the student does not achieve the minimum level of performance, more and/or varied instruction is in order. More drill may be required. Or review could be the type of instruction that is most appropriate. However, all too often teachers overlook the fact that a new and totally fresh instructional approach may better serve to meet the objective.

---

5. Let's take a quick check to see how you are doing. List the three components of a performance objective.

A.

B.

C.

Answer

___A. The situation.
___B. The behavioral term.
___C. The acceptance-level statement.

Answers A, B, and C, or similar answers, are acceptable. Did you list all three correctly? If so, very good. If you missed any, you should return to the beginning of Section I and review with more care the materials to this point.

---

6. Now let's construct some performance objectives. We'll start with the situation. Remember, the situation is an explicit definition of the conditions you will impose upon the student during the evaluation session. When first attempting to write performance objectives, it may be helpful to start with the words *after, given,* or *having.* However, it is not essential that these terms be used.

Do any of the following meet the definition of a situation?

yes   no

___   ___A. Given a list of ten United States presidents and a list of fifteen historical events in two different columns . . .

___   ___B. After reading the chapter on the United States presidents . . .

___   ___C. Given paper, pencil, and a list of ten names of United States presidents . . .

___   ___D. Having a list of United States presidents and while viewing a film strip depicting ten historical events . . .

___   ___E. After viewing a film strip depicting ten historical events, and without any additional materials . . .

Answer

A. Yes. Here we have clearly indicated the materials available to the student. He will have a list of ten United States presidents and fifteen historical events. As of yet, we do not know the behavior required of him, but we do know what he has to work with.

B. No. We know what the student has to do prior to being evaluated, but we do not know the conditions under which he must perform. Will he be asked to name ten United States presidents with his book open or closed? May he use notes to answer several essay questions? We stated earlier that the conditions during testing must be given in the situation. You can see that the conditions for evaluation are not clearly stated in item B. We'll have to restate it, but not now—we'll work on restating objectives later.

C. Yes. This answer tells us just what is available to the students: paper, pencil, and a list of ten United States presidents. We don't know what will be asked of the student, but his situation is clear. This is an acceptable situation.

D. Yes. Again, as in items A and C, we know the conditions for testing. In this item, the student will be asked to perform in some way while viewing this particular film strip.

E. Yes. This situation is acceptable because it states "without any additional materials," which satisfies our requirement of stating the testing conditions. It also notes the prior type of instruction ("After viewing a film strip depicting ten historical events"), which *may* be added but is *not required* to meet our definition of a situation.

---

7. Now it is time for you to try your hand at writing just the situation for a performance objective. Select your own topic. Remember to designate clearly the materials and/or the environment in which you expect to place the student. You may or may not desire to include the type of prior instruction given. You may wish to begin the situation with the words *given, after,* or *having,* but many others could be used instead.

Answer

See if you are correct by asking yourself if the situation is detailed in such a way that one of your students or a fellow teacher could establish the test conditions you intended. If so, you are doing a fine job. If you are not sure of your ability to write a situation, maybe you should review frame 6.

---

8. Now let's turn our attention to the behavioral term. The purpose of this term is to designate a behavior, an action that is observable and measurable. Not all words used in objectives express a performance required of the student. The teacher develops objectives in order to clarify. Using a nonbehavioral term results in ambiguity. Thus, it is most important that you use an unambiguous behavioral term when you write performance objectives.

Indicate which of the following are behavioral terms (B) and which are nonbehavioral (N).

__A. To know.	__H. To group.
__B. To select.	__I. To write.
__C. To identify.	__J. To have insight.
__D. To understand.	__K. To list.
__E. To appreciate.	__L. To match.
__F. To state.	__M. To feel.
__G. To learn.	__N. To name.

Answer

A. N	F. B	K. B
B. B	G. N	L. B
C. B	H. B	M. N
D. N	I. B	N. B
E. N	J. N	

---

9. You probably didn't miss more than one or two of the above terms. Nevertheless, we should look at behavioral terms some more. We stated earlier that a behavioral term must express some type of activity the student has to perform, something we can observe and measure. We can observe a student selecting, identifying, stating, or grouping. We cannot directly observe a student knowing, understanding, appreciating, or feeling.

Do we want our students to know, understand, appreciate, and feel? Certainly. But we also want to be able to determine to what extent they know, understand, appreciate, and feel. Thus, instead of using words that connote actions that cannot be measured directly, we simply employ behavioral terms that allow us to measure directly the degree of knowing and understanding.

Let's consider a performance objective written in such a way that when an understanding exists within a student, it can be observed. Which of these objectives dictates a need for an understanding of map reading, yet is expressed in performance terms? Read only the answer corresponding to your selection.

___A. Given a map that is color-coded to show differences in relief, the student should be able to label the height (given in feet above sea level) of five different areas.

___B. Given a map that is color-coded to show differences in relief, the student should be able to show an understanding of map reading.

Answer

A. If you selected item A, very good. You noted that in order to "label the height" an understanding of map reading had to exist. The degree of understanding can be measured directly. It is only in this way that the teacher can observe the varying degrees of understanding that exist among his students and make the needed adjustments in his instruction and procedure.

B. It was just stated that understanding is not a behavioral term. Your selection of item B means you do not possess the ability (behavior) to select a behavioral term. The phrase "to show an understanding" is ambiguous. We have no idea of the action or conduct that the writer of the objective would accept as evidence of an understanding of map reading. If you wish to review this further, return to frame 8.

10. The third component of the performance objective, the acceptance-level statement, is important because it specifies the minimum level of performance that is considered acceptable. In this way, both the teacher and student know just what the student must do to meet the minimum standards established. Since no two classes are made up of exactly the same types of students, the teacher must vary, from class to class, the minimum level of performance established in an acceptance-level statement.

Consider the following two performance objectives. Select the objective in which the acceptance-level statement is presented most clearly.

___A. The student, given a color-coded map and the key to the color code, should be able to name the height (in feet) of ten points on the map.

Acceptable performance would be naming the height of eight of the ten points within the altitude range specified in the color-code key. (Refer to answer A.)

___B. The student, given a color-coded map and the key to the color code, should be able to name the height (in feet) of ten points on the map. Acceptable performance would be naming the heights within the range of the color-code key. (Refer to answer B.)

Answer

A. Your selection is correct. The acceptance-level statement is very clear to all concerned.

B. Your selection is not wrong, but it does not spell out how many of the ten heights should be named to meet the minimum requirements. You might assume all ten are needed. If ten correct answers are desired, the acceptance-level statement should clearly say so.

---

11. It is not equally easy to write acceptance-level statements for all behavioral terms. Terms such as *compare, define, contrast,* and *evaluate* require more thought from the person writing the acceptance-level statement if the minimum performance is to be clearly indicated. However, do not let difficulty in writing a qualified acceptance statement deter you from using behavioral terms that require students to perform tasks that are more thought-provoking.

Let's examine some acceptance-level statements for behavioral terms that are more difficult to clarify. Consider the partial performance objective below. Immediately following it are several acceptance-level statements that were written for it. Read each and then mark the *yes* column if it clearly states the minimum level of performance expected and the *no* if it does not.

After completing a unit on the vertebrates, the student, given paper and pencil, will be asked to compare similarities and differences among any of the following classes: fishes, amphibians, reptiles, birds, and mammals.

yes   no

___   ___A. Acceptable performance would be comparing and contrasting all five classes with one another.

___   ___B. Satisfactory comparison is made when three similarities and three differences (morphological and/or physiological) are listed for each of the five classes being compared. Each of the similarities and differences needs to be stated in just one or two sentences.

___ ___C. Acceptable performance is listing (in a phrase or in one sentence) ten characteristics of each class.

___ ___D. Acceptable level of performance would be achieved when the student could compare each class on the basis of the following systems: (1) nervous, (2) circulatory, and (3) respiratory.

Answer

A. No, it is not clear what the writer means by "comparing and contrasting." Teachers' expectations would vary a great deal. Consider the responses expected from a fourth grader compared to that anticipated from a college zoology major. This acceptance-level statement does not tell us any more about what is expected from the student than what is given in the partial performance objective. The term *compare,* although behavioral, needs to be qualified by a statement that expresses what the student needs to do in order to compare.

B. Yes. You were quick to see that these statements do clarify the behavioral term *compare.* It is necessary to clarify this term if the student is to know his required performance level.

C. Yes. Again, it is clear what will be an acceptable level of performance. You may not feel that the mere listing of characteristics constitutes a comparison. I tend to agree. However, that is beside the point. This teacher has clearly indicated what the student must do to compare (as he views it) the classes of vertebrates listed.

D. No. This example points out the topic that must be covered in comparing the five classes, but nothing is said to clarify the behavioral term *compare.* What has been stated is fine. However, this writer needs to complete the job.

---

12. Now that you have examined all three aspects of performance objective, you should be ready to test your skill in constructing one. Select a topic that you teach or plan to teach, and in the space below write a performance objective dealing with it. Be sure to keep in mind the model we have been developing during this chapter. It may help first, to begin the situation with *given, after,* or *having.* Second, it might help to know the words that frequently precede the behavioral term. Refer to the objectives of Section I of this chapter (see page 99). Note that the words *should be able to* are generally given before the behavioral term. Knowing this will help the novice write performance objectives. However, you may prefer to use *will be able to, shall be able to,* just *will,* or just *shall.* This is a matter of personal preference.

Answer

Your performance objectives are written correctly if they meet these established criteria.

Performance Objective Checklist:

1. Does the objective contain a situation, a behavioral term, and an acceptance-level statement?
2. Does the objective contain a situation that specifies the conditions for testing in such a way that they might be established by another person?
3. Does the objective contain a behavioral term that connotes a behavior that can be measured directly?
4. Does the objective contain an acceptance-level statement that is totally clear as to how well the student must perform the described behavior?

Note that the checklist does not require you to write the three components of a performance objective in a certain sequence. Neither does the checklist contain any set of terms or phrases that *must* be included. The checklist thus offers a great deal of latitude in the style in which performance objectives may be written.

In constructing performance objectives, as in most activities, the competency of the performer increases with practice. Do not be discouraged if you are slow in formulating this type of objective or if the phraseology is not to your liking; you will overcome these difficulties as you gain experience. The important thing is not to give up your attempt to develop this type of objective for your lesson.

Before we leave this unit of Section I, we need to look at what is considered by some educators to be the fourth component of a performance objective—the *rationale*. Although the rationale is frequently not incorporated into the performance objective, it is exceedingly important.

The rationale explains, states, or justifies the relevance of the behavior being taught. That is, it expresses why the student should spend his time developing the stated performances. Some experts think that stating the rationale will aid the student by informing him of the use this particular learning will have for him, thereby motivating him to learn the stated behavior.

Possibly the most obvious impact that the rationale can have on classroom instruction is to force the teacher to justify the course content. Some of the sacred cows of the course may not stand the test and may have to be dropped. Teachers should be willing to examine each of their objectives on such grounds, since the resulting course would be of greater value to their students.

The rationale can be developed in two ways. First, a *topical rationale* may be written to cover a topic or behavior that can be easily subdivided into several subtopics or subbehaviors. In this instance, the rationale is developed for many performance objectives that have a common component on which the rationale is based. For example, a biology teacher decides to construct six performance objectives on the care and use of a microscope. Instead of repeating a like rationale for each objective, he elects to construct a topical rationale such as the one that follows.

> It is important for each person in the class to develop skill in the use of the microscope since this instrument will enable us to examine the world that our unaided eye cannot view. Not only will viewing this micro-world help our overall understanding of living things, but it is also both fascinating and just plain fun.

A second type of rationale is a brief statement in the objective that justifies the use of the objective. In this case, each performance objective has its own rationale. There may be times when the teacher will find this type of rationale more appropriate. Consider the following objective, in which the rationale has been italicized.

> Given a slide rule and a list of problems (involving multiplication, division, and the determination of square roots and squares), the student should be able to calculate the answers. Performance is acceptable if 95 percent of the answers are correct and the student uses only the slide rule to obtain the requested results. *The slide rule is a handy tool both in and out of the classroom. It is a great time saver for the person who is skilled in its use.*

Posttest

This measure should help you determine whether or not you possess the behaviors described in the objectives for Section I (p. 99). Read each question and answer it. After completing the questions, compare your answers with those given immediately following the test.

Posttest Questions

1. Apart from the rationale, name the three components of a performance objective.

   A.

   B.

   C.

2. Examine the following statements. Indicate whether or not they would be considered performance objectives.

yes   no

___ ___A. Given any resource materials, the case history, the laboratory test results, and an opportunity to examine five patients, each inflicted with a different disease, the student should be able to name the diseases and state reasons for his decision. Acceptable performance would be correctly naming each of the five different diseases and stating no less than two characteristics unique to each.

___ ___B. After completing the unit on Shakespeare, the student should demonstrate a knowledge of this material. Acceptable performance would be achieved if the student correctly answered 75 percent of the forty questions covering this unit.

___ ___C. After visiting the planetarium, the student shall name ten constellations. Eight of the ten must be named correctly to meet acceptable performance.

___ ___D. Given thirty-five preserved specimens of birds of the area, the student will be asked to identify each by writing its common name. Acceptable performance consists of correctly naming twenty-five of the specimens.

___ ___E. Given paper, pencil, and an audio tape of five musical selections that have not been played in class, the student must correctly identify the composer of each piece.

3. Examine the following objective. Identify the portion that constitutes (A) the situation, (B) the behavioral term, and (C) the acceptance-level statement.

Given a solution containing more than one ion and the assigned laboratory materials, the student should be able to identify the ion present. Acceptable performance consists of correctly identifying each ion within a two-hour period. Only one opportunity to identify the ion will be given.

A. Situation:

B. Behavioral Term:

C. Acceptance-Level Statement:

4. Change the following nonperformance objective into a performance objective.

The student should demonstrate his capability as a mechanic by being able to correct a set-up mechanical problem in less than twenty minutes.

5. Write a performance objective on any topic.

Posttest Answers

1. A. The situation.
   B. The behavioral term.
   C. The acceptance-level statement.
   Refer to the check list of performance objectives (p. 99) if you were unsure of any of your answers.
2. A. Yes.
   B. No. It lacks a behavioral term. The phrase "demonstrate a knowledge of" is nonbehavioral. We do not know if the student will be asked to match, select, write, or demonstrate some other behavior. Note, too, that the situation is given last. This is acceptable. Remember, we stated that the order in which the components of a performance objective are written is not important; we need only meet the requirements of the check list.

    C. No. The situation is lacking. We do not know which materials and/or conditions will accompany the testing.

    D. Yes.

    E. Yes. If you question whether an acceptance-level statement is present, ask yourself if the student knows at what level he must perform. The objective clearly implies that each student must meet a minimum standard of identifying all five composers.

3. A. The situation is "Given a solution containing more than one ion and the assigned laboratory materials."

    B. The behavioral term is "identify."

    C. The acceptance-level statement is contained in the last two sentences.

4. As always, several possibilities exist. When checking your answer, just be sure all three of the components of a performance objective are present. Refer to the checklist of performance objectives. You might have restated the objective in this way:

Given a complete set of tools and an automobile with a set-up engine problem, the student should be able to correct the problem within twenty minutes. The problem will be considered correct when the engine can be started and continues to run for two minutes with no outside aid.

5. Any objective is satisfactory if it contains all three elements of a performance objective. It should be stated so that it is not ambiguous to another person of comparable background and/or a student for whom the objective was prepared. Again, refer to the checklist if necessary.

Did you answer each question correctly? You should have scored 100 percent in order to meet the acceptable level of performance. But if you missed just one, you still did a fine job. So you missed more! Perhaps we should start again . . .

SECTION II:
IMPLEMENTING PERFORMANCE OBJECTIVES

The prior discussion focused on the formulation of performance objectives. Little time was spent on discussing the advantages to the classroom teacher of using performance objectives. In this section, I would first like to discuss the role of performance objectives in the classroom. However, the major portion of Section II will deal with a method of implementing performance objectives in the classroom.

Some people say that all we have to do to resolve most of our curriculum problems is to develop performance objectives. Others say that the presence of performance objectives causes the curriculum to become too structured and too limited; this results, they maintain, in an atmosphere that stifles creative thinking. *Neither is the case!*

Performance objectives are neither good nor bad. Their value, like that of the automobile, depends on the way they are used. Few of us want to give up the auto. It is virtually a necessity for most of us. However, when driven improperly the auto can cause damage. The performance objective is like the auto. When used properly it serves a vital role in planning classroom instruction. But if it is employed improperly by the teacher, it can be a detriment to learning.

In our discussion of the ways that a performance objective can be applied so that it is an asset to classroom instruction, we must not forget that performance objectives are written to include *specific* and *measurable behavior*. It is this characteristic of the performance objective that gives it its worth. Here are some of the ways that the performance objective can aid the teacher and the student.

1. *Motivation.* All of us desire to know where we are going and just how well we must perform to get there. Students are no different. Objectives that make clear the behaviors expected and how well they must be performed stimulate students to do better. A student who is more highly motivated should learn more.

2. *Establishing Problem Areas.* The use of performance objectives to spell out desired behaviors helps pinpoint more specifically problem areas that exist for the student, the teacher, and the curriculum.

3. *Instructional Design.* Once the teacher has determined the method of measuring the presence or absence of certain traits, instructional design becomes a matter of trying out various teaching styles and aids, and of sequencing these instructional variables to determine the best way for that teacher to enable his students to attain the desired behaviors. So, if we want to know the best instructional strategy, we need to know when the desired behavior has been attained. That requires clearly spelled-out performance objectives.

4. *Simplification of Evaluation.* To assess pupil progress, the teacher must determine the number of objectives the student has attained. The best way to do this is to develop a list of performance objectives that serves as a standard for both the teacher and the student. Once the performance objectives have been established, the construction of an assessment measure involves little more than the restating of the required behaviors.

Perhaps you have had some experience in implementing performance objectives. If so, there may not be any reason for you to continue with Section II. Read the objectives and take the Pretest. This will give you a basis for deciding whether or not you should continue.

Objectives

1. Without the aid of reference materials, the reader should be able to list three characteristics of a performance objective to be considered in *implementing* one. Acceptable performance would be listing worth, fit, and match (or words representing these characteristics).

2. Without the aid of reference materials, the reader should be able to list three characteristics of a performance objective to be considered in determining its *worth*. An acceptable level of performance is listing any three of the following: relevance, prerequisites, enrichment, interest (or words representing these characteristics).

3. Without the aid of reference materials, the reader should be able to list six characteristics to be considered in determining the *fit* of a performance objective to a student or class of students. An acceptable level of performance would be to list any six of the following: grade level, cultural background, academic background, maturity, reading comprehension, listening comprehension, writing ability, intellectual capability, psychomotor skill.

4. Given a performance objective, a résumé containing background information on a student or class of students, and a performance objective check list, the reader should be able to circle *yes* or *no* for each item listed under the headings of "worth," "fit" "match," and "level of thinking." Acceptable performance is doing so at a level of 90 percent consistency with the information on the résumé.

5. Given a performance objective, a résumé containing background information on a student or class of students, and a performance objective checklist already marked, the reader should be able to identify whether or not the performance objective has worth, fit, and/or match. Also, the student should be able to write a brief statement of one or two sentences indicating (a) whether the objective should be retained or discarded, and (b) a justification of the position taken. Acceptable level of performance would include (a) a clear indication as to whether the objective is to retained or rejected, and (b) any reasonable justification of the position taken.

Pretest

Questions

1. List three characteristics of a performance objective to be considered in implementing one.

A.

B.

C.

2. List three characteristics of a performance objective to be considered in determining its worth.

A.

B.

C.

3. List six characteristics to be considered in determining the fit of a performance objective to a student or class of students.

A.   D.

B.   E.

C.   F.

4. Tear out one of the performance objective checklists at the end of this chapter. Circle *yes* or *no* for each item in the list after considering the following performance objective and résumé for a class of students. The teacher wants the students to have the ability to copy a print.

Objective:

Given all necessary drafting equipment, and a detailed blueprint of the wiring specifications for an industrial plant, the student should be able to reproduce the print. Acceptable performance is a print nearly equal in quality to the original.

Résumé:

Class: first-year drafting, mostly high school juniors, elective course.
Time: early in the fall.

Academic ability: normal distribution of abilities for a junior class.
Interest: normal distribution.
Prior classroom experience with topic: none.

5. Refer to the performance objective checklist you completed for question 4. Write a brief statement of one or two sentences (a) indicating whether the objective should be implemented in the class, and (b) justifying the position taken.

Answers

1. A. Worth.
   B. Fit.   *(Other words representing these characteristics are*
   C. Match.   *acceptable.)*
2. Any three of the following are acceptable.
   A. Relevance.
   B. Prerequisites. *(Other words representing these characteristics are*
   C. Enrichment.   *acceptable.)*
   D. Interest.
3. Any six of the following are acceptable.

   A. Grade level.   E. Reading comprehension.
   B. Cultural background.   F. Writing ability.
   C. Academic background.   G. Intellectual capability.
   D. Maturity.   H. Psychomotor skill.
   (Other words representing these characteristics are acceptable.)
4. Compare the answers on your performance objective checklist with those below.
   A. Worth.

			Comments
(1) Relevance.	yes	(no)	Possibly in a more advanced course; there are more basics to learn first.
(2) Prerequisite.	yes	(no)	Skills needed at this early point in the year are lacking.
(3) Enrichment.	yes	(no)	
(4) Interest.	(yes)	no	It is likely that interest would be present, since the course is an elective. This interest would probably decline quickly, since the lack of skills would result in inability to reproduce the print.

B. Fit.

(1) Grade level.   yes   (no)
(2) Cultural.   (yes)   no
(3) Academic.   yes   (no)
(4) Maturity.   (yes)   no
(5) Reading
    comprehension.   (yes)   no
(6) Listening
    comprehension.   (yes)   no
(7) Writing ability. yes   (no)   Considering the special writing
(8) Intellectual   needed.
    capability.   (yes)   no
(9) Psychomotor
    skill.   (yes)   no

C. Match.

(1) Match between desired behavior   (yes)   no
    and specified behavior.

D. Type of performance objective.

(1) Motor skill.   (yes)   no
(2) Feeling.   yes   (no)
(3) Intellectual skill.   yes   (no)
    a) Repeating information.   yes   no
    b) Applying information.   yes   no
    c) Analyzing information.   yes   no
    d) Evaluating information.   yes   no

5. Reject the performance objective. Any justifiable reason is acceptable, such as (a) lack of worth (in terms of relevance, prerequisites, and enrichment) or (b) fit (in terms of grade level, academic background, and writing ability).

If you answered all five of the Pretest questions correctly, that is just great; consider yourself done with this chapter. If you missed only one, it is not critical that you work through Section II, but it might be a good review. A score of three or less correct indicates that you should work through Section II.

How To Implement Performance Objectives

Apparently, you have decided to read through this section of the chapter. Good! If implementing performance objectives is new to you, there will be a number of new ideas presented to you in the following pages. If you have had some experience, you will likely brush up on some of your present ideas and perhaps be introduced to some new ones.

Read each of the following frames carefully, and then answer the question(s) for that frame. Immediately following each frame are the answer(s) and an explanation of the answer(s). *Use a separate sheet of paper to cover the answer(s)* as you work. Always confirm your answers before going to the next frame.

---

13. Many teachers use curricula that include prewritten performance objectives. Some construct their own. Few evaluate the performance objectives they are implementing into the curriculum.

Why should one evaluate the performance objectives that are to be used in the classroom? For three reasons. First, we need to know if an objective has *worth*. Just stating an objective in performance terms does not automatically make it worth bringing into the classroom. The teaching of a skill, concept, or attitude that has little application or cannot be generalized probably has little value to the students. Such a skill, concept, or attitude should not be introduced into the classroom.

Any objective that is expressed in performance terms serves to enrich the curriculum.

___A. True. (See answer A.)
___B. False. (See answer B.)

Answer

A. You must have been thinking of things more exciting than performance objectives. Read frame 13 again.
B. Good. Move on to Frame 14.

---

14. I stated that three reasons would be given to answer the question, "Why evaluate performance objectives?" The first one we just gave. The second is that if we determine the objective to be of worth, then we need to evaluate it to decide if it *fits* the children in the classroom. For example, is it a reasonable objective considering the interests, abilities, and backgrounds of the students?

The third reason to examine a performance objective is to determine if the behavior specified truly measures the knowledge to be learned. The behaviors called for in the performance objective may not be a good measure of the skill or concept to be learned. If they are not, capable performance of the designated behaviors leaves no indication of the degree of learning that has taken place regarding the skill or concept to be learned.

Thus, it is necessary to determine if a *match* exists between the stated behavior and the skill or concept to be learned.

Using just one word, idenitfy three reasons for evaluating a performance objective. Review frames 13 and 14 if you like.

1. _____

2. _____

3. _____

Answer

You should have something like this:

1. Worth.
2. Fit.
3. Match.

---

15. *How does one measure the worth of a performance objective?* The worth of a performance objective is a subjective judgment, so it is possible —even likely—that disagreement will exist regarding some objectives. However, if the objectives are examined carefully, objectively, and in an orderly manner, the result will be a high yield of performance objectives worthy of use in the classroom.

Below are some suggestions for evaluating the worth of an objective and still staying within the time restrictions ever present in the busy life of a teacher.

1. *Identify* the objective for the unit of study.
2. *Consider* if the objective:
   A. Has *academic relevance* (that is, application or generalization) for the children, now and/or after they leave your classroom.
   B. Provides a necessary *prerequisite* for subsequent lessons.
   C. Provides an *enrichment* experience.
   D. Covers a topic that is reasonably *interesting* to the children.
   E. Is being selected primarily for the *teacher's* interest in and knowledge of the subject.
3. *Justify.* Construct a brief written or oral statement defending the use of the performance objective, a statement that would stand up under the

scrutiny of (a) yourself, (b) another colleague, (c) a curriculum specialist, (d) an administrator, (e) your students, and/or (f) a small group of parents.

If after careful consideration by you and one or more of the groups noted in item 3 you still feel the objective has worth, it is a strong possibility that it is justifiable to retain it in the curriculum.

Review the steps in this frame. Noting the words in *italics*, list the steps in determining the worth of a performance objective.

Step 1.

Step 2.

    A.

    B.

    C.

    D.

    E.

Step 3.

Answer

Step 1. List the performance objective.
Step 2. Consider:
    A. Relevance.
    B. Prerequisites.
    C. Enrichment.
    D. Student interest.
    E. Teacher interest.
Step 3. Justify.

---

16. Consider the worth of this objective for a sixth grade mathematics class.

Given paper and pencil, the student should be able to write consecutive whole numbers starting at 1 and ending at 5,000. This list must be completed in one day and with no more than three errors.

Select one of the following as your answer.

A. This assignment is a worthwhile objective. (See Answer A.)
B. This assignment is not a worthwhile objective. (See Answer B.)

Answer

A. Do you think that writing 1,2,3 . . . 5,000 is relevant? How many times have you actually had to write such a series of numbers? Consider the time it would take! Is this assignment a necessary prerequisite for learning to write numbers? There must be better ways to meet such a prerequisite. Certainly, few children would find writing that many numbers interesting. Here is an example of a performance objective that is best left in the academic trash can! Go to Frame 17.

B. Good! You quickly realized that this objective is lacking in several areas. It is highly unlikely that one would be asked to write such a series of numbers, so the objective is not relevant. It is not interesting, and there must be other ways to meet any skills prerequisite to later lessons. This performance objective leaves a great deal to be desired and should be rejected as not worthy of being included in the curriculum. Go to Frame 17.

---

17. Check the following performance objective for its worth in a second grade classroom.

Given a class member having a birthday, each of the remaining students in the class will state, orally and in turn, one good thing about him. Any positive statement about the class member is acceptable.

Worthwhile? *yes*   *no*

Why?

Answer

Surely this assignment is a worthwhile objective. It has relevance in that the children learn to express themselves. In addition, it is enriching to the student who is having the birthday since it builds self-esteem. Plus, it provides every class member with the experience of behaving positively toward another person and observing the results. Interest would certainly be present.

Most would agree that it is a worthwhile objective for a classroom of young children.

---

18. Here are two more objectives. Consider the worth of each to a high school life science class.

___ Worthwhile.   A. Given an organism with a size between 1 and 3
___ Not worthwhile.   centimeters, the student, while blindfolded, should be able to state the exact number of legs of the organism. An acceptable response is stating the exact number of legs of the organism on the first attempt.

___ Worthwhile.   B. Given a hand lens, paper, pencil, and a set of ten
___ Not worthwhile.   harmless organisms ranging in size from 1 to 3 centimeters, the student should be able to state the exact number of legs on each organism. An acceptable response is stating the correct number of legs of each organism on the first attempt.

Answer

A. Not worthwhile. The morphology of organisms, including the number of legs, has great significance in the identification of living things. There seems to be little value, however, in blindfolding the student. I would toss the objective out on that basis alone.

B. Worthwhile. Morphology has great value in identifying organisms. Thus, the objective is relevant since all students will have direct or indirect contact with living things. Depending on just what type of classroom instruction takes place, the objective should be relevant, serve as a prerequisite, provide enrichment, and interest the student. This objective appears to be justifiable.

19. Let us now turn our attention to *how to evaluate the fit of an objective* to a class of students with which it is to be used. Once the performance objective has passed the first hurdle by being determined of worth, it is necessary to consider if it should be used with a particular student, small groups of students, or a class of students.

Ideally, each performance objective is measured for fit against the background of each student in the class. For example, particular lessons or units may be treated instructionally on an individual basis. In such cases, the teacher can quickly judge whether or not a particular objective fits the student involved.

A more common situation faced by most teachers is that of judging the performance objective for fit against a small group of students or an entire class. The special problem here is that each student is different and therefore the teacher must take a compromise position in order to accommodate the variety of backgrounds.

The first step in evaluating fit is to develop a background statement. This may be done for each student, a small group of students, or an entire class. In all three cases it is necessary to consider (a) grade level, (b) unique cultural traits, (c) academic background, (d) maturity, (e) language skills (reading, listening, and writing), (f) intellectual capability, and (g) psychomotor skills.

Depending on the performance objective, certain of these background characteristics need to be weighed more heavily than others. Assume you have developed background information for each of your students. Consider the fit of the following performance objective.

After reading a novel of approximately 250 pages, the student will write a 200-to-500-word paper that includes (1) a summary of the novel, (2) a statement identifying the major theme of the novel, and (3) a personal reaction to the novel. Acceptable level of performance is to include all three items and make no more than five grammatical errors.

Identify two or three characteristics that should receive the most careful consideration when determining the fit of this objective.

1.

2.

3.

Answer

1. Grade level: It is recognized that extreme differences exist among students at a given grade level. However, considering grade level does help place the objective within the range of a few grades, and therefore it seems wise to consider grade level nearly every time fit is to be determined. This performance objective obviously does not fit children in the early and middle elementary school grades.
2. Language skills: Certainly, reading and writing ability must be a critical consideration when evaluating the objective. A fit must exist between the reading ability of the student(s) and the reading level of the novel.
3. Academic background: Since a maximum of five grammatical errors is the acceptable level of performance, the academic background in this area must be considered carefully.

You may have listed other background characteristics, which is understandable, since each does have an impact on the degree of fit between the objective and the students. We said the first step in determining fit is to *develop a background statement.* Next, one must *judge the objective for fit against the background characteristics.* Finally, the teacher must decide to *accept* or *reject* the performance objective.

---

20. After *worth* and *fit,* the third item to be considered in evaluating a performance objective is the *match.* It is necessary to determine if a match exists between the skill or concept to be learned and the behavior being measured. That is, does the behavior being observed truly measure the skill, concept, or attitude we wish the student to attain? There are three steps in determining if match exists:

1. *Identify* the skill, concept, or attitude you want the child to possess.
2. *List* the behavior(s) stated in the performance objective.
3. *Determine match.* Compare the listed behavior against the skill, concept, or attitude identified, to determine if a match exists.

---

21. At first glance, it appears easy to identify the skill, concept, or attitude we wish the student to attain. Sometimes it is and sometimes it isn't. But in either case it is very important that the teacher decide just what is primary in the lesson. Is it neatness and order? Is it learning a process skill, memorizing a passage, analyzing a problem, applying a rule, or developing an appreciation for a type of music, writing, or painting? It is essential that the teacher decide the skill, concept, or attitude that the student is to attain, whether using "homemade" or "store-bought" objectives.

Pick any performance objective you have written, worked with in the past, or plan to use in the future. Read it carefully, and then in the space below write the skill, concept, or attitude you would like the students to possess after having been exposed to instruction involving this objective. Be specific!

Answer

You may have a statement similar to one of the following:

1. Classify a set of objects into two or more groups.
2. Identify the major theme of a story.
3. Develop a desire to read more.
4. Interpret a set of data.

Did your answer identify a particular skill, concept, or attitude? If so, it is acceptable.

---

22. Pick one of the four statements listed in the answers to frame 21. List two behaviors that you feel could be used to judge whether or not the skill, concept, or attitude in that statement has been learned.

1.

2.

Refer to the performance objective you selected in frame 21.
List two behaviors that could be used to measure learning of the skill, concept, or attitude you identified in that performance objective.

1.

2.

Answer

Several behaviors could have been listed to demonstrate the desired outcome. Some suggestions are listed below for each of four statements listed in the answer to frame 21. You might wish to add other behaviors.

1. Classifying a set of objects: the student could (a) state, (b) place, or (c) list the objects in some fashion to provide observable evidence.
2. Identifying a major theme of a story: the student could (a) state it, (b) write it, or (c) select it from a list of themes.
3. Developing a desire to read more: the student could show this by (a) checking out more books, (b) reading more in the library, (c) subscribing to new magazines, or (d) electing reading over other free-time activities.
4. Interpreting a set of data: the student could (a) state (orally or in writing) three similar or dissimilar patterns in the data, or (b) state (or write) one or more inferences based on the data.

Several behaviors should be listed for your performance objective. They could be quite different from those in the above list.

---

23. Determine match. Ask yourself if the behavior(s) listed do in fact measure what you had hoped to accomplish. For example, does stating, placing, or listing show that the student can classify? Does stating, writing, or selecting demonstrate that the student has the desired ability to "identify a major theme of a story"? Does checking out books, reading in the library, subscribing to new magazines, or electing to read during free time show that the student has developed "a desire to read more"? Does stating or writing an inference demonstrate the ability to interpret data? Determining match requires asking these or like questions; if you are sure the answer is yes, match probably exists.

Test the performance objective you selected in frame 21 for match. Is the behavior desired for the student matched with a behavior that probably indicates that the behavior has been learned?

Check your ability to determine match by circling the behavior(s) that you feel match the following skill to be learned:

Determine the circumference of a circle.

1. Measure.
2. Calculate.
3. List.
4. Name.

Answer

Measuring and calculating certainly demonstrate that the student can determine the circumference of a circle, asuming that these behaviors are performed correctly. However, a student might be able to list or name the steps in determining circumference and still be unable to obtain the correct answer. Why then ask the student to list or name? Why not just focus on the behaviors of measuring or calculating, depending on which you want the student to be able to perform.

A few last comments before wrapping up this unit of Section II. Performance objectives are a great aid, but there exists a danger that you should be aware of. Performance objectives can be constructed more easily for some behaviors—such as naming, listing, constructing, and matching, many physical skills, such as running and jumping—than for others. As a result, these types of behaviors are frequently emphasized to a greater degree than perhaps they should be. Their overuse is due principally to the ease with which they can be qualified numerically in the acceptance-level statement.

Like most teachers, you undoubtedly want your students to develop behaviors that demand the use of higher levels of thinking, such as applying ideas to new and varied situations and analyzing, synthesizing, and evaluating problems of all types. You also want students to develop an appreciation for art, drama, books, life, and nature. Therefore, you must be sure to construct performance objectives that involve your students in the higher levels of thinking and that develop their appreciation in certain areas.

To aid you in your effort to prevent an overemphasis of one type of performance objective, we suggest that you classify your objectives according to the simple scheme suggested in Table 3-1.[2]

[2] Many readers will recognize that the three groups of performance objectives listed in this table—motor skills, feelings, and intellectual skills—are simplified representations of the psychomotor, affective, and cognitive domains commonly found in the literature and first mentioned by Bloom (1956). See Bloom (1956) and Krathwohl (1964) for a complete treatment of how to classify education objectives.

Table 3-1

	Type of Performance Objective	Type of Behavior
Type 1	motor skills	running, jumping, drawing, throwing, focusing
Type 2	feelings	appreciate, respect, love, value, attitude
Type 3	intellectual skills	definitions, concepts, theories, principles

Depending on the type of class you teach, you may wish to use more performance objectives from one of the three categories. For example, a teacher of industrial arts, physical education, or a science laboratory course may prefer to stress motor skills rather than feelings and intellectual skills. However, a teacher of literature, a foreign language, or a science lecture course may want to emphasize the intellectual skills. It is not necessary that the performance objectives for a class reflect an equal distribution among all three categories.

24. Classify the following three performance objectives according to the three types listed in Table 3-1.

1. Type ___ Given a picture of a student microscope, the student should be able to name all eight parts of the microscope as given in the student laboratory guide. Acceptable level of performance is naming all eight parts correctly.

2. Type ___ After completing the swimming class, the student should be able to swim continuously a minimum of two lengths of the pool in the crawl and two lengths in the backstroke. Acceptable level of performance is swimming two lengths of each stroke.

3. Type ___ Given a picture of a starving child, the student will write one paragraph responding to the question, "Do you think one country has a responsibility to aid the starving people in another part of the world?" Any paragraph is acceptable if it attempts to respond to the question.

Answer

1. Type 3. This is a check on learning parts of a microscope—an intellectual skill.

2. Type 1. The ability to swim is primarily a motor skill.

3. Type 2. Here a value judgment is being made; thus the objective is classified under feeling.

You may wish to practice a bit by classifying some of the performance
objectives you have written for this chapter.

---

25. To encourage higher levels of thinking in your students, each performance objective classified as type 3 in Table 3-1 needs to be further
categorized as one that:

1. Repeats information learned.
2. Applies information learned.
3. Analyzes information into its components and assesses their relationships.
4. Evaluates information and makes a judgment.

If you wish to demand higher levels of thinking from your students, then
a major share of your objectives must be in the applying, analyzing, and
evaluating categories. (See Table 3-2.)[3]

Table 3-2.   Intellectual skills

Level	Characteristic
Repeating information	Learns information as given and repeats it with little or no modification.
Applying information	Uses ideas, theories, principles, and concepts learned.
Analyzing information	Examines the components, and their inter-relationships, of a problem, report, story, or some other body of information.
Evaluating information	Calls for a judgment based on criteria.

Referring to Table 3-2, classify each of the following performance objectives as one in which the student is asked to repeat, apply, analyze, or
evaluate information. For the sake of brevity, the acceptance-level statement has not been included in these objectives.

_____1. Given a set of hypothetical experimental data, the student
will be able to select and use one of Mendel's laws of in-
inheritance to solve the problem posed.

[3] The four categories of intellectual skill level in Table 3-2 are simplified and
modified representations of Bloom's (1956) six levels of educational objectives in
the cognitive domain. See Bloom (1956) for a complete treatment of how to classify
educational objectives.

_____2. Given five Civil War battles, the student should be able to list (a) the generals for each side, (b) the location of the battle, (c) the date of the battle, and (d) the winning side.

_____3. Given a complete set of information on a patient, the student should be able to prescribe a drug and its dosage and state why it was selected over other drugs frequently used in similar cases.

_____4. Given an article from the newspaper, the student should be able to circle in red those statements that are based on observations and circle in blue those statements that are based on inferences.

Answers

1. Application. Here the student is asked to solve a problem by applying a principle to a new situation.

2. Repetition. This simply requires the student to repeat information previously learned.

3. Evaluation. In this case the student must make an evaluation and then a judgment as to which drug would best serve the patient.

4. Analysis. The article is being examined to determine which statements are based on observation and which are based on inference. Therefore, an analysis is taking place.

That does it! You should be ready for the posttest. Try it!

Posttest

1. List three characteristics of a performance objective to be considered in implementing one.

   A.

   B.

   C.

2. List three characteristics of a performance objective to be considered in determining its worth.

A.

B.

C.

3. List six characteristics to be considered in determining the fit of a performance objective to a student or class of students.

A.   D.

B.   E.

C.   F.

4. Tear out one of the performance objectives checklists at the end of this chapter. Circle *yes* or *no* for each item in the list after considering the following performance objective and résumé for a class of students. The teacher wants the student to have the ability to identify the heavy-metal ions found in an "unknown" supplied by the instructor.

Objective:

Given an unknown that might possess one or more heavy-metal ions, and given access to the chemical supplies provided throughout the course, as a part of the final examination the student should be able to state in writing which, if any, heavy-metal ions are present in the unknown solution provided him. An acceptable performance is 100 percent accuracy in listing the heavy-metal ions; also the correct symbol and charge must be given for each.

Résumé:

Class: College Introductory Qualitative Chemical Analysis, elective for majors.

Time: end of course.

Academic ability: normal distribution for undergraduate chemistry majors.

Interest: above average, since it is an elective in the major area.

Prior experience with this topic: topic fully covered during the course.

5. Refer to the performance objective checklist you completed for question 4. Write a brief statement of one or two sentences (a) indicating whether the objective should be implemented in the class, and (b) justifying the position taken.

Answers

1. A. Worth.
   B. Fit.   *(Other words representing these characteristics are*
   C. Match.   *acceptable.)*
2. Any three of the following are acceptable.
   A. Relevance.
   B. Prerequisites. *(Other words representing these characteristics are*
   C. Enrichment.   *acceptable.)*
   D. Interest.
3. Any six of the following are acceptable.
   A. Grade level.   E. Reading comprehension.
   B. Cultural background.   F. Writing ability.
   C. Academic background.   G. Intellectual capability.
   D. Maturity.   H. Psychomotor skill.
   (Other words representing these characteristics are acceptable.)
4. Compare the answer on your performance objective check list with those below.
   A. Worth.

			Comments
(1) Relevance.	(yes)	no	Relevant and essential.
(2) Prerequisite.	(yes)	no	Needed for future courses.
(3) Enrichment.	yes	(no)	Basic material.
(4) Interest.	(yes)	no	Likely with major.

   B. Fit.

(1) Grade level.	(yes)	no
(2) Cultural.	(yes)	no
(3) Academic.	(yes)	no
(4) Maturity.	(yes)	no
(5) Reading comprehension.	(yes)	no
(6) Listening comprehension.	(yes)	no
(7) Writing ability.	(yes)	no
(8) Intellectual capability.	(yes)	no
(9) Psychomotor skill.	(yes)	no

C. Match.
(1) Match between desired behavior
and specified behavior.   (yes)   no

D. Type of performance objective.
(1) Motor skill.   yes   no
(2) Feeling.   yes   no
(3) Intellectual skill.   (yes)   no
    a) Repeating information.   yes   no
    b) Applying information.   (yes)   no
    c) Analyzing information.   yes   no
    d) Evaluating information.   yes   no

5. An acceptable response would include something like the following. First, denote the performance objective as acceptable for this class. Second, justify it by stating that it has worth, fit, and match; in addition, it requires thinking on a higher level than just rote learning.

You probably completed all five of the posttest questions correctly. However, if you answered four correctly, that is fine and acceptable. If you had three or less correct, doggone! Maybe you need a little break, and then review the frames that relate to the questions you missed.

REFERENCES

BLOOM, BENJAMIN S., ed., *Taxonomy of Educational Objectives, Handbook I: Cognitive Domain*. New York: McKay, 1956.

KRATHWOHL, DAVID R., BENJAMIN S. BLOOM, and BERTRAM B. MASIA, *Taxonomy of Educational Objectives, Handbook II: Affective Domain*. New York: McKay, 1964.

Performance Objective Checklist

Student, Class, Group _____

Performance Objective _____

_____

_____

	Circle One		Comments
A. Worth.			
1. Relevance.	yes	no	
2. Prerequisite.	yes	no	
3. Enrichment.	yes	no	
4. Interest.	yes	no	

Justification:

B. Fit.			
1. Grade level	yes	no	
2. Cultural.	yes	no	
3. Academic.	yes	no	
4. Maturity.	yes	no	
5. Reading comprehension.	yes	no	
6. Listening comprehension.	yes	no	
7. Writing ability.	yes	no	
8. Intellectual capability.	yes	no	
9. Psychomotor skill.	yes	no	
C. Match.			
1. Match between desired behavior and specified behavior.	yes	no	
D. Type of performance objective.			
1. Motor skill.	yes	no	
2. Feeling.	yes	no	
3. Intellectual skill.	yes	no	
a. Repeating information.	yes	no	
b. Applying information.	yes	no	
c. Analyzing information.	yes	no	
d. Evaluating information.	yes	no	

Performance Objective Checklist

Student, Class, Group _____

Performance Objective _____

_____

_____

	Circle One		*Comments*
A. Worth.			
1. Relevance.	yes	no	
2. Prerequisite.	yes	no	
3. Enrichment.	yes	no	
4. Interest.	yes	no	

Justification:

B. Fit.			
1. Grade level	yes	no	
2. Cultural.	yes	no	
3. Academic.	yes	no	
4. Maturity.	yes	no	
5. Reading comprehension.	yes	no	
6. Listening comprehension.	yes	no	
7. Writing ability.	yes	no	
8. Intellectual capability.	yes	no	
9. Psychomotor skill.	yes	no	
C. Match.			
1. Match between desired behavior and specified behavior.	yes	no	
D. Type of performance objective.			
1. Motor skill.	yes	no	
2. Feeling.	yes	no	
3. Intellectual skill.	yes	no	
a. Repeating information.	yes	no	
b. Applying information.	yes	no	
c. Analyzing information.	yes	no	
d. Evaluating information.	yes	no	

Performance Objective Checklist

Student, Class, Group _____

Performance Objective _____

_____

_____

	Circle One		*Comments*

A. Worth.

1. Relevance.	yes	no	
2. Prerequisite.	yes	no	
3. Enrichment.	yes	no	
4. Interest.	yes	no	

Justification:

B. Fit.

1. Grade level	yes	no	
2. Cultural.	yes	no	
3. Academic.	yes	no	
4. Maturity.	yes	no	
5. Reading comprehension.	yes	no	
6. Listening comprehension.	yes	no	
7. Writing ability.	yes	no	
8. Intellectual capability.	yes	no	
9. Psychomotor skill.	yes	no	

C. Match.

1. Match between desired behavior and specified behavior.	yes	no	

D. Type of performance objective.

1. Motor skill.	yes	no	
2. Feeling.	yes	no	
3. Intellectual skill.	yes	no	
a. Repeating information.	yes	no	
b. Applying information.	yes	no	
c. Analyzing information.	yes	no	
d. Evaluating information.	yes	no	

4

Questioning Behavior, or, How Are You at P.R.?

ROGER CUNNINGHAM

Ohio State University

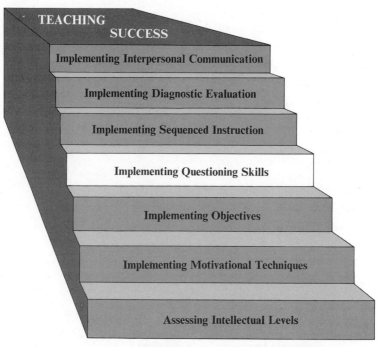

TEACHING
SUCCESS

Implementing Interpersonal Communication

Implementing Diagnostic Evaluation

Implementing Sequenced Instruction

Implementing Questioning Skills

Implementing Objectives

Implementing Motivational Techniques

Assessing Intellectual Levels

**"STEPS" TO IMPLEMENTING
TEACHING COMPETENCIES**

INTRODUCTION

We usually associate the abbreviation P.R. with public relations. This is not a chapter on public relations. The focus here is on questioning behavior. Of course, it is not difficult to argue the merits of good questioning in public relations activities. However, in this chapter we interpret P.R. to mean personal relations (or interpersonal relations). Specifically, the designation P.R. refers here to the many strategies and techniques for questioning described in this chapter and identified in Figure 4-1.

QUESTIONING AND HUMANISM

The cry for relevancy in education today includes a demand for adults who can interact with students in a more humanistic way. Effective communication is the key to understanding. Questioning, as a form of communication, is one of the most potent means of personalizing interaction.

With your questioning you can create the climate for students to emerge from their learning as valuing and thinking individuals. Questioning is one of the best ways for you to express humanistic attitudes involving respect for students' ideas, freedom of choice, self-expression, and honesty. Using appropriate questions, you can highlight uniqueness, clarify student needs, enhance an environment of spontaneity, and integrate feeling and thinking for understanding of self and others—sound bases for a humanistic relationship. Over a period of time, proper questioning should promote a positive self-concept within the student. It probably will also have a dramatic effect on your own self-concept. The high correlation between a positive self-perception and success has been proven time and again. Openness and trust are benefits often reaped from this emphasis. Most suggested approaches to teaching today encourage the teacher to act as a guide to learning. One does this primarily through questioning. Utilizing the P.R. questioning skills well will make a significant difference in your teaching.

CHAPTER ORGANIZATION

As you develop what we call the P.R. skills, you will learn to avoid the pitfalls characteristic of inhumane and impersonal teaching. The experiences here are intended to help you change your questioning behavior by using the P.R. skills in real but controlled instructional situations. The

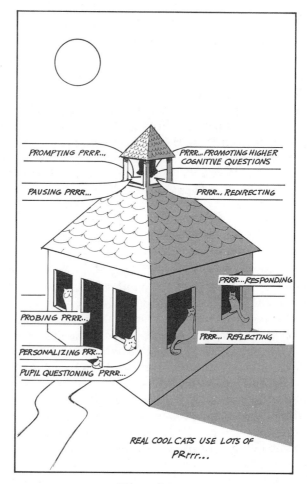

Figure 4-1

printed materials will give you the means to analyze and revise your questioning behavior both before and after a practical experience. Therefore, activities with students are an integral part of your work in this chapter.

This chapter is not designed to be completed in one sitting. It is organized so that you will study the printed materials to develop and practice a given strategy. When you feel you have a working knowledge of the technique, you may leave the printed materials and practice the skill in a real teaching situation—a micro-teaching context with a group of five to eight students. The next step to implanting the skill will be to analyze your questioning behavior on the basis of provided guidelines, model dialogues,

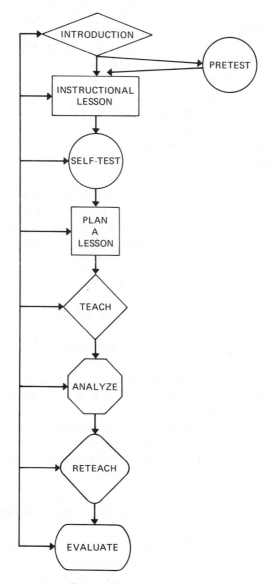

Figure 4-2

147

and feedback from your micro-teaching experience. Finally, you will be encouraged to make necessary modifications in the focus skill and reteach the lesson. Each of the four sections of this chapter is outlined according to the scheme shown in Figure 4-2.

Notice that this approach allows you to learn the skill in small steps; in addition, you have the option of retracing your steps where necessary. The chapter is divided into four modules:

 I. Promoting higher cognitive questioning.
 II. The P.R. strategies.
 III. Personalizing questioning.
 IV. Pupil questioning.

A module is a set of related experiences designed to help you learn a specific strategy or set of techniques. Although these techniques are interrelated, you should learn and practice them one at a time; by the end of the chapter you will be prepared to integrate them.

OBJECTIVES

Upon completion of this chapter, you will be able to:

1. Classify, construct, and use higher level questions to raise the cognitive operations of students.
2. Implement questioning strategies for pausing, redirecting, prompting, clarifying, refocusing, and reflecting in order to improve and extend the responding capabilities of students.
3. Demonstrate a capability for personalizing the questioning process and thereby help students clarify values and their value systems.
4. Use strategies in your classroom behavior that stimulate and sustain student questioning.

PROMOTING HIGHER COGNITIVE OPERATIONS

If you were asked, "What is the prime objective of education?" how would you respond? If you are like most teachers, your answer would be a quick and firm "The ability to think!" However, what goes on in classrooms? What was your own school experience like? If you teach, how are you proceeding toward your goal of encouraging thinking? If you are like most teachers, you need help. Although nearly all teachers stress the importance of high cognitive products, such products are seldom the outcome of questioning in their classrooms.

Teachers have been guilty of placing an almost exclusive emphasis on low-level, factual questions at the expense of other intellectual skills. What kinds of questions are you asking or would you ask? If you're not sure, you should really start thinking about it. Deprived of the opportunity to think, students become distracted, bored, and frustrated, fail or give up, and become dull-minded. Some students are cheated more than others. Biases against slow learners and disadvantaged children have been observed by researchers. These students are not given the opportunity to deal with thought questions, although they have proved they can perform when their teachers' questioning patterns are changed to encourage higher cognitive skills. Like many other teachers, you can improve your questioning behavior to include more thoughtful questions and, as a consequence, reap the benefits of success.

Teaching for thinking means placing students in thinking situations. They need regular opportunities to "test their wings," to try for the intuitive leap, to make guesses, and to have time to contemplate and assimilate experiences. A teacher who respects students creates an atmosphere where these opportunities are available. He avoids judgments and spends time listening, providing alternatives, allowing divergence, and encouraging discussion as a means of enhancing thinking.

MODULE I:
PROMOTING HIGHER COGNITIVE QUESTIONING

Ready? Here we go! Because too much emphasis is placed on lower cognitive questioning in teaching, we will concern ourselves only with the upper levels. The purpose is to help you modify your teaching behavior to include a greater number of thought-provoking questions. If you feel uncomfortable with the lack of attention to lower-level questions, you might refer to the sources listed below for help:

Carin, Arthur, and Robert Sund, *Developing Questioning Techniques.* Columbus, Ohio: Charles E. Merrill, 1971.

Hunkins, Francis, *Questioning Strategies and Techniques.* Boston: Allyn & Bacon, 1972.

Saunders, Norris, *Classroom Questions: What Kinds?* New York: Harper & Row, 1966.

Before proceeding with this module, it might be helpful to find out where you are in your knowledge of questioning for cognitive purposes. The pretest that follows will help you find your starting point.

Pretest

In the questions below, label the lower-level ones with an *L* and the higher-level ones with an *H*.

___ 1. What is the main idea of this chapter as you see it?

___ 2. What is the meaning of the word *accountability?*

___ 3. What are some of the things that might happen if teachers were evaluated on the basis of their students' test scores?

___ 4. Why do people disobey speed limits even though they know slower speeds are safer?

___ 5. What do you think is the most serious domestic problem in the United States today?

___ 6. In what ways is owning a condominium like owning your own home?

___ 7. What are the differences between no-fault divorce and regular divorce?

___ 8. How might the institution of marriage be different if divorce were not permitted?

___ 9. What is your opinion on the granting of the right to vote to eighteen-year-olds?

___10. What are some of the fallacies in the speaker's thinking?

___11. What kinds of changes in our society might assure a greater number of successful marriages?

___12. Divorce is on the rise in this country. What evidence can you give to support this statement?

___13. What country has the most people and a current growth rate of 2 percent?

___14. How do you feel about the issue of sterilizing mental retardates?

___15. Name the three different ways of reporting news.

Check the next page for the correct responses.

If you answered more than 85 percent, or thirteen, correctly, you might skip this module and proceed directly to Module II. We assume that you have a good grasp of questioning at different cognitive levels. However, if you feel that you were lucky and guessed correctly or that you need a review, then you may still find this module useful.

If you answered fewer than thirteen correctly, don't be discouraged. The topic is probably very new to you. It is also easy to be confused at times. We expect that you will do quite differently later.

Please proceed to the next step in the module.

Answers to Pretest

1—L	6—H	11—H
2—L	7—H	12—H
3—H	8—H	13—L
4—H	9—H	14—H
5—H	10—H	15—L

Items 1, 2, 13, and 15 are low-level questions because they require a factual answer. Why the others are higher-level questions will become clear to you as you proceed through this module.

One way of conceptualizing the higher categories for cognitive questioning is outlined in Figure 4-3. Note the operations involved in each category.

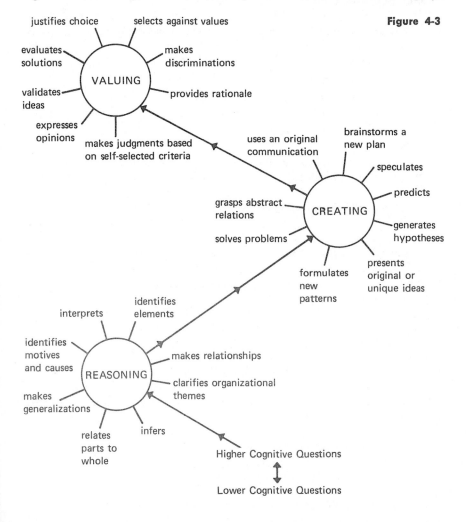

Figure 4-3

It will be helpful for you to compare these operations with the key phrases used in the questions that follow below for each category.

Reasoning Questions

We cannot assume that students will automatically engage in reasoning. To see something in terms of its parts requires experience with materials, events, and ideas. When a student engages in reasoning, he explains cause-and-effect relationships or identifies motives; he gives evidence or reasons for outcomes or actions; he supplies a rationale for compared events. Inferences and interpretations are also common operations. Refer to Figure 4-3 to identify all the operations involved. "Why" questions are typical, and, consequently, they are often used as probing questions. Examples of reasoning questions follow:

1. Why do you think the author's explanation in the following paragraph is appropriate?
2. What are some of the reasons why teachers do not let students ask more questions in the classroom?
3. Why do you think Carl grouped the objects the way he did?
4. How do rock concerts reflect the changing nature of our times?
5. How do the diverse ways of polluting our air suggest ways of eliminating the problem?
6. Divorce is on the rise in this country. What evidence can you give to support this contention?

Note that some of the common phrases for the wording of the questions are:

1. How does _____ relate to _____?
2. What is the meaning of _____?
3. Why do you think these are organized this way?
4. What are some of the reasons for _____ ?
5. What information do we need _____?
6. Why did _____?
7. What evidence can you give for _____?
8. What are some of the factors involved in _____?

Which of the following are reasoning questions? Check those you think fit the criteria.

___ 1. Why is the right of free speech included in our constitution?
___ 2. What state has a new "get tough" shoplifting law?

___ 3. How does news reporting in the United States compare with that in the USSR?

___ 4. Do you think Jack Anderson was right in the way he obtained his information?

___ 5. What is the difference between no-fault divorce and regular divorce?

___ 6. Why do you think the tough style of the marines no longer appeals to young men of today?

___ 7. What reasons can you give for the large number of school dropouts volunteering for the army?

___ 8. What causes a tidal wave?

___ 9. What do you see as the advantages and disadvantages of legalizing marijuana?

___10. What information do we need to judge the effectiveness of his conclusions?

Answers

1, 3, 5, 6, 7, 9, and 10, are examples of reasoning questions.

If you did not identify these examples correctly, there will be opportunities for you to identify others. It might be helpful, however, to review the criteria, examples, and phrases and construct your own examples.

If you had no difficulty identifying the reasoning questions, you are tuned in. Good for you!

Creating Questions

Creating questions encourage speculating, predicting, and hypothesizing. In responding to this kind of question a student represents something in a new form, constructs a plan to solve a problem, or elicits a different communication. Relating the parts to their whole is a common operation. Some examples of creating questions follow:

1. How do you think your life might change when we have fully functioning robots?

2. How do you think our energy situation might change once we are able to tap the geothermal resources in the earth?

3. What kind of plan might the people of Africa use to eliminate the destruction of animal life?

4. What are some ways to reduce racial prejudice?

5. If you were concerned about its effect on the ecological balance in a certain environment, where would you locate a new factory?

6. What alternatives to strikes might be used to solve disputes between labor and management?

Some of the phrases common in the wording of creating questions are:

1. How would you _____ if _____?
2. What would you do if _____?
3. Suppose _____; how might you _____?
4. If _____, what would _____?
5. What will happen if _____?
6. Draw a cartoon _____?
7. Write a story to _____.
8. Play the role _____.
9. How could we improve _____?
10. What kind of plan _____?

Which of the following are creating questions? Check those you think fit the criteria.

___ 1. What is the relationship between spiders and insects?
___ 2. How do you think our government might function differently with a woman as president?
___ 3. How do you feel about Israel's rights to hold onto conquered land?
___ 4. What are some ways we could record changes in the plant as it grows?
___ 5. How are isopods maintained in a terrarium?
___ 6. Draw a cartoon that depicts women's liberation.
___ 7. What are some reasons for the great increase in crimes against government officials.
___ 8. If you were mayor, what kind of plan would you use for urban renewal?
___ 9. Do you think the news media have the right to report any and all news?
___10. How does man adapt himself to living in outer space?

Answers

2, 4, 6, and 8 represent creating questions.

If you succeeded in identifying the creating questions correctly, you are making great progress. Keep it up!

If you did not label all four correctly, don't be dispirited. Review the criteria for phrasing creating questions. We think it will become easier for you to identify this type of question when you have seen all three categories. Stick to it!

Valuing Questions

When a student responds to valuing questions, he makes selections against a set of values, makes discriminations, provides rationales, expresses opinions, or takes a self-selected position on an issue. In so doing, he may also justify choices, judge the validity or quality of something, and evaluate solutions. Study the following examples:

1. How do you feel about the offering of a sex education course taught by classroom teachers in the public school?
2. Do you feel that competition is a deterrent to effective learning?
3. What do you think is the best way to raise children in this modern world?
4. How effective are price controls in curbing inflation?
5. Which of the local issues do you find most disturbing?
6. What experiences in your life make you the proudest?
7. Do you think you have the right to criticize a friend for something personal?
8. Who do you think is the most successful person in the entertainment field today?

Note the phrases common to valuing questions.

1. Do you agree _____?
2. What is your opinion _____?
3. How do you feel about _____?
4. Which is the best _____?
5. How might _____ be better?
6. What is your reaction to _____?
7. Do you think _____?

Which of the following are valuing questions?

___ 1. For what reasons might you not buy Christmas gifts?
___ 2. If you were given a million dollars, how would you use that money to change the lives of others?
___ 3. If you wanted to communicate a human relations problem, what kind of game would you design?

___ 4. Which method of solving your budget problems do you think would be the most efficient?

___ 5. Who do you think is the greatest athlete of modern times?

___ 6. What is your reaction to the practice of using animal waste as an additive to cattle feed?

___ 7. How does a dog's foot compare with a cat's?

___ 8. How many basic foods are there?

___ 9. How do you feel about enforcing strict birth control techniques for families on welfare?

___10. Why do you think different cultures follow different practices in the same set of circumstances?

Answers

4, 5, 6, and 9 belong to the valuing category.

If you were successful, you're really with it—move on!

Using the letters *R, C,* and *V,* label the list of questions below according to their appropriate category—reasoning, creating, or valuing.

(SELF-TEST) ___ 1. Who do you think were the most heroic, the astronauts or the servicemen in Vietnam?

___ 2. If your school were to change its name, what do you think it could be called?

___ 3. Your semitrailer truck loaded with umbrellas overturns on the side of the road. What are some ways you can use your cargo to get the truck out of the ditch and upright?

___ 4. From what you have learned of your examination of the magazines, how would you rank them?

___ 5. What are some reasons why the Alaskan pipeline is so important?

___ 6. How do you feel about engaging in premarital sex?

___ 7. What evidence can you give in support of having pets in a family?

___ 8. What are some ways we could make your classroom a happier and more comfortable environment for learning?

___ 9. What do you think would be the most unusual way to celebrate your birthday?

___10. What do you predict will be our major problems in this nation by the year 2000?

___11. What is the best way to help students develop a positive self-concept?

___12. Why do you think the ancient Egyptians were such great worshipers of animals?

___13. What is your reaction to the prospect of creating life in a test tube?

___14. Why do you think nonwhites are more often identified by their race in news reports of violent crimes than their white counterparts?

___15. What are some ways you might measure the width of a river?

Refer to page 159 for the correct answers.

Apply Your Skill

The ability to classify questions correctly represents one level of skill. Constructing your own questions requires a higher level of skill. Brainstorm questions from the three different higher cognitive categories (reasoning, creating, valuing) for the following passages.

Auto Theft

People often leave their cars unlocked when parked near their own homes. Don't do it, advises the Administration of Justice Committee, a nonprofit criminal reform agency in Cleveland, Ohio. A committee study indicates that 28 percent of cars stolen in the Cleveland area during a six-month period were taken from driveways. Other observations from the agency: An alarm system deters thieves. So does leaving your dog in the back seat on shopping trips. A spokesman says: "We've never had a case where a car was stolen when a dog was in the car." Valuables should be locked in the trunk. Spare keys shouldn't be hidden beneath the hood or under a bumper.[1]

Questions:

[1] © *U.S. News and World Report,* July 8, 1974, p. 8.

Some examples of questions that could be raised from the content of this passage are listed here by categories:

Reasoning:
Why do you think some people steal cars?

What values are promoted by our society that motivate a person to be a thief?

Some people ask to have their car stolen. What evidence can you give to support this statement?

Creating:
How would you plan a campaign to reduce the number of car thefts?

What are some ways that the energy crisis might reduce auto thefts?

What effect do you think so many car thefts will have on our economy?

How would you make a car theftproof?

Valuing:
Do you think the penalty for auto theft is harsh enough?

Do you think that an insurance company has the right to withhold payment if your car was not locked when it was stolen?

Do you agree that the problem of car theft is of major importance?

Repeat this brainstorming activity for the following passage.

World Population

It has been estimated that the human population of 6000 B.C. was about five million people, taking perhaps one million years to get there from two and a half million. The population did not reach 500 million until almost 8,000 years later—about 1650 A.D. This means it doubled roughly once every thousand years or so. It reached a billion people around 1850, doubling in 200 years. It took only 80 years or so for the next doubling, as the population reached two billion around 1930. We have not completed the next doubling to four billion yet, but we now have well over three billion people. The doubling time at present seems to be about 37 years. Let's examine what might happen on the absurd assumption that the population continued to double every 37 years into the indefinite future.

If growth continued at that rate for about 900 years, there would be some 60,000,000,000,000 people on the face of the earth. Sixty million billion people. This [would be] about 100 persons for each square foot of the Earth's surface, land and sea.[2]

2 From Paul R. Ehrlich, *The Population Bomb*, rev. ed., © 1968, 1971 by Paul R. Ehrlich. Reprinted by permission of Ballantine Books, a division of Random House, Inc.

Questions:

Answers to Self-Test

1–V	6–V	11–V
2–C	7–R	12–R
3–C	8–C	13–V
4–V	9–V	14–R
5–R	10–C	15–C

If you were unsuccessful in answering at least 80 percent, or twelve of the questions correctly, review the criteria and try writing several questions in each category using the topics listed below.

1. Extraterrestial life.
2. Drugs.
3. Vanishing wildlife.
4. Fuel crisis.
5. Cigarettes and smoking.

If you did achieve at least 80 percent, CONGRATULATIONS! "You've come a long way, BABY!"

If you are gaining more confidence in your ability to ask higher cognitive questions, you might try brainstorming questions on a topic without any additional information—a still higher level of skill. Some possible topics are:

1. Pollution.
2. UFOs.
3. Clothes.
4. Population explosion.
5. Nudity in movies.
6. Television and children.

PLAN A LESSON Identify a group of from five to eight students. Decide on a topic for which you can plan a lesson. Consider carefully the potential of the topic or content for higher cognitive questions. Write out the questions emphasizing the higher levels that you will ask in the lesson. Plan for about a ten minute lesson. Consider carefully the wording of your questions—quality is better than quantity.

TEACH Make a tape recording of your lesson for analysis. Restrict yourself to questioning concerns. This is your "trial" lesson.

ANALYZE After completing the lesson, listen to the tape. Carefully match student answers with the questions. Consider the following in judging the appropriateness and effectiveness of the questions:

1. How many responses did you obtain for each question?
2. Who was responding?
3. How did the cognitive level of the responses match the level of the question?
4. Were the answers in complete sentences?
5. Did you use any distracting cues, such as "Right" or "OK"?
6. Did you change the wording or intent of the questions from their planned form?
7. Did you revert to lower-level questions in tight situations?

RETEACH Correct areas that seem to be problems for you. Rewrite questions where necessary. How will you encourage longer answers? What will you do if you get one-word answers? Identify a different group of children and teach your revised lesson.

EVALUATE What were noticeable areas of improvement? Identify specific outcomes. How did rephrasing questions affect the outcome? How did you manage the phrasing of questions for different cognitive levels? What were the responses to the rephrased questions like? Identify areas that still remain problems. If you are still having problems or seem to need more practice, we suggest you return to the module at a point you deem best for yourself.

After that roller coaster ride, this may be a good time for you to take a break from this material—stretch your legs or get your stomach back. Of course, you may want to take additional rides later.

Proceed to Module II.

MODULE II:
THE P.R. STRATEGIES

What do you do after you have asked a question? "It depends on what I get for answers" is probably your response. The questioning strategies to be discusssed here deal primarily with the moves the teacher makes to manage pupil responses. Therefore, they are responding procedures. There is some real P.R. in practicing these strategies. Sometimes it is difficult to get children to see the merit in responding and therefore to respond adequately. Some students have been driven to finding unique ways to escape involvement. They may also give responses based on misconceptions or misunderstandings. However, seldom does a student give wrong answers by design. Students need help in building suitable answers.

Try This

Sit in a classroom and listen to the kinds of answers students give during a lesson. Do not be surprised if you find mostly one-word answers, "I don't know's," or other very brief responses.

The P.R. skills (pausing, redirecting, prompting, refocusing, and reflecting)[3] are planned to increase the number of good and thoughtful answers given by your students. They are divided into two general groups: (1) those designed to *increase* the number of pupil responses and (2) those that *extend* responses. The expected outcome is a more personalized interaction. The personal attention built into these strategies reinforces the student's confidence in you and himself. The consequence can only be a more positive kind of understanding. Although these skills will be described under one heading, you might find it quite useful to practice them independent of one another in a micro-teaching situation with students.

Increasing the Number of Responses: Pausing and Wait-Time

INSTRUCTIONAL
LESSON

Elsewhere,[4] we have described the rapid-fire technique of questioning. Because of its question-answer-question-answer pattern it is considered an undesirable activity, one that discourages thoughtful involvement by students. Research continues to support this position. Teachers ask too many questions. Consequently, students are not given time enough to think. If a teacher's purpose is to evoke longer and more thoughtful responses, it will be necessary to provide time for them. It has been found that an average of fourteen seconds is required for high-ability ninth graders to respond to an open question. Yet studies [5] show that teachers generally do

---

[3] Adapted from Walter Borg, Marjorie Kelley, and Philip Langer, *Effective Questioning: Mini Course I,* Far West Laboratory for Educational Research and Development (Beverly Hills, Calif.: Macmillan Educational Services, Inc., 1970).

[4] James Weigand, ed., *Developing Teacher Competencies* (Englewood Cliffs, N.J.: Prentice-Hall, 1971), p. 120.

[5] See, for example, Mary Budd Rowe, "Science, Silence and Sanctions," *Science and Children,* National Science Teachers Association, Washington, D.C., March 1969, p. 11.

not pause more than one second after a question. As a result, all children are cheated of the opportunity to use and develop their intellectual skills. Classroom observations reveal that the slow learner is expected to respond faster and given less time and encouragement for his answers than the average or fast learner.

In one study, Mary Budd Rowe [6] and her associates experimented with an increased wait-time of three to five seconds. The consequences were revealing and exciting. Some of the outcomes were that:

1. Students gave more answers and answers that were longer, more thoughtful, and more complete in linguistic structure.
2. More pupils responded and gave more hypothesizing or postulating types of answers.
3. They seemed more confident in their responses.
4. Even more important, students began to ask more questions.
5. Teachers found that students who were usually turned off about learning suddenly became excited about contributing.
6. Teachers changed their questioning behavior by increasing the variety of questions and the number of thought-provoking questions.
7. The learning process was not deterred by too much teacher talk, which resulted in more of a student-centered approach.

The advantages for the teacher in using wait-time effectively are that he gets to know his students better because he does more listening, he is allowed time to think and to do a better job of directing the learning, and his overly optimistic expectations for learners change drastically. As a consequence of knowing his students well, a teacher is in a better position to make and interpret evaluative statements about their performance and progress. Pausing ultimately results in two main outcomes:

1. It stimulates more of an open-discussion interaction context.
2. Students develop an ability to use the pausing time to construct more complete answers. [7]

However, even though you may have mastered the technique, students will not immediately change into more responsive individuals. You have to help them understand the purpose of the pause by using words or phrases that draw attention to the pausing (verbal prompts) in conjunction with an indication that you expect them to use the time to think of answers. Some possibilities for prompts follow:

---

[6] *Ibid.*
[7] Borg, Kelley, and Langer, *Effective Questioning,* p. 31.

1. I'm going to ask a question that I want you to really think about, so don't rush your answer.
2. This question is a toughie, so think about it before you answer.
3. I know that in the questions that follow you might be anxious to give answers, but let's hold back for a little while and give everyone a chance to think.

Try Some.   Construct some examples of prompts you might use. List three to five below.

Another example might be: "When I ask questions, I am going to pause so you can get your thoughts together and give complete answers."

Obviously, in using pausing and its related prompting strategies, you will ask more open questions. It would be impractical to pause after a factual question. After a time, the prompting can be abandoned. It must be clear to the student, however, that using the pausing time is expected of him. Reinforcing longer, more thoughtful answers will insure its implantation. It is also a good idea not to reinforce short or incomplete answers.

A classroom dialogue in which a teacher uses pausing is illustrated here. Note the student responses.

T. What were some of the things Lightning Joe told Tom about? (PAUSE)

S. He told him about the big woods and that there were so many rabbits in the big woods that you could step on 'em. (REDIRECT)

S. And he told them when he shot the gun or aimed the gun Jennie had better luck with it. (REDIRECT)

S. And he told them about a cave near the river bank that Indians used to live in and about how the trees reached clear down to the river. (REDIRECT)

S. And that there were so many fish they could shake a stick at them. (REDIRECT)

S. They talked about the prairie chicken. (REDIRECT)

S. And about the frogs that ran across the road.

T. We know that Tom was very anxious to see Ma and Pa, but suppose Tom had wanted to stay in Maryland and go to school—how would this have changed our story? (PAUSE)

(Seven complete-sentence answers followed the last question.)

Plan a brief lesson using the pausing strategy. Record your lesson as you work with a small group of children. Note the number and length of the responses.

Increasing the Number of Responses: Redirecting

The strategy used by the teacher in the dialogue above is relatively simple. Nevertheless, it is an effective procedure for increasing pupil participation and reducing teacher talk. When a pupil redirects, he nods, calls the name of another student, or uses some phrase to indicate recognition of another student. When you initiate this strategy, however, you will have to use more sophisticated prompts. Inform the students that you expect more than one of them to respond: "Mark, what else might you add to that answer?" "How do you respond to her answer, Jeff?" "When I finish with this question, I want more than one answer. I will give each of you a chance." At all times remember that your main goal is to increase the number of pupil responses. The advantage is that you are laying the groundwork for them to do more responding to one another. It is also a way to eliminate choral responses. The longer prompts should be dropped after a short time. Notice that our teacher in the dialogue didn't use any verbal cues. If the prompts are not dropped, you run the risk of doing too much talking.

An important consideration in redirection is the kind of question you ask. Certainly, a question that does not allow more than one or two acceptable answers is not suitable. Be sure to avoid repeating your questions. An open-ended or multiple answer (listing) or an opinionated question is good for redirecting. Most high cognitive questions fit the need, and their use will help improve question quality.

Which of the following would be good questions for redirecting?

1. What is the main crop of Argentina?
2. What are some of the events that led to the Civil War?
3. What is a pesticide?
4. What are some ways of improving the quality of the product?
5. Who is the advertiser?
6. Why did John react the way he did?

If you chose questions 2, 4, and 6, you're right! An additional consideration is that using questions that allow several answers will produce two advantages:

1. Students have more time to think.
2. Hearing all the different answers will permit more relationships to be made and will help clear up misconceptions held by students. It is also an appropriate step toward building lengthier answers.

Write a question sequence that illustrates redirection.

Extending Responses:
Prompting and Clarifying

Students should learn that not all answers are acceptable. The number of times that teachers allow students to get away with giving one-word, brief-phrase, or incomplete answers, or even an "I don't know," is appalling. Accepting any and all answers is not a justified means of reinforcing students; you only cheat them if you do so. Partial answers reflect fragmented thoughts, and if the learner is allowed to continue responding in this fashion, he will become incapable of complete and logical thought. A teacher has an obligation to inform the student of the status of his response on an acceptability scale. This can be done without being punitive. It is possible to tactfully inform a student that his answer is only partly correct or is partly unacceptable—accentuate the positive.

We have observed that the two previous pedagogical moves—pausing and redirecting—were fairly simple strategies to employ. However, using the probing strategies (new P.R. word) of prompting and clarifying will be more challenging. You need to make a judgment about the quality of the response and find a verbal prompt that fits with what you know about the student and the purpose of the question. Yes, there is a personalizing quality about it. Your task is to build inadequate responses into longer and more thoughtful responses.

In prompting, you first need to inform the student about the quality of his response. We don't mean a judgment of good or bad, but something more in terms of acceptability. Reinforce the correct portion of his answer and then seek to modify the incorrect or incomplete part. Some examples:

1. Your answer isn't too far off, but you really need to rethink the last part. Give it some thought—it'll come back to you in a minute.
2. Your answer is about four-fifths right; how would you correct the other one fifth?
3. Bill's answer is about 33 percent correct; how would you help him boost that up to 100 percent?

Try This

List other statements you might make as prompts in order to obtain a more complete response from the student.

What do you think you might do if a student says, "I don't know"?

One strategy is to start asking the student lower-level questions to help him gather information so that he can build himself to where he can respond to a more divergent question. In any case, he should learn that you expect him to give complete answers and that you are sincere about helping him. Calling his attention to relationships with your questions helps.

The exact questions to be used as prompts depend on the answers given to the original question. The key is to inform the student of the quality of his answer in a tactful and a nonrepulsive manner. Negative reinforcement can only have a short-term effect. *Never pit students against one another.* Allow time for a student to reconstruct his answers. Others can become accustomed to giving this much attention to one member for a few minutes. If you don't pursue a student's misunderstanding immediately and clear it up before moving on, it is likely never to be cleared up. Besides, such failure to follow up tells the student you don't really care that much about his answers, and this defeats your purpose.

Clarifying is also a move used to have the student improve the quality of his response. The student's response may contain the idea of an appropriate answer but lack organization. It may be incomplete, or it may reflect shallow thinking, misconceptions, or misunderstandings. But at least the student has demonstrated a willingness to respond. Using verbal prompts (questions), the teacher seeks to have the student add his own information so as to improve his response. Some examples are:

How might you add to your answer?
What else could you tell us about it?
How could you improve your answer to make it more understandable?

Clarifying may also be applied to someone else's answer. If a student is unable to respond to a clarifying question, it then becomes necessary to start prompting him with lower-level questions and then ask him clarifying questions. For example:

T. What else can you tell us about it?

S. I don't know.

T. Did it have more than one part?

S. Yes.

T. What was the outer shell like?

S. Shiny—like metal.

T. What are some other things you noted about it?

S. It had strange-colored lights, oddly shaped windows, and was oblong in shape.

The clarifying strategy is also employed when you know the student is guessing. In this case, you usually ask him to justify his answer or to provide a rationale. For example: [8]

T. Mark Twain says that Tom Sawyer was not the model boy of the village. What are some things that Tom did that would support that statement?

S. He was really mischievous.

T. In what way?

S. Like he played hookey from school and he was able to trick lots of people into doing what had to be done.

[8] Meredith Gall, Barbara Dunning, and Rita Weathersby, *Higher Cognitive Questioning: Mini Course IX*, Far West Laboratory for Educational Research and Development (Beverly Hills, Calif.: Macmillan Educational Services, Inc., 1971), pp. 143–45.

T. What kind of person is Tom?

S. A sneaky one.

T. What do you mean?

S. He tricked his aunt. First he tricked her into coming out in the open; out the door. Then he told her to look around.

S. He's tricky.

T. How?

Some additional clarifying questions might be:

1. What are your reasons for that answer?
2. What do you mean by that statement?
3. I'm not sure I quite understand; would you restate it for me?

Try This

Construct some other examples of clarifying questions you could ask to help students extend their answers. What criteria did you use to word the questions?

Extending Responses: Refocusing and Reflecting

Students do give "right" answers. By "right" we mean responses that match with what the teacher wanted, not what he was willing to accept as close. We are talking here about what to do when you receive good or acceptable answers, not something that faintly resembles a right answer. Refocusing basically relates to the cognitive domain, whereas reflecting is an affective-domain operation.

When you ask refocusing questions you request the student to expand his conceptual base by relating his answer to previous learnings and to respond with a more comprehensive answer. This is what you would do if you were taking a child through a sequence leading to higher cognitive questions. This process is much more demanding of the teacher, however, because he must have a thorough knowledge of several topics simultaneously and how they may be related. The refocusing process is what you do to lead children to abstract thinking, for refocusing is an important step in concept development. The dialogue below illustrates one example of refocusing.

T. What words do you know that have the long sound of "o"?

S. (several students respond) "Coal," "Oh," "Comb," "Moat," and so forth.

T. What words can you group together because they are alike in some way?

S. (several illustrations)

T. Why do you group those words together?

S. Because they have a T on the end.

T. Thinking of the reasons, what are some of the labels for these groups?

S. (several rationales given)

T. What is a good label for this group?

This dialogue is representative of the model formulated by Hilda Taba.[9] In this model, questions require (1) enumerating, (2) finding bases for grouping, (3) identifying common characteristics, (4) labeling groups, and (5) subsuming items under labels.

Some examples of refocusing questions are:

1. How does that relate to the story we read yesterday?
2. What relationship do you see between the school dropout rate and the increase in volunteers for the army?
3. How is the life of the people of Hyku different from or similar to the people of Nabre?
4. What comparisons do you see between the green plant and a factory?
5. How does your answer help explain the problem we were trying to solve yesterday?

Obviously, each question must respond directly to an answer just given by the student. You can probably recognize answers that might stimulate the above questions.

Reflecting is a responding procedure used to cause a student to reconfirm a position he has taken, clarify a feeling he has, test the duration of a belief he holds, and/or justify a choice. In using reflecting questions to respond to the student's original answer, the teacher might create dissonance. He might also challenge a student's position, distort his previous response, raise a moral issue, make negative assumptions, and cite incon-

---

[9] Hilda Taba, *Teachers Handbook for Elementary Social Studies* (Palo Alto, Calif.: Addison-Wesley, 1967).

sistencies. However, moralizing, preaching, or imposing values is not involved. Rather, a brief encounter with a student is used merely to stimulate his thought. The burden of action or decision lies with the student.

The teacher uses the reflecting procedure with no expected outcomes or goals other than to get the student to know himself better. The questions used are open-ended—there are no right answers—and are always directed to an individual. Reflecting is a very personalized activity related to the attitudes, beliefs, feelings, and goals of the person being questioned. It can help the student clear his thinking of ambiguities and confused ideas. The student has to reexamine those things he cherishes or values. There is no pattern for the teacher to follow in questioning for reflection. Therefore, this procedure can be creative and extremely responsive to the individual. You need to know your students well. You must also be unbiased and accepting. Here are two examples of the use of reflecting:

S. I believe that all men are created equal.

T. What do you mean by that?

S. I guess I mean that all people are equally good and none should have advantages over others.

T. Does this idea suggest that some changes need to be made in our world, even in this school and this town?

S. Oh, lots of them. Want me to name some?

T. No, we have to get back to our spelling lesson, but I was just wondering if you were working on any of those changes, actually trying to bring them about.

S. Not yet, but I may soon.

T. I see. Now, back to the spelling list.[10]

T. You say, Glenn, that you are a liberal in political matters?

Glenn. Yes, I am.

T. Where did your ideas come from?

Glenn. Well, my parents I guess, mostly.

T. Are you familiar with other positions?

Glenn. Well, sort of.

T. I see, Glenn. Now, class, getting back to the homework. . . .[11]

[10] Louis Raths, Merril Harmin, and Sidney Simon, *Values and Teaching* (Columbus, Ohio: Charles E. Merrill, 1966), pp. 52–54.
[11] *Ibid.*, p. 55.

It is impossible to list all possible reflective responses. For a comprehensive set you might study the book, *Values and Teaching*.[12] A few sample responses from this book are listed below:

1. *Is this something that you prize?* . . . The response could, of course, be in a different form and have the same intent, e.g., "Are you proud of that?" "Is that something that is very important to you?" "Is that idea very dear to you; do you really cherish it?"

2. *Did you consider any alternatives?* Note how this tends to widen or open up the thinking of children. With this response, as with all the others in the list, teachers will need to accept whatever the student replies without judgment. After he answers the question, leave him with an honest "Oh, now I see," or "I understand," or "You stated your views clearly," or "I appreciate hearing what you say," or some non-judgmental phrase or gesture.

3. *Have you felt this way for a long time?* Questions that get at the same thing are, "When did you first begin to believe in that idea?" and "How have your ideas or understandings changed since the time you first considered this notion?" Here the person is pushed to examine the history of his beliefs or attitudes, to look at their origins, and to see if they are really his or if they have been absorbed unthinkingly.[13]

Try This

Brainstorm questions that could encourage reflective responses.

Some other possible reflecting questions: [14]

"Do you do anything about that idea?"
"How does that idea affect your daily life?"
"Have you thought much about that idea?"
"Do you have any reasons for [saying or doing] that?"

The P.R. strategies for extending student responses just explored can be defined as a continuum:

---

[12] *Ibid.*
[13] *Ibid.*, pp. 55–62.
[14] *Ibid.*

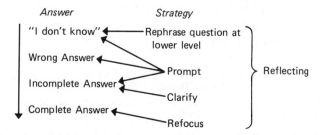

Reflecting stands somewhat apart from the continuum. It might be considered a free-floating strategy that is inserted when the situation permits.

A. Pausing.
B. Prompting.
C. Redirecting.
D. Clarifying.
E. Refocusing.
F. Reflecting.

Identify the activity by letter.

___1. Asks probing questions to help the student improve the quality of his answer.

___2. Asks the student to relate his answer to previous learnings.

___3. Counters the rapid-fire technique and tends to establish a question-answer-answer-answer pattern.

___4. Encourages more student participation by having several students respond to the same question.

___5. A strategy used along with most of the others to help the student give more complete answers; it uses statements of encouragement.

___6. A strategy that causes the student to look at the value implications of his responses.

Key

1—D	4—C
2—E	5—B
3—A	6—F

If you identified all six correctly, you have done well to sort out the differences and similarities.

If you did not match them correctly, it might be good for you to review each strategy. There were several to keep in mind.

PLAN
A
LESSON
Consider carefully the information given and develop a learning experience to use with a small group of children. Plan the use of the P.R. strategies. You might, however, focus only on one strategy at a time (wait-time). Therefore, you might conduct more than one lesson. Try to insert others as the occasion allows.

TEACH
Critique the tape of the activity. Consider the following questions:

1. How long were your pauses?
2. How did students respond to the use of the pauses?
3. To what did the students respond?
4. What kinds of responses resulted from the wait-time?

ANALYZE
5. Did you ask questions that allowed for redirection?
6. How many times were you able to have the students refocus?
7. How could you improve the use of redirection? How many and what kinds of prompts were necessary?
8. Were you able to employ the appropriate prompts to different answers?
9. How could you improve this technique?
10. How might the content studied affect the outcome of the lesson?

Reconsider the phrasing of your questions. Did you take advantage of opportunities to have students clarify their answers? Construct other criteria from the discussion of the strategies to evaluate your lessons.

RETEACH
On the basis of your analyses and the feedback from the lesson, reteach the same lesson to different students, and/or revise the lesson to include other strategies or plan a new experience. You might test a new strategy or apply the familiar strategies to different content.

EVALUATE
What difficulties might you have in using these strategies in a regular classroom situation? Identify areas that you will need to spend more time developing. You may have found the refocusing and reflecting procedures quite difficult unless you had previous contact with the same students you have now. What did you discover about your own behavior?

If you feel comfortable about these strategies, move on to Module III.

MODULE III:
PERSONALIZING QUESTIONING

The critical difference between impersonalized and personalized learning is the teacher. Studies confirm the impact of the teacher's behavior. We maintain that the teacher who will swing the pendulum to the positive side is the teacher who can use effective questioning. Appropriate questioning permits the teacher to create the open and flexible atmosphere conducive to positive interpersonal relations. Humaneness is a quality of interaction. Questions are usually the stimulus for this interaction.

Probably the most unreal aspect of the educational scene is the preponderance of failure. Failure must be one of the most inhumane and debilitating experiences that can happen to a person. Yet, for many students it is an everyday occurrence. They don't lack intellectual ability. They have been the victims of a highly impersonal world that is reflected in questions used to test for factual knowledge. As a consequence, they perceive themselves as incompetent and incapable of reasoning. In addition, they are confused by value conflicts, threatened by adult intervention, and reluctant to be involved, or committed. The learner's perception of himself is by far the greatest determinant for success. If he distrusts his own experiences, he becomes more dependent, less responsible, and increasingly dull-minded. As a result, he feels inadequate and incompetent.

Teachers who challenge students to think stimulate them to use their intellectual powers, encourage them to extend their thinking to abstract levels, and restore their confidence. Teachers who allow students to practice freedom and cooperation promote understanding. Teachers humanize and personalize the teaching-learning process when they set forth value concerns for unbiased study by the class. Teachers who lead students to self-understanding through questioning are effective practitioners of humanism. Humanizing and personalizing is bringing students to realize their own potential. Great power for accomplishing this lies in their skill in questioning.

Learning how to clarify values should be an integral part of the classroom activity. It can be done through subject matter or conducted as a separate activity. Questioning on the part of both the student and teacher is the main mode of presenting issues for clarification. We do not propose to determine values for the student. The purpose is to help him better understand his own values and the process involved in evolving values as a way of making sense out of a very confusing world. Value clarification is a highly personalized set of moves that serves the following purposes: awareness of values, exploration of alternatives, consideration of consequences, measurement of actions against beliefs, and dealing with options. A few strategies of value clarification are described in this module.

Values Voting [15]

This is a quick and easy means of posing value-oriented questions and having students make a public confirmation of their beliefs. It illustrates

[15] Adapted from: Sidney Simon, Leland Howe, and Howard Kirschenbaum, *Values Clarification: A Handbook of Practical Strategies for Teachers and Students* (New York: Hart Publishing Company, 1972), p. 38.

very vividly how people view issues differently. The teacher asks a series of questions that begin with the phrase "How many" or "Which of you." For example, "How many of you like to daydream?" Affirmation is demonstrated by a show of hands. Those who want to respond no give a thumbs-down sign. If undecided, a student can fold his arms. Those who wish to pass may do nothing at all. Specific values can be highlighted, and a discussion of different outlooks is an appropriate follow-up. Some examples of questions for value voting follow:

1. . . . wish you could be someone else?
2. . . . think you should be able to express your own ideas at all times?
3. . . . enjoy talking to people?
4. . . . would not buy products made in a foreign country?
5. . . . feel threatened by some people?
6. . . . would leave a party if some others were smoking marijuana?
7. . . . think students lack respect for their teachers?

Try This

Add to the list of questions started above. Consider specific value concerns that might be introduced to the group you are concerned with. Construct as many questions related to these issues as you can in ten minutes.

TIME OUT

Many of your previous activities were conducted with small groups of students. It might prove more fruitful to try values voting strategies with a whole class. Identify a class of students you can work with, and spend some time raising value questions on which they can vote. Consider the basis for discussion. Note reactions carefully. However, you might want to wait and try more than one values clarification strategy.

Decision making is an important part of everyday life. We constantly have to make choices between options. For some this is much more difficult than for others. Some simple examples:

1. Shall I go to the store now or later?
2. Shall I wear a halter or blouse?
3. Should I pay this bill now or spend the money on groceries?

Rank ordering helps students to deal with situations in which options are available and to defend their choices to others. They see why they must be open-minded about the content of the thought that they give to several possibilities when they are considering value concerns.

The teacher presents the students with a question and three to four answers that they must rank in order of preference. In so doing they are reflecting their value system. After asking the question the teacher writes the options on the chalkboard and calls on five to seven students to give their rankings. A follow-up discussion may be used to have students explain why they took the position they did in their rankings.

Some examples of rank-ordering questions are listed below:

1. What kind of person do you like best?
   __One who makes you feel good.
   __One who has clear objectives and follows through.
   __One who is popular with other people.
2. What would you like to change about yourself?
   __Your appearance.
   __Your ability to do things.
   __Your life style.
3. If you had a free morning, which would you rather do?
   __Sleep in.
   __Do something for someone else.
   __Work on your hobby.
   __Watch TV.
4. How would you prefer to obtain your spending money?
   __Have it given to you.
   __Earn an allowance.
   __Get a job on your own.

[16] *Ibid.*, p. 58.

5. Where would you like most to live?
   __On a farm.
   __Near a lake.
   __In the inner city.
   __In a suburb.
6. Who would you most want to be like?
   __Your mother (or father).
   __A friend.
   __A TV star.

Try Some

Put together some of your own rank-ordering questions. Brainstorm as many as you can in a ten-minute period. Surely you should be able to identity some other critical issues.

Values Continuum [17]

Using the values continuum helps students explore a range of alternative responses. They realize that issues are not clearly delineated and that there are varying attitudes about them. When students respond to the value continuum questions, they will have to expose their attitudes and opinions to others.

Construct a line the length of the classroom or in the hallway. Use string or tape and mark the line off in seven equal parts.

Present the question to the class and have them write down the position they would take. Now have them position themselves on the line accord-

[17] *Ibid.*, p. 116.

How far would you go to win someone's friendship?

Would do anything at all,
even if it meant losing
another friend

Would do
nothing
at all

1   8

How do you feel about going to school in the summer?

Sluff-off Sammy
would prefer not
to spend any time
in school

Enthusiastic Eddie
would spend
weekends in school
if he could

1   8

What kind of relationship would you most like to have with your teachers?

Chummy,
complete freedom

middle of the
road; lets several
things go

complete
disciplinarian; lets
you get away with
nothing

1   8

How sanitary are you?

Dirty Denny chews
gum from under the
desks

Germ-Proof
Peter washes hands
constantly 18

1   8

How much responsibility do you assume?

Need to be told
almost everything
you must do

Volunteering Viola:
You do everything of
your own volition

1   8

ing to their selection. This will discourage a decision based on peer action. While the students occupy these spots, conduct a discussion about why they took the position they did. Some examples follow:

Try Your Own

Plan and write out some of your own questions for a question continuum.

18 *Ibid.*, p. 125.

Percentage Questions [19]

Forced-choice responses have some limitations. Usually, our decisions are not of an either-or nature. The use of percentage questions helps students qualify their feelings and beliefs. It allows them to examine the direction and nature of their priorities. When you use this strategy with students, present them with a number of questions one at a time so that they can record their responses. Arrange the class into small groups of three to five students and have them discuss their responses with the other members of the group. Some examples of percentage questions follow:

1. What percentage of your time do you give to helping others?
2. What percentage of your allowance do you think you should save?
3. What percentage of your allowance do you save?
4. What percentage of your time is spent helping around home?
5. What percentage of your time is spent watching TV?
6. What perecntage of your time is spent reading or working on a hobby?

Try Your Talents

Construct some percentage questions of your own. We are sure you can improve upon the quality of the above list.

<hr>

[19] *Ibid.,* 224.

TIME OUT

If you have worked on value clarification with a specific group of students before, it might be more useful to continue with the same group. If this is your first attempt at value clarification, identify a class you can work with. Explore the value classification strategies with the students by using questions you have constructed yourself. Observe carefully the patterns displayed by individual students. You may communicate your own value system to students, but avoid doing so in such a way that their responses are influenced by yours.

Simon et al.'s excellent *Values Clarification* contains seventy-nine different proven effective techniques. We encourage you to obtain a copy of this book and to explore these strategies as a way of improving your capabilities for personalizing learning. The idea for the four techniques described in this module originates with this book. The authors report proven success in several areas. Students become more involved, enthusiastic, and thoughtful about themselves and others. The book's greatest impact has been in reversing the trend for students who have difficulty in school.

Values clarification is only one dimension of personalization. However, helping a student feel comfortable about his beliefs and attitudes and knowledgeable about why he acts the way he does, thereby making him feel good about himself, has to be a very humanistic and personalized approach. Perhaps this is the way to help the thousands of individuals who are confused about life, who are unmotivated and uninvolved, who seek escapes, and who are unsettled about their life goals or their work life.

Proceed to Module IV.

MODULE IV:
PUPIL QUESTIONING

INSTRUCTIONAL
LESSON

It seems almost criminal that students sometimes do not have the opportunity to ask questions in classrooms. It is a fact that this occurs: students may not be given the opportunity to question before, during, or after a learning activity. How can one really be considered a learner without being able to ask questions? What is learning? If learning is defined as the consumption and regurgitation of factual information, then the student does not need to question. If, however, it is defined as a change in behavior resulting from interaction (with materials, people, and events) in which the learner plays an active role, then questioning by the student is crucial.

When not allowed and required to ask questions, students are being cheated of their means of becoming rational, inquiring individuals capable of dealing with problem situations, acting independently, considering logical consequences, and establishing effective channels of communication with other human beings. Preschoolers and kindergarten children inundate adults with questions. However, the farther they go in school, the less inclined they are to ask questions.

If they are given the opportunity to ask questions, students tend to participate more. They strive to improve their own questions if they can see the importance of learning. It is crucial for the teacher to show enthusiasm for the questions students raise. Students attach value to their peers' questions according to the importance given their own. This is an excellent means of building respect and understanding. The teacher must reveal to his students a genuine interest in their questions. As a teacher, you have a responsibility to establish an environment that communicates a need for questioning by the students. Tell them you expect them to ask questions; then structure activities that both stimulate and allow time for student questioning. This questioning will not occur without reinforcement on your part.

Here are some advantages of turning the questioning over to the pupils: [20]

1. It can revitalize their curiosity and allow them to express their interests.
2. It can open new lines of communication between adults and children and between students.
3. Students are not nearly as threatened by asking questions as they are by giving answers.
4. The kinds of questions asked and the pattern used by the students reveals information about thinking, feelings, attitudes and values, and cognitive skills.
5. Students will do more conversing with one another.
6. They are more responsible for their own learning.
7. It matches more with the reality of everyday life.[21]

Activity. Brainstorm other advantages.

---

[20] John Warren Stewig, "Instructional Strategies," *Elementary English* 50 (April 1973), 46–48.

Try This

Plan and conduct a lesson in which you purposely emphasize student questioning. Your topic and technique will make a difference. Evaluate the lesson on the basis of the following criteria: [21]

1. How and how often do you encourage students to ask questions on any phase of the topic?
2. How patient are you in allowing students to formulate and ask questions?
3. To whom do the students direct their questions?
4. How do you help students resolve solutions to questions that bother them?
5. Who answers the questions posed by students?
6. How do you treat a question once it is asked?
7. How do you follow up with the student who asked the question for evidence of its resolution?
8. What criteria do you set for the questions students ask?
9. What do you do with questions that represent dissent or matters of opinion?

Activity: On the basis of your observations and lessons, brainstorm other questions to ask about the way to handle student questioning.

Activities for Pupil Questioning

Students need to have the opportunity to explore alternatives by means of questioning. Critical thinking is widely recognzied as a valuable skill. Some of the elements of critical thinking include interpreting the meaning of statements, identifying ambiguity in reasoning, seeing contradictions in positions, recognizing appropriate authority for information, and judging the feasibility of conclusions. Questioning has proved effective in developing these skills. The activities that follow represent a few ways to involve students in the role of question asker. Certainly, you will generate ideas or modifications as you read.

[21] Reprinted courtesy of *Business Education World* magazine, copyright May/June 1970.

Brainstorming Questions

Although this is a fairly simple technique, it does allow students to initiate something with which they have not had much practice. If used properly, it can set the stage for a number of more involved and challenging activities. Describe a situation for which students might brainstorm questions. One approach is to present them with a provocative passage, such as the one below. To assure more success with the question-raising process, use a topic that is close to their interests. Other bases for brainstorming include controversial topics, current or local issues, pictures, discrepant events, problem situations, critical incidents, and behavioral problems. Instruct the students to try to be creative and to record questions as quickly as they come to mind.

Try It Yourself! Take five minutes and brainstorm as many questions as you can for this passage.

Over 23 million Americans 18 years of age and older have completed less than 8 years of schooling. Eight million adults 25 and over have completed less than 5 years. At least the latter and many of the former are likely to be, for all practical purposes, illiterate. Those who have not completed high school are only 46 percent of the total labor force; yet they account for 64 percent of the unemployed. Sixty-two percent of the jobless fathers of children receiving aid to dependent children have no education beyond elementary school. Forty-five percent of all families with less than $2,000 annual income have a family head with less than an eighth grade education. The link between lack of education and the over $4.5 billion now spent annually on welfare payments to 7.25 million persons is beyond dispute.[22]

As a follow-up to the brainstorming session with students, you might:

1. Examine questions on the basis of similarities, differences, intent, feelings, or cognitive levels.
2. Use questions as a basis for organizing the study of a unit or area.
3. Utilize the questions for a group discussion of the situation or related concerns.
4. Use questions as a way of extending learnings.
5. Look for misconceptions or misunderstandings.
6. Consider a more structured analysis of questions.

[22] Grant Venn, ed., *Man, Education and Manpower* (Washington, D.C.: The American Association of School Administrators, 1970), p. 123.

Analysis of Questions

We have found that students at most age levels can become very involved in analyzing questions in terms of cognitive function. They learn to apply the taxonomy of cognitive levels and construct questions for the different levels. This has been especially successful with upper elementary and junior high school students. The following procedures might be employed:

1. Provide a question-answer situation (utilizing printed dialogue and/or an audio- or video-taped lesson in which the students were participants) and have them react to questions and answers from a general base, perhaps using their own criteria for evaluating the lesson. Some criteria that might be used are:
   A. Intent of the lesson.
   B. Fit of questions to content.
   C. Relation of questions to materials used.
   D. Phrasing of questions.
   E. Relation of questions to values or feelings.
   F. Timing of questions.
2. Involve students in developing skill in categorizing and constructing questions for different cognitive levels.
3. Provide students the opportunity to analyze questions from the affective domain. Criteria related to feeling, attitudes, values, and value clarification may originate from their own questions. In this situation and the previous one students find it fun to contrive circumstances in which they can try out their questions on one another.
4. After a question-raising and exploring experience using an existing transcribed dialogue of a classroom lesson, have the students trace the pattern or sequence of the questions and answers.
5. Analyze question-answer lessons for logical patterns and response quality.

Situations in Which To Encourage Questioning

1. From their analyses of questions students might construct and use surveys to test the effectiveness of their questions.
2. Pictures have merit at all levels, but they are particularly useful with young children for both cognitive and affective questions.
3. Role playing can be useful for both the application and the raising of questions, for it encourages involvement.
4. Students enjoy making and analyzing their own tape recordings of questions and responses.

5. Questioning skills may be applied and tested in interviews.
6. Construct and use "brain teasers."
7. Students might analyze questions in textbooks or other printed materials.
8. Stories and poems prove helpful in stimulating student questions.
9. A number of games and game-oriented activities are now on the market. Simulation games, self-created games, and other commercial games are extremely interesting. Questioneze, Queries and Theories, and Explanation are games specific to questioning. The Caribou Game, Road Game, and Star Power represent some of the many games that encourage interaction.

Here is an example of an instructional situation in which questioning is encouraged.

Have each person in a group write down five or six things about himself, such as traits, possessions, recent experiences, and physical features. A coordinator collects the papers and redistributes them, making sure no one gets his own. Then each person moves about the room questioning others in an attempt to find the individual with the attributes listed on his paper. Questions would best be phrased as yes-no questions. A questioner cannot ask directly for identification of the attribute. For example, if the item was "I got a parking ticket," the questioner should not ask, "Did you get a parking ticket?" He must ask questions whose answers allow him to infer this conclusion.

TIME OUT

Plan an activity with students that would involve one or more of the procedures so far described. Record the outcomes.

One of the most prominent applications of student questioning is contained in Richard Suchman's *Inquiry Development Program*.[23] You might locate and study this technique. Suchman also presents some excellent ideas for evaluating student progress in developing cognitive operations and inquiry skills by an analysis of their questions.

Directing Questions to Other Students

As a teacher, you can assure positive outcomes in pupil questioning if you employ strategies for directing their questions to peers. It must, of course, be clear that this is not side-stepping on your part. The students must realize that you genuinely want them to interact with one another in their questioning activities rather than participating only in two-way con-

[23] (Chicago: Science Research Associates, 1966.)

versations with the teacher. An example might be, "John, Bess has a pretty good question; how would you respond to it?" Or, "Before I react to the question let's hear how some of you might answer it." We are sure you can devise even better prompts to use in directing student questions to others.

Try Some Here!   Write as many different prompts that come to mind.

Reinforcing Pupil Questions

You need to be a good listener. A teacher who is more concerned with moving on in the subject matter will squelch student questioning. Respect unusual ideas and questions. What appears strange initially may be very creative. Be sensitive to the intent of a student's questions, and try to read into the questions interpretations of feelings or attitudes that may require follow-up. Try to help students deal with problems, concerns, or uncertainty by assisting them in breaking down their questions into comprehensible parts. Students need to know that their ideas and questions have worth. They see this more readily when others respond to their questions and when their questions are used for some purpose. Provide periods of unevaluated practice and unrestricted experiences in self-initiated learning. In structuring the learning environment it is important to provide students with materials with which to interact as they begin to question. Research demonstrates a high student dependence on such materials.

Activity.   Spend some time just listening to students. Force yourself to listen carefully to what they are saying or implying. Creating a situation in which students are free to talk about a topic at length would probably serve your purposes best.

PLAN
A
LESSON   Utilizing some of the questioning situations described above, plan a learning experience that will allow a small group of children to become involved in the question-raising process.

TEACH   The use of an audio or video tape will be important in this situation. The students will be anxious to comment on their questions. We expect you will find that one teaching experience will not be enough to see change.

ANALYZE   The criteria you use to analyze the pupil questions will depend on the situation. However, we are sure you will find that it is possible to analyze the questions in several ways. On the basis of the data presented in the instructional lesson, devise a plan for improving or extending the pupil questioning. You may consider cognitive level, number or length of questions, student attitudes, speaking time of pupil versus teacher, or using student questions to further discussion.

RETEACH   Plan a second experience either to explore a new area of student questioning or to improve upon your previous lesson.

EVALUATE   Apply your previously established criteria and reconsider areas that you will have to work on if you are to develop skill in this area.

SUMMARY

The purpose of this chapter has been to help you master a competency for implementing questioning as a means for personalized interaction with students. We have isolated the strategies so that you could study and practice them one at a time. However, we are sure it is apparent to you by now that reality requires you to call on all of these skills, sometimes simultaneously. Your challenge now is to integrate these techniques and apply them where the situation demands. We are confident you are ready to meet this challenge. Your next major step will be to practice these questioning skills in a whole-class situation. This will be more problematic. With continued study and practice you should also be able to master this situation. Implanting effective questioning is like learning to play golf with some degree of skill. If you don't persist, you'll remain a duffer. Behavior changes slowly. However, the success you achieve in applying the ideas of this chapter should stimulate you to continue modifying your behavior toward becoming a better teacher and person.

The crux of any communication between persons lies in their ability to ask appropriate questions. Becoming a sensitive, responsive, and loving human being is important to youth today. A teacher who is conscious of this in his questioning will be more successful. A teacher who uses the more personalized questioning strategies helps the individual build self-esteem, develop security and identity, develop his cognitive skills, and acquire confidence in his own abilities. Students respond to the empathic and aware teacher, attitudes made viable through good questioning. To help the learner to become more responsive and to contribute actively to the learning process has to boost his ego. Respect, acceptance, and trust are enhanced in an atmosphere that allows self-expression. Helping the student clarify his feelings, beliefs, attitudes, and value system promotes his understanding of others, self, and learning. The guidance you provide in these areas by utilizing appropriate questioning must be one of the most humanistic activities in which you can engage.

We hope you will continue to broaden your competency for effective questioning. Periodically, you will find it helpful to return to this chapter and review the questioning strategies. We wish you continued success.

5

Implementing the Competency of Sequencing Instruction

DORIS A. TROJCAK

University of Missouri—St. Louis

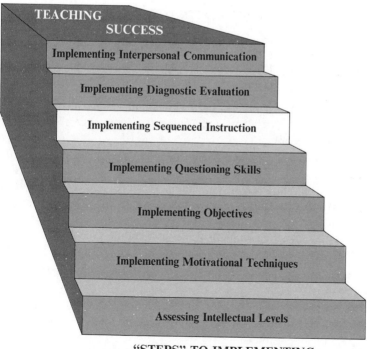

TEACHING
SUCCESS

Implementing Interpersonal Communication

Implementing Diagnostic Evaluation

Implementing Sequenced Instruction

Implementing Questioning Skills

Implementing Objectives

Implementing Motivational Techniques

Assessing Intellectual Levels

**"STEPS" TO IMPLEMENTING
TEACHING COMPETENCIES**

INTRODUCTION

Suppose you had just been given a special kind of trifocals for viewing the process of organizing and sequencing instruction. But these trifocals would be special in that they would enable you to scan the instructional scene in terms of past, present, and future events. With such trifocals you would be better equipped to view teaching and learning as a continuous process that can be diagramed very simply here.

TEACHING-LEARNING CONTINUUM

Actually, we know comparatively little about when and how learning really begins and ends. We certainly can *infer* that it is an ongoing process. However, in an attempt to formalize the learning process many educators have tended to divvy up learning into specific grade levels. The learning process has now come to look like this diagram.

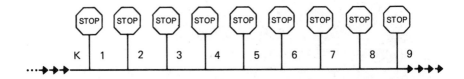

This stop-and-go arrangement has both its advantages and disadvantages. It is advantageous if all students are "going the same speed." It can be hazardous if they are not.

Let's say you are a sixth grade teacher meeting your class at the beginning of the school year. Will all of your students be at the same starting point on the sixth-grade learning continuum? Hardly! Some might still be struggling with basic arithmetic while others can handle basic calculus. Every day you face those children you will also have to face several extremely important questions dealing with instruction:

1. Where are we right now (academically, psychologically, physically, socially, and so forth)?
2. Where are we headed?
3. How do we get there?
4. Are we on the right track?
5. Have we arrived?

Answering these five questions in terms of the *entire* year's curriculum would be an enormous and perhaps overwhelming task. Some teachers tend to avoid this difficulty by thinking of instruction *only* in terms of small segments called daily lesson plans. What is needed is a compromise. Both teachers and learners need to see continuity in their experiences. Both need to be striving toward specific payoff achievements rather than wandering about aimlessly.

The general purpose of this chapter is to help you become better able to organize and sequence specific components of the teaching-learning continuum. The scope of the component you eventually select to develop is unpredictable. However, in order to provide some general guidelines try to utilize your strategies for a period somewhere between a minimum of one week of instruction and a maximum of whatever time is needed to complete a unit of instruction.

You should be able to demonstrate that from this chapter you have learned to:

1. Specify the desired payoff behavior(s) you expect your learners to eventually demonstrate. *(Where are they headed?)*
2. Hypothesize the learners' present abilities—that is, their entry behaviors. *(Where are they right now?)*
3. Outline the tentative task analysis—that is, identify the sequence of steps that are needed to get *from* the entry behavior *to* the desired payoff behaviors. *(How do they get there?)*
4. Design an instrument (pretest) or method for checking your initial plans. *(Are they on the right track?)*
5. Administer the pretest and analyze the results to determine if you need to modify your task analysis. *(Are they on the right track?)*
6. Specify as instructional objectives the sequence of behaviors identified in your task analysis. *(How do they get there?)*
7. Present your instructional sequence to your students and evaluate the results. *(Have they arrived?)*

The flow chart in Figure 5-1 summarizes these steps.

Wait a minute! If we're not careful, this whole chapter may evolve into a monologue. *You* need your chance to interact. So let's use some different procedures from here on. When instruction or directions are presented,

the symbol of 🯅 will appear. When your direct participation is re-

quested, the symbol 🯅 will appear. The symbol 🯅 will indicate a suggested solution to a problem.

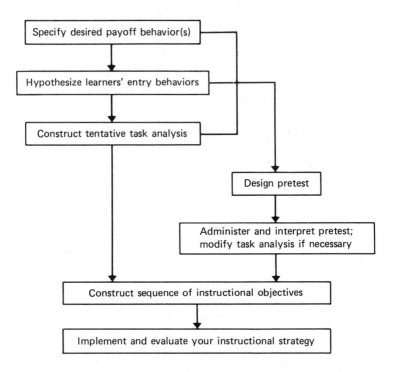

Figure 5-1.   **Steps in the teaching-learning continuum (adapted from Trojcak, "Designing a Strategy for Long-Term Instruction,"** *School Science and Mathematics,* **December 1972, pp. 811-16)**

STRATEGY FOR SEQUENCING INSTRUCTION

1. Specify the Desired Payoff Behavior(s)

The desired payoff behavior is the end product the students should be able to demonstrate for each segment of instruction. Usually, this expected behavior requires the learners to acquire a specific concept or concepts, principles, or psychomotor skill or skills. The extent of time and instruction needed to reach the payoff behavior can vary immensely. It depends greatly on how close or distant the learners already are to that particular performance. Remember the idea of the learning continuum? Suppose the desired payoff behavior is at point X on the continuum. The learners might be at any of the other lettered points shown below.

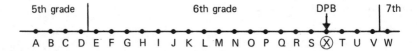

You might possibly experience some difficulty in selecting an appropriate payoff behavior toward which you hope to guide the learners. You will have to confront that most elusive question, "What should I teach?" or, more important, "What's worth teaching?" or, in terms of relevance, "What do the learners need to learn?" An escape hatch is often provided by following the course outline, or what is "to be covered" next in the text, or what has been suggested or determined by the principal, department chairman, or another subject matter specialist. Often, however, the "answer" provided by these sources may not be the best decision for the students. It's interesting to speculate on how much more meaningful education might be if the choices for various end-product objectives were made mutually by the teacher *and* the students. Or if this sounds too revolutionary, consider the possibility and the effects of students being better informed of what is expected of them and *why* such a payoff behavior is worth achieving.

Whether the desired payoff behavior is decided dictatorially or democratically, it should be both observable and measurable if it is to be truly recognizable. Otherwise, there is no way of clearly determining the achievement of the desired objective. (If this is not clear to you, stop and read Chapter 3 before continuing with this chapter.)

Periodically in this chapter, you'll encounter places where you will be asked to put theory into practice. Sometimes you'll be asked to spend some time out in a school setting. A time out in a sporting contest is usually more than a rest period. It might be used to analyze performances or to plan the next strategy. Often, the effective use of time outs can influence the player's success. That will certainly be true in terms of your learning from this chapter.

TIME OUT

Spend some time analyzing the presence or absence of desired payoff behaviors in various curricular materials of your interest and/or in classroom settings. Try to answer the following questions:

1. Was it obvious that the curricular materials or teacher was headed toward specific payoff behaviors? Why or why not?
2. Were the learners aware of these objectives?
3. Were the desired behaviors actually achieved? Why or why not?
4. What were the differences between teachers and classes in situations

where the objectives were clearly known and in situations where they were not known or were known only vaguely?

TIME OUT

Explain the importance of specifying clear end-product or payoff behaviors.

When you are able to determine the desired payoff behavior(s), you are in a much better position to provide direction and specificity to the learning continuum. This makes instruction more purposeful and manageable. You now have a basis for evaluation. However, some teachers are more accustomed to think in terms of where the students are heading than where they are right now. Therefore, the next point we need to examine is the learners' entry behavior.

2. Hypothesize the Learners' Entry Behavior

As we said, many teachers tend to overlook this point. Reflect for just a few moments on your own experiences or on observations you have made in classrooms. How often have students jumped into or been pushed into supposedly new segments of learning without the teacher determining if the subject matter or task is really new or appropriate? Have you ever observed a class respond, "Oh, we've had this before!" and then watched the seemingly deaf teacher plunge on as planned, with full determination, oblivious of the students' interests and/or present capabilities? Wouldn't it be far more advantageous for the teacher to determine what the students actually know already about the topic to be presented?

If an initial attempt is not made to determine the present ability of the learners, the desired payoff behavior might well be far too easy or far too difficult. In either case, learning would not readily occur—that is, if we view learning as a *change* in behavior or capability.

It is difficult to consider a suitable end-product objective without considering almost simultaneously the learner's entry behavior. The two are inseparable when we construct an instructional strategy since they represent the beginning points and the end point of a particular learning segment. The distance between these two points gives us some general indication of the time needed and the number of learning steps necessary to reach the expected behavior. For example, if one is in a large city, he certainly needs to know where he is presently situated before he attempts to travel to a new location—that is, if he wishes to reach the new location most efficiently. The more accurately he knows his present location in relation to the new one, the better he can plan his maneuvers, anticipate obstacles, and gauge his time.

What's that I hear you saying? That moving about in a city is far easier and more predictable than leading students through a learning sequence? That you're still not clear on how to establish the learners' entry behavior?

Those are good concerns! One thing you must learn to do is to become more specific in your assumptions of prerequisite skills related to the payoff objective. Suppose your payoff objective involves writing a paragraph for the first time. Which of the following are prerequisites related to this desired behavior?

___1. The ability to spell words correctly.

___2. The ability to write a complete sentence.

___3. The ability to divide fractions.

___4. The ability to read a map.

Certainly, items 3 and 4 are "honorable" abilities, but they are not directly related to the specific objective of paragraph writing. Items 1 and 2, however, are.

Remember the title of this section—*"Hypothesize* the Learners' Entry Behavior." The word "hypothesize" was chosen very deliberately. It does not mean to declare definitively, but rather to make a *tentative guess*. Based on what you know about the learners, what can they do now that relates to the desired behavior? Certainly, students of all ages already possess almost countless skills and facts, but which of these (and *only* these) are related to the end product expected? Your selection at this point will be just a hunch. You'll learn how to verify your hunch later when we discuss *pretesting*.

But before we explore the topic of pretesting, we need to discuss the "middle component." What do we mean by that? The next section will provide some answers.

3. Construct a Tentative Task Analysis

So far we've been thinking about starting points (entry behaviors) and end points (desired payoff behaviors). If you know where you are and where you want to go, the next question becomes, "How do I get there?" It seems most reasonable to attempt to take the most direct route possible. The process of determining the necessary steps or components to reach a desired payoff behavior is called task analysis. In other words, you simply attempt to analyze the task to identify what skills or understandings are necessary to reach your goal. Task analysis involves the outlining of enroute behaviors or prerequisites in a meaningful manner.

"Meaningful manner?" you're asking skeptically. "What constitutes a meaningful manner?"

A few teachers seem to know intuitively how to sequence instruction. They either have an innate talent for ordering learning experiences or are extraordinarily sensitive to the reactions and responses of their students. Others, however—especially the inexperienced—need some kind of instructional models or learning hierarchies to follow in sequencing teaching-learning events. These models are provided chiefly by learning psychologists, theorists, or curriculum developers such as Skinner, Gagné, Piaget, Bloom, and Taba.[1] Your selection of the most appropriate instructional model depends primarily on the type of end-product objective you selected as well as the learners' entry behaviors. For instance, if the payoff behavior requires some type of creative writing, such as synthesizing a great many previously learned facts and skills, then Bloom's taxonomy might be the most appropriate model to employ. Whether or not you need to begin the instructional sequence at the basic knowledge level depends on what the learners already know—in other words, their entry behavior. Your se-

---

[1] Five learning hierarchies or instructional strategies are described by the author in the chapter, "Developing a Competency for Sequencing Instruction," in James Weigand, ed., *Developing Teacher Competencies* (Englewood Cliffs, N.J.: Prentice-Hall, 1971).

quence might include only activities at the application and analysis levels as prerequisites for the payoff behavior of synthesis. If the payoff behavior requires problem solving, then Gagné's model would be an appropriate choice. Again, where you begin instruction according to his model (whether at specific responding, motor or verbal chaining, multiple discrimination, concept formation, or at a level as complex as principle formation) will depend on the learners' entry behaviors. You will need to examine your final objective very critically in terms of the *kind of performance* it specifies. Once you define this performance clearly, you can better select the model—perhaps a hybrid model—that can best be used to bridge the gap between entry behavior and payoff behavior.

At this point you may be saying, "I'm not sure all of this really answers my question about that 'meaningful manner' business. I need more 'nitty gritties'!"

Basically, when you attempt to outline en-route behaviors or prerequisites in a meaningful manner, you try to arrange them most logically in terms of their *order of difficulty*. New learnings always build on old learnings. It is highly unlikely that a learner can master a more difficult skill until he has achieved a simpler, subordinate skill. You can identify these subordinate skills by applying task analysis. Suppose Ⓩ is the desired payoff behavior and you assume V̱ to be the entry behavior. The key question becomes, "What must the learner know or be able to do to achieve Ⓩ?" A variety of sequences might be possible, such as the diagrams of task analysis shown in Figure 5-2.

In (a), the subordinate skills W , X , and Y represent three distinct levels of difficulty or understanding that are prerequisite to achieving

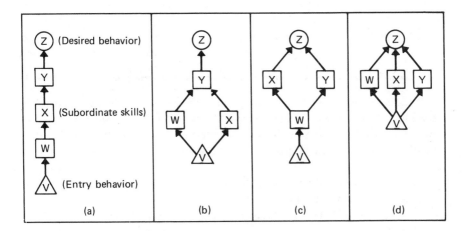

Figure 5-2. Task analysis examples

(Z) $\boxed{W}$ is a prerequisite of $\boxed{X}$, which in turn is a prerequisite of $\boxed{Y}$ In (b), $\boxed{W}$ and $\boxed{X}$ are both at the same level of difficulty and are both prerequisites of $\boxed{Y}$. In (c), $\boxed{W}$ is the prerequisite of both $\boxed{X}$ and $\boxed{Y}$, which are at the same higher level of difficulty, and (d) shows all three of the subordinate skills at the same level of difficulty.

"Theory! Theory! Theory!" you say. "It looks as simple as A–B–C when you use only V–W–X–Y–Z! But what's it like in the real world?"

Let me give you an example dealing with a common science topic, magnetism. Suppose students were given the following as a desired payoff behavior:

> Given two identical-looking iron rods, one magnetized (therefore a magnet) and the other not (but nonetheless magnetic since it is also iron), the learner should demonstrate which rod is the magnet by using ONLY the two iron rods.

"Wait a minute! I don't know if even I can figure that out! It seems impossible to do if one can use *only* the two different iron rods."

That's all right. Just tell me what you *do* know about magnetism that might be relevant to solving this problem.

What I know about magnetism. . . .

Here are a few principles of magnetism in general. Some are relevant to solving the rod problem and some are not. Reread the rod problem objective. Then mark the principles you think the student would need to know or learn in order to solve this specific problem.

___1. Magnets are used in many machines.

___2. Magnets attract objects made of iron.

___3. There are different degrees or strengths of magnetism.

___4. Magnetism is strongest at the ends and weakest at the middle of a magnet.

___5. Magnets will not attract copper.

___6. Magnetism will pass through paper.

The statements *most* necessary for solving the rod problem are 3 and 4. (Certainly, principle 2 is also related; but it is implied in the objective that the learner already knows this.) The learner can solve the rod problem by applying principle 4 especially. How? He could place the end of one rod at the middle of the other rod [(a)] Figure 5-3 and see what happens.

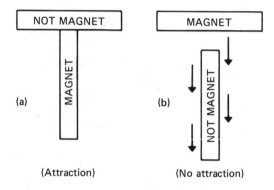

Figure 5-3

Since magnetism is weakest at the middle of a magnet, the magnet rod will not attract the nonmagnet rod, as shown in (b). Principle 3 is also related to principle 4 and, of course, to solving the rod problem.

TIME OUT

Now let's attempt to organize these ideas into some kind of sequential order or task analysis. The task to be analyzed is the rod problem objective. The most important question to be asked next is, *What must the learner know in order to achieve the objective* (or desired payoff behavior)?

At this point, the task analysis would look like Figure 5-4.

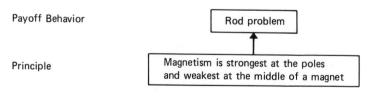

Figure 5-4

The next question becomes, *What must the learner know in order to understand the principle?*

Every principle consists of a combination of at least two or more *related concepts*. The main concepts involved in the principle, "Magnetism is strongest at the poles and weakest at the middle of a magnet," are *magnetism,* the *degrees* of magnetism, and the *location* of magnetism. You can see more clearly the relationship among the learnings subordinate to the desired payoff behavior in the task analysis diagram shown in Figure 5-5.

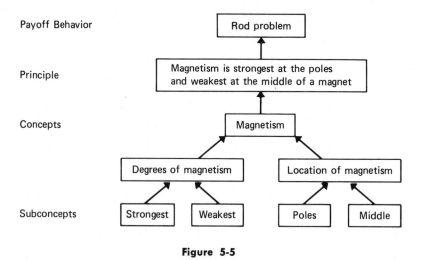

Figure 5-5

Whether or not additional task analysis is required will depend on the entry behaviors of the learners.

TIME OUT

Let's check signals. What does task analysis mean to you?

Your answer should contain these aspects:

The process of outlining a learning hierarchy of subordinate skills or under-standings.
Analyzing the desired payoff behavior and "working backward" by answering at each segment the question, What must the learner know or be able to do . . . ?
Arranging the segments from the most difficult to the simplest subordinate tasks.

Again, it is important that you recall the title for this section: "Construct a *Tentative* Task Analysis." Why the inclusion of the word "tentative"? Just as in the discussion on hypothesizing the learners' entry behaviors, here too we can only speculate on the most suitable outline of subordinate tasks. What we need to consider next is how to actually determine the entry behaviors.

4. Design Pretest

Before we begin, let's have a time out.

TIME OUT

What do you think should be included in a pretest, an instrument to check your initial plans? (It would probably help to think also about the *purpose* of a pretest.)

The primary purpose of a pretest is to obtain concrete evidence of what your learners can or cannot do and what they know or do not know *in relation to the desired payoff behavior*. Everything we have considered so far can be used in constructing your pretest. What have been our major considerations?

1. Desired payoff behavior.
2. Hypothesized entry behavior.
3. Task analysis.

Or, in question form:

1. What major objective are you leading the learners toward?
2. Where do the learners stand in relation to the payoff behavior?
3. What are the learnings between the entry behaviors and the desired payoff behavior?

In constructing your pretest, you'll need to draw from these three considerations to formulate your questions or tasks. Try to include the most economical selection of test items or the items you are most interested in verifying. It would also be helpful to *code* the test items drawn from the three sources. Identify which items verify abilities from the three main sources. (For example, entry behavior items might be labeled EB1, EB2, EB3, and so forth; components of the task analysis could be labeled TA; and items dealing with the desired payoff behavior might be labeled PB.)

Construct your pretest succinctly yet thoroughly. It should be a diagnostic tool rather than a cumbersome ordeal. Try to avoid constructing any questions or tasks that allow for chance guessing (especially avoid yes-no questions) or that require an undue amount of writing or time from the students. If at all possible, try to provide the opportunity for the students to *demonstrate* their abilities by *doing* (that is, by some sort of "hands-on" manipulation) rather than just by verbal or written expressions of their understandings. Good command of the language does *not* necessarily equal clear understanding! The adage, "I hear . . . and I forget; I see . . . and I remember; I do . . . and I understand," still makes a great deal of sense. Use it to your advantage in constructing the pretest.

"My turn to say 'Stop!' " "What do I do about students who are test-shy or who freeze up when given tests?"

5. Administer and Interpret Pretest Results

There is no need to "play games" with the students and try to trick them into taking the pretest or frighten them into a state of near panic. It is far more important that you simply be as honest with them as you can. Explain the purpose of the instrument as it really is—not a test in the usual sense, but rather a "tell me or show me what you know" situation. Help the students realize that no letter grade will be attached to their score; on the contrary, from their scores you will be able to arrange the learning sequence better to fit individual needs and abilities. Older students will be especially pleased with this opportunity. The "young uns" will enjoy the chance to show off what they know or can do. Generally, they're not bothered by what they don't know.

If you have coded your pretest items as was suggested, you will be able to diagnose each student's present capabilities. You will be able to determine what percentage of the learners already possess "x" percentage of the entry behaviors, the intermediate tasks, and the desired payoff behavior. You will be able to verify what up until now have only been hunches. You might even have some rather startling revelations. For instance, if 80 to 90 percent of the students respond to the pretest with 100 percent accuracy, you will realize that you underestimated your initial plans and assumptions. Or the opposite might occur. In either case some major revisions are needed. But such extremes are not likely to occur unless you have been careless in your planning or unless you are completely unfamiliar with either your students or the subject matter to be presented. Usually, some students will respond correctly to some questions or tasks and incorrectly to others. When you interpret the pretest results, look for trends. Determine what should be omitted from the suggested sequence of the task analysis and/or what should be included. After interpreting the pretest results carefully, you should be able to plan for individual pacing or for grouping the students according to similar abilities. One discovery that you will most surely make is that instruction geared toward a "twenty- or thirty-headed child" is totally unsuitable. It is unrealistic to believe that all students can perform to the same degree at the same time. Thus, the critical interpretation of the pretest results can provide invaluable information for sequencing instruction for either individuals or groups of students.

"I wonder if this business of pretesting is really worth all of the effort? Could this step be eliminated?"

TIME OUT

Try answering your own question. What do you think are the advantages and/or disadvantages of pretesting?

Advantages? Lots of them! You can find out if the students can do what you thought they could do (that is, verify entry behaviors). You can determine which students can already perform the desired payoff behavior. (This could do wonders for preventing boredom or indifference in the classroom.) You can know who can perform specific subordinate tasks. This will help you plan for individual differences and/or grouping according to abilities. In general, you will see how accurate or inaccurate your speculations were and whether the payoff behavior was appropriate or inappropriate.

Disadvantages? Pretesting is time consuming—but just about anything worth pursuing takes time. Pretesting may injure the students psychologically—but isn't it more offensive to bore students stiff or expect from them performances that are beyond their capabilities? If you don't collect some objective data to support or disprove your initial plans, how will you know if you're on the right track? Perhaps this will become clearer in the next section.

6. Modify the Task Analysis if Necessary and Construct a Sequence of Objectives

After you have interpreted the data from the pretest, you will know whether you need to modify your task analysis or whether you can retain it as originally conceived. Once you have completed your skeletal outline (task analysis) of subordinate skills and sequenced them according to levels of difficulty, your remaining task is to "add the meat to bones." You can accomplish this by translating the components into specific performance objectives. The more clearly you have constructed the task analysis, the simpler this procedure becomes. The level of mastery expected in the form of the desired payoff behavior will dictate the degree of performance acceptable for the specific subordinate objectives.

AN APPLICATION

Before we begin discussing the final step in sequencing instruction, let's review the steps we've studied so far.

Review

The six steps discussed so far for sequencing instruction are:

1.

2.

3.

4.

5.

6.

The six steps we have discussed up to this point are:

1. Specify the desired payoff behavior(s).
2. Hypothesize the learners' entry behaviors.
3. Construct a tentative task analysis.
4. Design a pretest, an instrument for checking your initial plans.
5. Administer and interpret the pretest results, and modify your task analysis if necessary.
6. Construct your sequence of instructional objectives to achieve the desired payoff behavior.

Now let's see if we can start applying these steps. Here's a goal that might be suitable for intermediate grade children. Notice how a motivational setting has been incorporated so that the goal becomes one that children would more likely consider worth achieving.

You have just received word that a bomb has been planted somewhere near your school. You recall the secret fallout shelter at school. You must get word to all of the neighbors on how to find the fallout shelter; but the telephone wires have been cut, and giving face-to-face directions would take too long. So you'll need to learn how to make a map.

This goal is motivational and would probably stimulate the learners. But it leaves much to be desired in terms of giving clear directions toward achieving the payoff performance(s) desired. In other words, it lacks specificity. You know the general area of the ensuing instructions—map making —but little more. The following addition would help make the goal more observable and concrete to both the teacher and the learner.

The map will have to be constructed on graph paper, and the sides must be labeled. The streets, houses, and other landmarks should be drawn to metric scale. A key identifying all parts should also be included.

Write a suitable objective for this desired payoff behavior.

 I'll try, too.

After hearing the motivational story and receiving instruction on making maps, and given pencil, metric measuring instruments, and graph paper, the learner should construct a map showing the position of the school's fallout shelter. The map should (1) include labeled axes or sides, (2) be drawn to metric scale, (3) show the position of landmarks, and (4) include a key for interpreting the parts.

By writing your desired payoff behavior (or *any* instructional objective) as clearly as possible, you are actually beginning to specify the components of instruction. And, most certainly, you will be greatly simplifying the process of evaluation since you will have ready answers to these questions: Where are my students headed? What precisely do I expect them to be able to do or understand? How well have they attained the goal?

The next question will be tougher, but see what you can do with it! What are some assumed entry behaviors you might expect of the learners? (Remember, these are fourth, fifth, or sixth graders.)

I think the learners should know:

Again, there are no right or wrong answers to this question. But here are some feasible assumptions of what the students might know:

1. What a map is and how to read one, but not necessarily how to construct one.
2. How to use a ruler, at least in standard English units (inches and feet), but not necessarily in metric units.
3. How to locate positions along a number line, but not necessarily when two lines intersect (that is, not necessarily by coordinates).

4. How to locate the directions of north, south, east, and west on a globe.
5. How to represent real objects by means of symbols (for instance, knowing that the numeral 5 represents five of something), but not necessarily how to use a key.

Oops! I threw a curve at you! Which one of the above is *not* related to the desired payoff behavior?

If you answered "4," you've really got the point of selecting only those assumed entry behaviors that relate *directly* to the *specified* payoff behavior.

Your next task is to develop a tentative task analysis for the desired payoff behavior. Remember to keep asking and answering that key question, What must the learner be able to know or do in order to . . . ? Begin with the payoff objective and continue with that questioning technique until you reach the assumed entry behavior.

Desired payoff behavior:

Subordinate goals?

You guessed it—no strictly right or wrong answers here either, but the outline in Figure 5-6 represents one suitable tentative task analysis. (This particular task analysis is based on Taba's model for concept formation, interpretation of data, and application of principles and facts.)

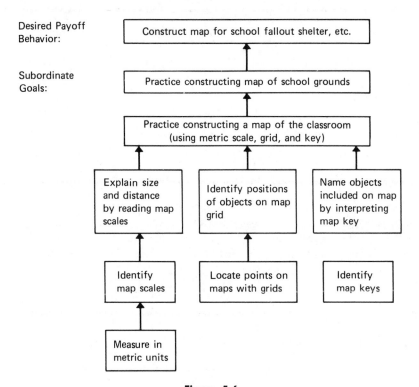

Figure 5-6

Why do we keep referring to the task analysis as tentative?

Because at this point we are still working only at the hunch level. We now need to verify our hunches by means of a pretest.

Briefly recall what you need to include when constructing the pretest.

Yes, you need to consider the "big three"—desired payoff behavior, entry behaviors, and task analysis. Let me do some of the groundwork this time. I'll give you some sample pretest items, and you decide whether they deal with entry behaviors, components of the task analysis, or the payoff behavior. (To simplify, use just the initials EB, TA, and PB for your designations.)

___1. Examine this simple map carefully.

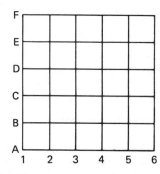

How far apart are the two tree trunks?

___2. Place an X on points 2D, 4A, 1B, and 5E.

___3. Which of these are symbols?

___4. Draw a symbol for a house.

___5. What is the length of each line in metric units?

A. _____

B. _____

C. _____

___6. What is the length of each line in English units (inches)?

A. _____

B. _____

C. _____

___7. Describe how you would go about making a map showing our school and each street surrounding it.

Have you labeled the seven items according to EB, TA, or PB? If not, please do so now.

Now, it would be helpful for you to justify your selection of coded items by completing the following chart:

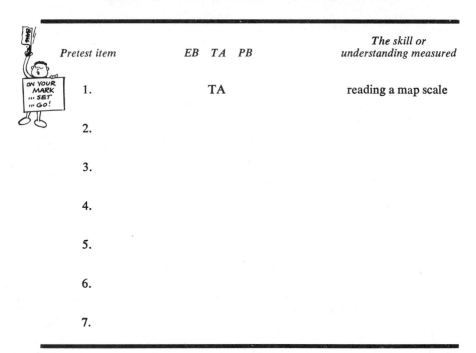

Pretest item	EB	TA	PB	*The skill or understanding measured*
1.		TA		reading a map scale
2.				
3.				
4.				
5.				
6.				
7.				

Please *don't* examine the answer chart until you've completed your own. Ready for the unveiling? See page 213.

See how sharp you're becoming! But get ready for another toughie. One very important component has been deliberately omitted from the pretest. Which one is it?

I detect the missing link to be:

Right! It's the use of a key for naming objects included on the map. Were an item to be added on this topic, the pretest would be fairly complete. Whether or not to add still more items seems to be a personal decision based on the particular class for whom the pretest is intended.

Answer Chart

2.	TA	locating points on grids
3.	EB	recognizing symbols
4.	EB	representing an object as a symbol
5.	TA	measuring in metric units
6.	EB	measuring in English units
7.	PB	describing how to map

In what ways does this pretest violate or support good pretesting procedures as discussed previously?

There's more evidence of good pretesting procedures here than poor. The poorest item might be 7, since it requires writing skills rather than the actual making of a map. However, it does economize on time, as is true of the entire pretest. Some other good techniques used are:

1. Avoidance of chance guessing.
2. Opportunity to demonstrate understandings rather than merely recall memorized facts or misconceptions.

3. Brevity and ease in both administering and scoring.
4. Adequate thoroughness in drawing from the "big three": EB, TA, and PB.

After interpreting the results of this pretest, you should have sufficient information for sequencing the instructional objectives according to the learners' capabilities. And, to go back to the beginning of this chapter, your original fuzzy view of the instructional process through those special trifocals is undoubtedly much clearer now.

Sometimes you might wonder if we will ever remove all of the "fuzzies" from the teaching-learning process. It's highly doubtful (and perhaps undesirable) that the state of our art will ever become like the status of automobile automation. (Would we even want this?) In very few of our teaching situations do we have a computerized diagnostic service center where we can run through our instructional strategy just as we would our cars. Analyzing the pros and cons, the strengths and weaknesses of sequenced instruction is much more difficult. There are far too many variables for us to handle effectively. However, if you were to attempt to design some kind of diagnostic criteria or check list to evaluate the sequencing of instruction, what important questions or considerations would it contain? Discuss this question with your peers and then with other teachers. Also examine curriculum guides in terms of how the authors determine, justify, or even view the importance of sequencing instruction. Educational magazines might also be of some help.

TIME OUT

Organize your ideas and the suggestions you value from others. Then construct some kind of diagnostic instrument or checklist for evaluating the sequencing of instruction.

HERE GOES

The following checklist is one attempt to help you confront the more obvious factors of sequencing instruction that are within your control. Compare this checklist with the instrument you designed. After doing so, perhaps you can develop a compromise that is better than either alone.

Checklist for Evaluating Your Sequenced Instruction

1. Desired Payoff Behavior.
   1.1. Can I justify the importance of this behavior?
   1.2. Can the students also comprehend its worth?
   1.3. Is it within the students' conceptual capabilities—for instance, according to Piaget?
   1.4. Have I considered possible negative reactions to or consequences of presenting this behavior?
   1.5. Is the behavior achievable within my present learning environment (in terms of space, equipment, social climate, and so forth)?
   1.6. Will I be able to recognize when the students have achieved it?
2. Entry Behaviors.
   2.1. Do I have some firm basis for my assumptions?
   2.2. Have I made a thorough coverage?
   2.3. Is each ability related specifically to the desired payoff behavior?
   2.4. Do they include the total range of the students' abilities?
   2.5. Are they stated so that I can identify them?
3. Task Analysis Components.
   3.1. Are they sequenced according to levels of difficulty?
   3.2. Are they all related to the desired payoff behavior?
   3.3. Do they represent the most important steps toward the achievement of the payoff behavior?
   3.4. Can their attainment be readily recognized?
   3.5 Do they allow for a broad range of capabilities?
4. Pretest.
   4.1. Does it include items designed to verify key entry behavior assumptions?

4.2. Does it include items designed to verify key components of the task analysis?

4.3. Does it include at least one item comparable in difficulty to the desired payoff behavior?

4.4. Can it be easily administered and scored?

4.5. Does it avoid the opportunity for chance guessing?

4.6. Does it require demonstration of understandings rather than merely recall of information?

4.7. Is the reading or listening level suitable to the students' abilities?

5. Sequence of Instructional Objectives.

5.1. Do they correspond to the selected task analysis?

5.2. Do they require observable and measurable behaviors?

5.3. Do they require the students to be involved in a variety of learning experiences?

5.4. Do they adequately describe the learning conditions needed?

5.5. Do they specify suitable levels of mastery?

5.6. Can they be communicated clearly to the students?

5.7. Will the students be motivated to perform them?

What would the educational scene look like if all teachers could answer yes to all thirty questions? Or how greatly would your own teaching-learning events be improved if you could respond with more yeses each time you moved along the learning continuum?

However, there is another "earthy" matter you need to consider. A great many of the desired behaviors presented throughout the school months or years deal with the cognitive (the knowing) level of learning. That is good and often very necessary but *not totally* good and necessary. We have previously discussed viewing the teaching-learning process through the trifocals of past, present, and future. We need also to consider the threefold makeup of our learners. A complete person is one who not only thinks but also acts and feels. He operates more fully when he combines his head, hands, and heart. Educators often refer to these as the three learning domains: cognitive (he thinks), affective (he feels), and psychomotor (he acts). Periodically, you should analyze your instructional strategies and especially the desired behaviors in terms of these three areas. What percentage of time and effort do you spend on guiding the learners to cognitive goals compared to affective and psychomotor goals? Do you direct enough effort toward attitudinal and skill development? (That would be worth investigating in another Time out).

Another practice you might investigate is using your evaluative checklist *both before* and *after implementation.* (By the way, you could try using the checklist with both your own instructional strategies and whatever you use that is "straight from the book." Your initial positive response to any one of the checklist questions may have been incorrect; were you incorrect consistently, you might discover a trend or even a number of trends of false assumptions. If you discovered that the opposite is true—that is, that your evaluations are virtually the same both before and after implementation— your growth in self-confidence should be rewarding. However, we need now to discuss the final step of organizing and sequencing instruction.

7. Implement and Evaluate Your Instructional Strategy

Once you have completed and evaluated the steps of (1) specifying the desired payoff behavior, (2) hypothesizing the learners' entry behavior, (3) constructing the tentative task analysis, (4) designing the pretest, (5) administering and interpreting the pretest, and (6) modifying the task analysis (if necessary) and constructing the sequence of objectives, you should be ready to begin presenting optimal conditions in which learning can occur.

"Isn't that a bit presumptuous?" you question. "Aren't you being guilty of ignoring or at least deemphasizing the most important variable here—the learners? Aren't you making this sound a bit like magic or some kind of 'plug 'n chug' automatic process?"

Those are excellent criticisms! Certainly, the person *most* responsible for learning is the learner himself. The person most responsible for arranging the optimal conditions in which learning can occur is you, the teacher. True, you cannot cause or force the learner to learn, but you can *facilitate* the learning process. That is what this chapter is all about, and that is what your own sequencing strategy should do.

But although your efforts may look perfect on paper or in your own mind, you will not realize how effective or ineffective they are until you observe and evaluate the actual performances of the learners. If the learners do not achieve each instructional objective, it is highly unlikely that they will reach the desired payoff behavior. It will benefit no one to discredit the learners and grumble, "I simply have a dumb class this year!" However, everyone will profit if you reexamine and reevaluate your plans. The need to plan and sequence instructional strategies is continuous, and so is the need to evaluate and often revise these plans. The latter might seem disheartening, especially in regard to the effort required to construct a sequenced strategy as described in this chapter. You, then, must face these questions: Is it worth it? Will the students benefit? And only *you* can determine the answers.

We hope you are now ready to implement the competency of organizing and sequencing instruction. How effective will your first attempt be?

and your second?

and your third?

and your fourth?

and your . . . ?

You'll never know until you try.

6

Diagnostic
Evaluation

JAMES R. OKEY

University of Georgia

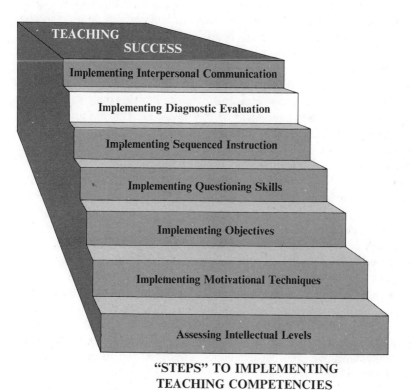

**"STEPS" TO IMPLEMENTING
TEACHING COMPETENCIES**

Usually, evaluation is thought of as an activity done when teaching is completed. When the study of a unit is finished, a test or evaluation is given by a teacher to find out how much each student learned. Scores on the test are used to rank students and as a basis for grades. This is a common and important kind of evaluation, but there are other types as well.

The type of evaluation you will learn to use in this chapter is done before, during, and after instruction. Its purpose is neither to rank students nor to give grades. Instead, this evaluation is used by teachers to collect information that they can use in making instructional decisions. For example, teachers can use evaluation to determine what students know and what they don't know, how well students liked a particular topic, or whether students retained what they learrned. Each of these pieces of information will help a teacher plan activities in a classroom with some confidence and assurance of success. If used properly, evaluation can be a positive force in your classroom, one that makes you a better teacher and your students more effective learners.

The evaluation you will learn to use is called *diagnostic evaluation.* The term "diagnostic" sounds medical and precise. Perhaps you can imagine yourself as the academic equivalent of the physician. But the analogy of a teacher diagnosing intellectual illness in the manner of a physician is unfortunate if we think of the teacher as dealing with sickness or illness. If a teacher uses diagnostic evaluation to find out what a student doesn't know, we should be cautious about calling this lack of knowledge a weakness or a problem. The teacher has simply determined what the student doesn't know and what he or she needs to learn.

Perhaps a conception of diagnostic evaluation that 'is more appropriate for teachers comes from Webster's dictionary, in which diagnosis is defined as "careful examination and analysis of the facts in an attempt to understand or explain something, a decision or opinion based on such examination." This gets to the heart of the problem: teachers need to collect information about students' abilities and attitudes and to make decisions based on this information. And that is precisely what you should learn to do in this chapter, if all goes well. You will learn to collect information by asking five different evaluation questions and to make decisions based on the information you collect.

OBJECTIVES FOR THE CHAPTER

After completing the exercises in this chapter, you should be able to:

1. Identify purposes and procedures for using diagnostic evaluation in the classroom.
2. Describe what information to collect and how to collect it when given a teacher's question about student achievement or attitude.
3. Describe a plan of action for a teacher to follow when given pupil data obtained for the purpose of answering a diagnostic evaluation question.

A short test at the end of the chapter will determine if you have achieved the three objectives. You may take the test now, after you do the chapter exercises, or both before and after completing the chapter. Follow the procedure that seems best to you.

THE EFFECTIVENESS OF DIAGNOSTIC EVALUATION

Teachers are often skeptical about the vast claims made for teaching innovations—and they ought to be. Many of the ideas touted by the experts as *the* way to improve student achievement and attitude simply do not work. Any teacher who reads this chapter should be skeptical too!

Does the use of diagnostic evaluation make any difference? Bloom and his colleagues [1] think that diagnostic evaluation should lead to "marked improvement" in pupil learning.

Two efforts to use diagnostic evaluation will be described; you can determine for yourself if the improvement was "marked." Collins [2] reports on the achievement of two groups of eighth graders studying mathematics; the two groups received different amounts of diagnostic evaluation and remedial work. Figure 6-1 shows the achievement of students in the Collins study. When diagnostic evaluation and remedial instruction were used, the number of students mastering the unit approximately doubled.

In another study, Burrows [3] showed that over 60 percent of the students who received diagnostic tests followed by remedial instruction achieved

[1] B. Bloom, J. Hastings, and G. Madaus, *Handbook on Formative and Summative Evaluation of Student Learning* (New York: McGraw-Hill, 1971).

[2] K. Collins, "A Strategy for Mastery Learning in Modern Mathematics," in *Mastery Learning: Theory and Practice*, ed. J. Block (New York: Holt, Rinehart & Winston, 1971).

[3] C. Burrows, "The Effects of a Mastery Learning Strategy on the Geometry Achievement of Fourth and Fifth Grade Children" (unpublished doctoral dissertation, Indiana University, 1973).

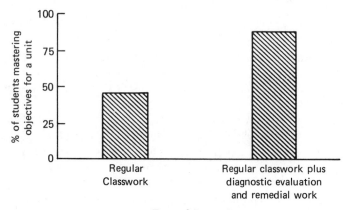

Figure 6-1. Achievement of students in classrooms using and not using diagnostic evaluation

mastery of objectives. Fewer than 20 percent of the students who received regular instruction reached the same level of achievement. Thus, more than three times as many students were able to master the material from a course when their teachers used diagnostic evaluation.

Both Collins and Burrows were able to show that diagnostic evaluation had a positive effect on learning, just as the experts had predicted. Their efforts, and those by a number of other teachers, to improve student achievement have been encouraging enough to warrant more work—*and work it is.* Without question, it is more difficult to teach using diagnostic evaluation. To evaluate frequently adds another task to a teacher's already full schedule. But the extra work should be compared with the benefits to students and the satisfaction to teachers when more of their students do well.

FIVE DIAGNOSTIC EVALUATION QUESTIONS

The remainder of this chapter describes five diagnostic evaluation questions a classroom teacher may wish to consider. The intention of these questions is to show teachers some practical steps they can take to increase student achievement: the discussion of each of the five questions includes an explanation of what the teacher does and why he or she does it. Each question is illustrated further by a case study. Examples of some of the types of evaluation instruments you may wish to prepare are also provided.

The five questions are:

1. Did they learn what I tried to teach?
2. Do they know it before I teach?
3. Do they know what I think they know?
4. Do they remember what they learned?
5. Do they like what they learned?

Teachers ask these five evaluative questions in order to gain information that they can use in making classroom decisions. They ask some of the questions before students begin studying a unit, some during the unit, and some afterward, because a teacher has decisions to make about students before, during, and after they study the unit.

After studying this chapter, teachers should be able to use diagnostic evaluation in their teaching. To keep this idea in mind, keep asking yourself, "How could I do this in my own classroom?" as you read the remainder of the chapter.

1. Did They Learn What I Tried To Teach?

When you teach, you want pupils to learn. Some might argue that if there is no learning, no teaching took place. A teacher asks the question "Did they learn what I tried to teach?" to find out which pupils learned and which didn't. The information obtained from pupils in answer to this question is used to identify faulty instruction as well as pupils who are experiencing learning difficulties.

The procedure used in answering this question is quite simple: give pupils one or more questions concerning the objectives of the lesson as soon as instruction is over.[4] Call these questions a self-help or diagnostic quiz, if you like, but make sure the pupils understand that your purpose in asking them is to find trouble spots and not to compare them with other pupils or to grade them.

Note that diagnostic tests must be given frequently to be of much value. Several short diagnostic tests given during a unit will help a teacher more than one long test given at the end. By frequently asking the question, "Did they learn what I tried to teach?" you can identify minor learning difficulties of pupils before they grow into major ones.

---

[4] It is assumed that readers can prepare evaluation items that test specific performance objectives. If you cannot, one of the following may help: R. Anderson, "Developing a Competency for Evaluation in the Classroom," in *Developing Teacher Competencies, ed. J. Weigand* (Englewood Cliffs, N.J.: Prentice-Hall, 1971); N. Gronlund, *Preparing Criterion-Referenced Tests for Classroom Instruction* (New York: Macmillan, 1973).

Average scores for the class or total scores for each pupil on diagnostic tests are of little value. The teacher needs information about individual pupils, not about group performance. A teacher needs to find out, for example, that Mary, Tom, and Sue missed the test item for objective 1; Julian and Beth answered the questions correctly for each objective; and Walt, Henry, and Joan missed the test items for objective 2. With this information about specific pupils, the teacher can plan remedial work. Peer tutoring, group instruction, teacher tutoring, rereading, or doing more practice problems are all choices that a teacher may then make to help pupils achieve objectives they have missed.

The following example shows how a teacher used diagnostic evaluation to find out which pupils mastered the objectives in a mathematics unit and which ones didn't.

Mrs. Sanders is teaching a unit on multiplication and division to the twenty-six pupils in her class. There are a number of specific objectives for the unit; on Monday and Tuesday the students worked on two of the objectives. Near the end of the period on Tuesday, Mrs. Sanders had each pupil complete eight practice problems related to the two objectives. She told them the purpose was to find out if more practice was needed with problems of this type. Figure 6-2 is a copy of the diagnostic test she used with the eight practice problems each pupil completed.

Math—Mrs. Sanders   Name_____

Multiplication and Division   Date _____ Room #____

1. $5 \times 5 = \Box$ 2. $4 \times 5 = \Box$ 3. $3 \times 6 = \Box$ 4. $2 \times 6 = \Box$

5. $8 \div 4 = \Box$ 6. $\dfrac{12}{3} = \Box$ 7. $24 \div 6 = \Box$ 8. $\dfrac{16}{4} = \Box$

Figure 6-2

After a few minutes, Mrs. Sanders put the answers to the eight problems on the board and all the pupils corrected their own papers. The results from a few pupils are shown in Figure 6-3. A check mark means that a student answered the problem correctly. A blank means that the practice problem was missed.

UNIT <u>Multi. & Division</u>

PROBLEMS

	Mult.				Division			
	1	2	3	4	5	6	7	8
Elmer B.	✓		✓	✓		✓	✓	
Bruce B.	✓	✓	✓	✓	✓	✓	✓	✓
Joan C.	✓	✓	✓	✓	✓			
Marge E.	✓	✓	✓			✓		
Will G.	✓	✓	✓	✓	✓	✓	✓	✓
Nora I.	✓	✓	✓	✓		✓		✓
Penny J.				✓				
Wayne L.	✓	✓	✓	✓	✓			
George P.		✓	✓	✓			✓	✓

Figure 6-3

Mrs. Sanders found that twenty-one of the twenty-six pupils missed at least one division problem. Only seven students, however, missed any of the four multiplication problems.

What would you do if you were Mrs. Sanders? Briefly describe how you would use this diagnostic test information to plan classroom activities.

Because nearly everyone in the class was having problems with division, Mrs. Sanders decided to work with the entire group by explaining the division process again, doing some sample problems at the board, and, finally, assigning practice problems for each pupil to complete. Because Penny J. seemed to have had considerable trouble with all eight problems, Mrs. Sanders worked individually with her. For the remaining six students who missed multiplication problems, Mrs. Sanders arranged for another student in the class to help them practice. After this practice with a fellow student or the teacher, the seven pupils were to complete a set of practice problems on their own.

By asking the question, "Did they learn what I tried to teach?" Mrs. Sanders acquired important information that she used to help her students learn. She found out which students needed additional study and which ones didn't.

2. Do They Know It Before I Teach?

Sometimes we fool ourselves as teachers. Not only do we fail to teach what we think we teach, but we take credit for teaching what pupils already know.

To answer the question, "Do they know it before I teach?" a teacher prepares a pretest to find out what students already know before they begin to study. The pretest includes one or more test items for each objective. Before pupils start to study a unit, they complete the test to see which objectives, if any, they have already achieved.

Preparing and administering pretests obviously consumes valuable time for both teachers and pupils. Is it worth it? Consider what information you might obtain and how it might be used.

Some Benefits of Pretests

1. Pupils often feel they know all about a topic if they have ever heard about it or studied it before. It's the old "We studied China *last* year" syndrome. It sometimes helps to show pupils that they don't know some things by having them take a pretest. If the unit is then studied and the pupils do well on the posttest, it is rewarding for them and the teacher to compare the two records of achievement.

2. Pupils differ greatly as to what they know at the start of a unit. One goal of individualized instruction is to help pupils work on tasks that they need to learn. If given before instruction starts, a test on the objectives of a unit allows a teacher to match pupils with tasks appropriate for them. Instead of all pupils beginning with the first objective, they may start at different points, depending on their pretest performance.

3. Pupils sometimes do know a great deal about a topic before the teacher

teaches it. If there are ten objectives for a unit and a pretest shows that everyone can already accomplish half of them, the teacher can alter plans and save time and effort.

The following example describes how a teacher used the question, "Do they know it before I teach?" to make some important decisions about her teaching and about her pupils.

Before she began teaching a social studies unit to the thirty-three students in her ninth grade social studies class, Miss Horowitz gave a pretest. Questions on the test related to each of the major objectives of the unit. Only the test is shown in Figure 6-4, but you can readily infer the objectives by examining it.

Social Studies   Name_____

Miss Horowitz—Room 116   Date_____

Answer each of the questions on a separate sheet of paper.

1. Give brief definitions for these words or terms: minority, prejudice, civil rights, separate but equal.

2. Explain why many white Americans of the Civil War era believed that black people were inferior.

3. Read the editorial taken from a 1920 New York newspaper and describe the writer's attitude toward minority groups.

4. Describe 2 legal events of the last 25 years that affected the civil rights of minority groups.

Figure 6-4

Miss Horowitz corrected the pretests herself and recorded the achievement of each pupil on each objective. The form in Figure 6-5 shows the results for some of the students in the class.

Miss Horowitz found that four persons (Joe Adams and three others) answered every question correctly. Fifteen students, including Martha Babcock, were unable to answer any of the questions. The remainder of the class answered some questions but missed others.

TOPIC *Attitudes Toward Minority Groups*

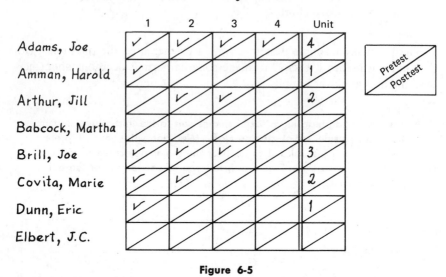

	1	2	3	4	Unit
Adams, Joe	✓	✓	✓	✓	4
Amman, Harold	✓				1
Arthur, Jill		✓	✓		2
Babcock, Martha					
Brill, Joe	✓	✓	✓		3
Covita, Marie	✓	✓			2
Dunn, Eric	✓				1
Elbert, J.C.					

(legend: Pretest / Posttest)

Figure 6-5

How would you use this information if you were the teacher of this class?

Of course, there is no *one* right way to act in this situation; different decisions could be made by different teachers. For example, one teacher might decide that everyone should study all the objectives in the unit; the pupils that already know some of the objectives can help other students. A teacher who has facilities and màterials for a highly individualized class could start each student on objectives that he or she has not yet achieved. The four students who missed no pretest questions could do optional work, start the next unit, or spend their time doing work for other classes. A third teacher could adopt tactics intermediate to either a group or highly individualized approach. He could plan both individual and group work: pupils would work alone sometimes, work in small groups at other times, and tutor fellow students occasionally.

Pretesting students by asking the question, "Do they know it before I teach?" can provide teachers with valuable information that can help them make classroom decisions. Teachers can find out how to spend their own time wisely and how to direct their students to appropriate activities.

3. Do They Know What I Think They Know?

Teachers make assumptions about what pupils have learned before arriving in their classes. Usually these assumptions remain untested and sometimes they are wrong. Imagine a teacher trying to teach long division only to find later that some pupils didn't know how to multiply. Since the skill of multiplication is a critical prerequisite of learning long division, there was little chance of pupil success.

Much of knowledge is cumulative: achieving a complex objective depends on achieving simpler ones first. For this reason, it is helpful for teachers to examine their assumptions about what their pupils already know when they begin a unit. The teacher needs to ask the question, "Do they know what I think they know?" If teachers find that pupils do lack assumed initial or prerequisite skills, they may be able to do something about this. The result may be less frustration for both teachers and pupils and more learning.

There may be some confusion between pretests ("Do they know it before I teach?") and tests on prerequisites ("Do they know what I think they know?"). Both tests are used by teachers before students begin studying a unit. They are used, however, to obtain different information. The former tests for achievement of objectives that will be studied during a unit. The latter determines whether students are ready to begin a unit by testing them on knowledge and skills they should already know.

To find out if students "know what I think they know," teachers need to first set out the objectives for a unit. Then they should list the prerequisite knowledge that they expect the pupils to *already have* in order to successfully begin study of the unit. Tests for the prerequisites are then prepared and administered to the students.

To see how a teacher can identify students that lacked prerequisite knowledge, examine the following case study.

"This year I'm not going to make that mistake again," said Mr. Burton, who teaches chemistry. Previously, he had assumed that his pupils had learned and remembered certain skills studied earlier in the year that were prerequisite to a unit on chemical calculations taught in the spring. For some students this was true, but for many it wasn't. So this year he decided to find out which pupils were ready to learn to perform calculations with chemical equations and which ones needed to review the prerequisites. So he listed the skills he expected pupils to *already know* that were essential to learning the new topic:

Unit Objective: Calculate the amounts of products formed when several chemicals are combined.

Prerequisite Skills. Determine the molecular weight of compounds.

Balance equations.

Solve proportion problems.

Next, Mr. Burton made up a short test on the prerequisite skills and had the twenty-eight pupils in his chemistry class complete it. See Figure 6-6. (You should be able to match the test items to each of the three prerequisite skills Mr. Burton identified.)

CHEMISTRY   Name_____

DIAGNOSTIC QUIZ   Date _____

The problems below represent skills you will need in order to perform calculations with chemical equations. If you learned these before fine, if not, special instruction will be available before starting the new unit.

1. Determine the molecular weight of these compounds.

H_2SO_4 _____ $CaCO_3$ _____ $Al(OH)_3$ _____

2. Balance these equations.

_____ $N_2O_5 \rightleftharpoons$ _____ NO_2 + _____ O_2

_____ $KClO_3 \rightleftharpoons$ _____ NCl + _____ O_2

3. Solve these problems for x.

$$\frac{1.226}{2(36.50)} = \frac{x}{3(32.00)} \qquad \frac{46.7}{x} = \frac{2(314.6)}{3(17.5)}$$

Figure 6-6

Results from some of the pupils in the class are shown in Figure 6-7.

Just as Mr. Burton had suspected, a number of pupils (such as G. Bramer) did not have the prerequisite skills for the unit. Mr. Burton's experience told him that this would lead to some serious learning problems.

UNIT __CHEM. EQNS.__

	ACHIEVEMENT								
	Prerequisites			Unit Objectives					
	A	B	C	1	2	3	4	5	6
Bend, J.	✓	✓	✓						
Bramer, G.									
David, H.	✓		✓						
Donnetti, A.		✓	✓						
Espara, M.	✓	✓	✓						
Everett, L.	✓	✓							
Ewell, J.	✓	✓	✓						
Farney, B.	✓	✓	✓						
Fell, V.	✓	✓							
Heller, J.	✓	✓	✓						

Figure 6-7

If you were Mr. Burton, what would you do about the eight pupils who lack one or more of the prerequisite skills?

The eight pupils need some kind of special instruction so that they can begin the unit with a fair chance for success. This will take time, a commodity most teachers have too little of, so there is probably no easy solution to the problem. The teacher can direct the eight pupils to special work in textbooks, work with them in a small group during free time, arrange for other pupils to help them, use a short programmed instruction sequence, or just move ahead to the new unit and let them suffer the consequences.

Sometimes, deficiencies in assumed knowledge (for instance, the ability to read) can be so substantial that to attempt to remedy them alone is futile. A teacher may need to request special help with such problems. But many deficiencies in prerequisites can be easily identified and treated. By asking the question, "Do they know what I think they know?" and then remedying gaps in assumed knowledge, the teacher greatly increases the chances for pupil success.

4. Do They Remember What They Learned?

Not only do you want students to learn, you want them to remember as well. Even if a student scores perfectly on a "multiplication through fives" test today, a teacher must be concerned about how well the student will remember the multiplication facts next week or next year. The fourth diagnostic question is concerned with how well students remember what they have learned.

More than the remembering of facts is involved here. In addition, teachers need to know if students remember how to use skills, where to look up information, what rules to apply, and so on. Retention of learned information is an important concern for both teachers and students.

The purpose of asking the question, "Do they remember what they learned?" is to find out if learning lasts. If it doesn't, the teacher may have to reteach some topics. Many texts are written on the assumption that topics must be encountered several times in order to be learned and remembered. Thus, a topic is introduced early in the year and then periodically restudied. Each time the topic is reintroduced, old material is reviewed and new material is added.

A teacher can use a retention test to find out what students need to restudy. Read the following case study to see how an elementary school teacher collected and used information about student retention of materials.

The thirty-two students in Mrs. Billings's class completed a unit two weeks ago on punctuation and capitalization. At the time, every student but two scored 80 percent or higher on the final unit test. Mrs. Billnigs decided to give the students another exercise to see if they remembered what they had learned two weeks before. The second exercise the students completed is shown in Figure 6-8. It required the students to use the same skills they had learned previously on a paragraph they had not seen before.

The table in Figure 6-9 shows the scores for the first test on punctuation and capitalization and the exercise that was completed two weeks later. A maximum score of 25 was possible each time.

Name _____

Date _____

Correct all errors of punctuation and capitalization in this letter.

dear mom

    i have been enjoying my week at camp we stayed in denver

on the way up here have you ever seen the mountains in colorado

the name of our leader is joe and he has a dog the dogs name is

willie

    when you come up on friday to see me bring my cap will you

remember what i look like

                        your son

                        bill

Figure 6-8

If you were Mrs. Billings, how would you use the information from the two tests?

Clearly, Mrs. Billings has identified some problems. For many students in the class, the answer to the question, "Do they remember what they learned?" is a resounding *no*. Many students apparently forgot punctuation and capitalization skills that they had used correctly two weeks before. Of the twenty-three students in the class, two had higher scores on the second exercise, six had the same score on the two exercises, and fifteen had lower scores on the second exercise.

Mrs. Billings decided to include more instruction on punctuation and capitalization in her teaching. She reasoned that the skills were vitally important and that many students had obviously not learned them. She also

Punctuation and Capitalization

March

	First Exercise	Second Exercise		First Exercise	Second Exercise
Paul	18	18	Ed	22	19
Marty	20	19	Fred	20	20
Jane	21	22	Lance	15	15
Jose	25	21	Laura	19	4
Mata	23	20	Hans	18	12
Claudia	23	23	Jim	19	23
Joan	24	14	Carole	16	10
Jan	23	11	Don	23	20
Jill	25	25	Bud	17	13
Bruce	17	5	Francis	17	15
Linda	18	13	Donna	25	25
Tom	22	11			

Figure 6-9

decided to have the nine students who had scored 20 or higher on the second exercise tutor the students who were having problems.

Students vary a great deal in how quickly they learn and how well they remember. Some students require repeated exposure to a topic; others learn and remember the first time. A teacher can use the diagnostic question, "Do they remember what they learned?" to find out what needs to be taught again and which students require additional attention.

5. Do They Like What They Learned?

Each of the four previous diagnostic questions has been directed toward the question of cognitive learning by pupils. But teachers work toward affective goals [5] too, and it is important to find out if their instruction achieves these goals. The fifth diagnostic question is asked to find out how well students liked what they learned.

Mager has written a concise and useful book [6] on attitudes toward learning. He talks about "sending students away from your instruction anxious

[5] Affective goals are concerned with the feelings and attitudes of people.
[6] *Developing Attitudes Toward Learning* (Palo Alto, Calif.: Fearon Publishers, 1968).

to use what you have taught them—and eager to learn more." Of course, that is what every teacher wants—but does it really happen? Teachers can fool themselves about how a lesson is liked by students. Sometimes a teacher will concentrate too much on sour looks and comments from just a few students. And sometimes they weigh too heavily the laudatory comments from one or two vocal students while the silent majority are seething. The several procedures for determining the attitudes of pupils in your classes are simple—they require a minimum of your time and effort—and they are potentially of great help to you in your teaching.

The basic procedure for finding out if students like what they have studied is to ask them just that: "How did you like the lesson on toads today, Jane?" Most students will be honest in their answers, sometimes brutally so. Because it is difficult to question each student individually, it might be wise to solicit written responses. To insure frank and candid comments, it is probably best to ask for anonymous answers.

How can teachers make use of information about student attitudes toward their learning? They can try, within reason, to make adjustments in such matters as course content, class organization, room arrangement, their own actions, and instructional materials that may affect their pupils' attitudes and perceptions.

One way to create positive pupil attitudes is to operate a classroom in which pupils are successful learners. Using diagnostic evaluation to identify learning difficulties and then reteaching as necessary is an excellent way to accomplish this. In other words, a successful instructional program seems to create positive attitudes—and one element of a successful program is diagnostic evaluation.

Figure 6-10 shows a sample attitude questionnaire used by a teacher to find out about student attitudes after the completion of a unit on local elections. Notice that some questions are about the content of the unit and some are about the teaching procedures.

Special procedures may be needed to measure the attitudes of very young children. Some authors suggest using faces that range from smiles to frowns as an aid to young children who might have trouble reading.[7] Teachers read the attitude statements aloud and pupils make a check mark beside the face that shows how they feel. An example of an attitude-measuring instrument of this type is shown in Figure 6-11.

How often you use measures to ask the question, "Do they like what they learned?" depends on what you wish to find out. The same logic applies to each of the five diagnostic evaluation questions described in this chapter. The teacher asks questions in order to obtain information, not because someone says that it's a good idea to evaluate frequently. Thus,

[7] See, for example, R. Fox, M. Luszki, and R. Schmuck, *Diagnosing Classroom Learning Environments* (Chicago: Science Research Associates, 1966).

Answer the following questions about the unit on *Local Elections*.

1. Compared with other units we have studied, this unit was:	better than most	about the same	poorer than most
2. The amount of work I had to do in this unit was:	too much	about right	too little
3. Working in study groups of 3 or 4 students on this unit was:	a good way to learn	OK some of the time	not right for this unit
4. Indicate the amount of teacher help you received in this unit:	too much	about right	too little

5. What did you like most about studying this unit?_____

_____

6. What one thing would you like most to change about this unit?_____

_____

_____

7. Write any other comments you would like to make about the unit. Use the back of the sheet if you need to.

_____

_____

_____

Figure 6-10.   A student attitude questionnaire

you should ask the questions (either verbally or in written form) as often as you need to know the answers in order to plan your teaching.

Attitude measurement can be done at the end of a unit (perhaps every two or three weeks) or more frequently. Figure 6-10 is an end-of-unit attitude measure. Figure 6-12 shows an attitude measure a teacher used to obtain students' reactions to the activities during a single lesson.

Read the following description of a teacher's use of diagnostic tests. See if his way of collecting information about student attitudes would help you.

Mr. Adair teaches a history class. In the past he has used a number of films, a regular textbook plus two supplementary books, some individual project work, and considerable group discussion in his teaching. This year, Mr. Adair has changed the way he teaches the course but has kept the topics nearly the same. He has adopted an individualized instruction approach. Occasionally a film is seen by all students, and a group discussion is held about once a week, but students work primarily on their own or in pairs.

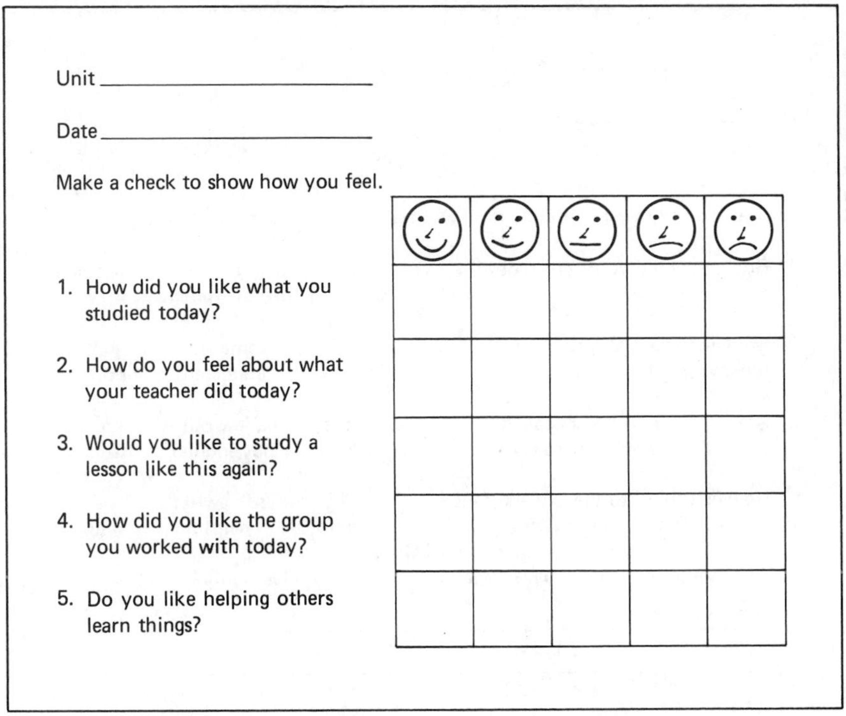

Unit _____

Date _____

Make a check to show how you feel.

1. How did you like what you
   studied today?

2. How do you feel about what
   your teacher did today?

3. Would you like to study a
   lesson like this again?

4. How did you like the group
   you worked with today?

5. Do you like helping others
   learn things?

Figure 6-11.   An attitude measure for young children

To find out how students responded to his individualized history course,
Mr. Adair prepared the attitude measure shown in Figure 6-13. Whenever
a student completed the activities for a unit, which was about every two
weeks, he was asked to complete the attitude form.

The results from twenty-five students in Mr. Adair's class are shown in
Figure 6-14. This was the third unit in which they had followed an individualized instruction format.

If you had the information that Mr. Adair collected, how would you
use it?

Unit _____

Date _____

Answer the following questions to show how you feel about class today.

1. How much did you learn today?	a lot	quite a lot	not much	nothing
2. How important to you is the topic we studied today?	very important	somewhat important	not important	
3. Were you given enough chances to participate in class today?	just right	a few but not enough	no chances	
4. How helpful were the explanations of the teacher in class today?	very helpful	somewhat helpful	no help	

5. What could the teacher have done today to help you learn more?

_____

_____

Figure 6-12.   An attitude questionnaire for a single lesson

Mr. Adair decided to do several things as a result of the responses to the attitude questionnaire:

1. Questions 2 and 6 showed that many students were concerned about either objectives or materials. A few questions to students showed that the problem was mainly with resources that were scattered about and unlabeled. Mr. Adair decided to place all the resources for a unit in one place so that students could find them more easily. He also decided to talk to all the students about returning the materials quickly so that others could use them.
2. The responses to questions 4 and 6 showed that students wanted more help from the teacher. Mr. Adair decided to spend more time moving about the room and helping the students instead of waiting for them to come to him for help.
3. Mr. Adair noticed that one pair of students had never really started on the unit. By means of some discreet questioning he found that they were

Unit _____

Date _____

Fill in the name of the unit you just completed and answer the following questions. There are no right or wrong answers, just say how you feel.

	Agree	Undecided	Disagree
1. I learned a lot studying this unit.	_____	_____	_____
2. The objectives for this unit were clear and learning materials were easy to find and use.	_____	_____	_____
3. Studying mostly on my own was a good way to learn in this unit.	_____	_____	_____
4. The teacher gave me as much help as I needed in this unit.	_____	_____	_____
5. More group work with the teacher should have been done in this unit.	_____	_____	_____

6. What could be done to make the study of this unit better for you?

_____

_____

Figure 6-13

the students who had marked "Disagree" for questions 1 and 3. He decided to separate these two students during the next unit and have each one work with another partner.

You may have made different decisions. Of course, Mr. Adair had other information about the pupils and the class that is not available to you. But, student responses on a simple six-item attitude measure helped this teacher make decisions that could affect learning in his classroom.

Unit _Central America_

Date _Sept.- Oct._

Fill in the name of the unit you just completed and answer the following questions. There are no right or wrong answers, just say how you feel.

	Agree	Undecided	Disagree
1. I learned a lot studying this unit.	⊬⊬ ⊬⊬ ⊬⊬ ////	////	//
2. The objectives for this unit were clear and learning materials were easy to find and use.	⊬⊬ /	⊬⊬ //	// ⊬⊬ ⊬⊬
3. Studying mostly on my own was a good way to learn in this unit.	⊬⊬ /// ⊬⊬ ⊬⊬	⊬⊬	//
4. The teacher gave me as much help as I needed in this unit.	⊬⊬ //	/ ⊬⊬ ⊬⊬	⊬⊬ //
5. More group work with the teacher should have been done in this unit.	////	⊬⊬ /	⊬⊬ ⊬⊬ ⊬⊬

6. What could be done to make the study of this unit better for you?

can't find materials to use ⊬⊬ ///   more time to talk to the teacher ⊬⊬ ⊬⊬ // Make students share books ⊬⊬ // scattered requests for: rugs for the floor, longer breaks, a quieter room, etc.

Figure 6-14

SOME FINAL CONSIDERATIONS

By this time, the topic of diagnostic evaluation should be quite familiar to you; you should have some clear ideas in mind as to how you could ask one or more of the five diagnostic evaluation questions in your classroom and how you would use the responses of your students. The only thing that remains is to *go and do it*. Then you can find out whether diagnostic evaluation is another of those fancy ideas that sound good but don't work, or whether it does make a difference in your students' achievement or attitudes.

Before you begin the difficult (but rewarding) job of using diagnostic evaluation, a few suggestions may be helpful.

1. Keep it simple. Don't try to implement a complete diagnostic evaluation program all at once; the job is too big. Instead, select one of the diagnostic questions and concentrate on it for a few weeks. Then, if you and your students are comfortable with that, include another question. The main idea is not to overwhelm yourself or your students with new classroom procedures. If students are not accustomed to diagnostic tests, it will take them a few days or weeks to understand their operation and value.

2. Use all the help you can get. To be of help in making classroom decisions, diagnostic evaluation should be done frequently. Second, information is needed about all students, so problems of record keeping naturally arise. No classroom will be improved by overloading the teacher with paper work. It is critical, therefore, to plan how the diagnostic evaluation records can be kept. One suggestion is to have others help you. Other students in the class, cadet teachers, pupils from other classes, mothers and fathers, and clerical workers are all possible sources of aid. The most likely sources, however, are the students in the class. They have an interest in the program, and, indeed, their interest level may rise if they can do much of the diagnostic testing and record keeping for themselves or for one another. In addition, the participation of students in the evaluation process will increase their commitment to make it effective.

3. Be flexible. Written evaluation has been emphasized in this chapter, but verbal procedures are good too—perhaps better in some cases. So don't feel that you must always use one kind of diagnostic test. Perhaps you should have students invent ways to show what they have learned, remembered, or need to learn before starting a unit. Some of their ideas may be excellent, and using them will have a good effect on class morale. You can be flexible as to when you use diagnostic tests, how you use them, who corrects them, how the results are recorded, and so on. There are no known best ways to do any of these things, so the wise teacher shouldn't feel tied to any one procedure.

4. Don't expect miracles. Be patient with your students and with yourself. You should expect difficulty, resistance, and misunderstanding when you first use diagnostic evaluation. Ultimately, a more satisfying and effective classroom may result because of skillful diagnosis, but almost surely it won't begin that way. Both you and your students should expect some difficulty until the bugs are worked out. *Be prepared for failures before the successes begin.* Then be prepared to work hard to continue the success.

The questions in this test are based on the three objectives of this chapter. Use the test as a pretest, posttest, or both. Some sample answers and explanations of questions are given at the end of the test.

1. Check each statement that describes a purpose of diagnostic evaluation in the classroom.

__A. Determine pupils' attitudes toward lessons or topics.

__B. Gather data that allow careful comparisons among pupils.

__C. Find out which pupils have achieved which objectives before, during, or after studying.

__D. Motivate pupils to try their best.

__E. Find out if pupils remember what they have learned at some later time.

__F. Find out if pupils have appropriate background knowledge and skills.

2. Check each statement that describes a procedure for obtaining diagnostic information in a classroom.

__A. Select and administer a standardized test (such as an IQ test) to all pupils.

__B. Prepare and give a surprise quiz occasionally to keep motivation and effort high.

__C. List all pupils and their test scores on a bulletin board.

__D. State objectives in performance terms and prepare specific test items for each objective.

__E. Administer tests to all pupils before, during, and after a unit of study.

__F. Use pupil help in administering and scoring tests.

3. Mr. Dinstock is planning a social studies unit in which pupils will use the library extensively on their own. He knows that in the previous year the pupils studied such skills as using the card catalog and locating items in the library on the basis of their card catalog number. The success of the present unit depends on these skills. Describe the information Mr. Dinstock should collect about the library skills, how he should collect it, and how he should use the collected information in planning the unit.

4. Following an intensive two-day practice session on metaphors, Miss Davis gave all the pupils in her class a ten-minute quiz to see if they could distinguish metaphors from observations, identify mixed metaphors, and write metaphors. The results from ten pupils in the class are tabulated below. A check mark means that the objective was achieved; a blank means that it was not. (*Note:* The quiz covered only objectives 3, 4, and 5. Previously, all ten of these pupils had achieved objectives 1 and 2. At this time no work had been done on objectives 6 and 7.)

	1	2	3	4	5	6	7
Mary B.	✓	✓	✓				
Bill B.	✓	✓	✓	✓			
Jean D.	✓	✓	✓	✓	✓		
Alfred E.	✓	✓					
Tim F.	✓	✓	✓	✓	✓		
Jill H.	✓	✓	✓				
Mona H.	✓	✓	✓	✓			
Debbie J.	✓	✓	✓	✓			
Bob K.	✓	✓	✓				
Alta L.	✓	✓	✓	✓	✓		

Describe briefly how Miss Davis could use this information to plan classroom activities.

COMMENTS ON THE "TEST ON OBJECTIVES"

1. Here are the items I would check and my reasons for doing so. You may have checked different ones for other reasons.

___A. This is one of the five kinds of diagnostic evaluation studied in this chapter.

___B. Comparisons among pupils may be done for other reasons, but they provide little help when the purpose of evaluation is diagnosis.

___C. This is the *major* purpose of diagnostic evaluation.

___D. You may have checked this, but you have to be cautious about using evaluation as a motivator. If evaluation helps students do better work, then their success becomes a motivator.

___E. This is another of the five kinds of diagnostic evaluation studied in this chapter.

___F. This is the "Do they know what I think they know?" question.

2. Some comments on procedures.

___A. Most standardized tests provide little diagnostic information because they rarely match your objectives.

___B. Some teachers use surprise quizzes effectively. But more often they fail to produce good study efforts by students; instead, they just cause anxiety.

___C. You need to be cautious about this. Failure on a diagnostic test should serve as an aid to improved work, but public discloseure of failure may have other effects.

___D. This is a key procedure in diagnostic evaluation.

___E. To obtain information about everybody you have to test or ask everybody.

___F. This is a good idea for busy teachers.

3. Mr. Dinstock needs to find out if students "know what I think they know." You might also consider it a long-range retention or memory problem. In any event, his present instruction depends on prior knowledge. A series of steps such as the following could be used:

A. Set out the objectives for the social studies unit.

B. Identify all the prerequisite skills and knowledge that students will need in order to start the new unit.

C. Prepare test items for all the prerequisites, and administer them to the students.

D. Examine student performance in regard to the prerequisites. If only a few students are having difficulty, plan individualized, small-group, or peer tutoring sessions. If many or most students are having trouble with the prerequisite skills, plan some special lessons for the students before beginning the new unit.

4. Only Alfred E. missed objective 3, so plan special study just for him. (Special tutoring, individual practice, or working with a peer are all possibilities.) More pupils failed objectives 4 and 5, so small-group instruction or repeat instruction for the entire class may be in order here. The students who have already learned the skills represented by objectives 4 and 5 may help with the instruction or work on other things.

7

Implementing Interpersonal Communication in School Environments

DeWAYNE KURPIUS

Indiana University

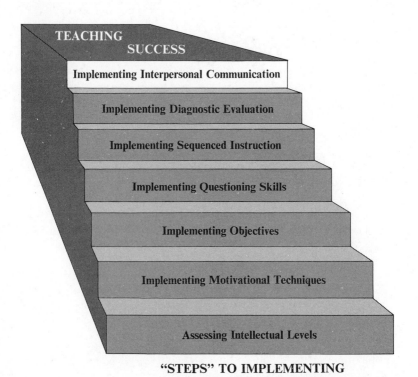

**"STEPS" TO IMPLEMENTING
TEACHING COMPETENCIES**

This chapter will focus on interpersonal communication within the classroom as well as among adults who work within a school. The format will follow two basic steps that the teacher or teacher trainee might logically follow: what the teacher already *knows* about interpersonal communication and what the teacher *does* in order to develop and implement a positive interpersonal approach to teaching and learning.

Each reader already possesses a wealth of experience about interpersonal communication. What an individual knows, however, may not always be accessible to him for direct application in a given interpersonal situation. Therefore, in this chapter we will attempt to:

1. Present a framework for helping the reader develop a point of view based upon a conceptual model of interpersonal communication.
2. Describe the basic issues related to this conceptualization.
3. Simulate the implementation of the concepts and facts in the classroom.

To do this we have selected one of the most widely accepted definitions of human growth and development, which states that, basically, humans are interrelated by a set of basic needs and desires that they strive to satisfy. These needs are innately similar among all humans and tend to be organized in a hierarchy. That is, certain needs must be at least partially satisfied before other, higher-order needs become important.

This developmental sequence of need satisfaction is commonly referred to as Maslow's hierarchy of needs and is often presented in the form of a pyramid. We have symbolized the developmental sequence through a stairstep approach. As you will notice in Figure 7-1, there is overlap between stages. However, at the level where one becomes conscious of striving to meet such needs, the stages tend to merge in a less conscious and more spontaneous manner.

To further explicate the need-satisfaction approach, we have set forth each need separately. Each is defined briefly and then illustrated in the form of a specific classroom or school behavior.

DEFINITION

PHYSICAL NEEDS   These are the first needs humans strive to satisfy. In some cases the needs are for food, shelter, and clothing—the most basic physical needs. In other situations a physical need might be proper classroom temperature or comfortable furniture. Certainly, the coffee and Coke breaks and teacher work areas are linked to this basic need.

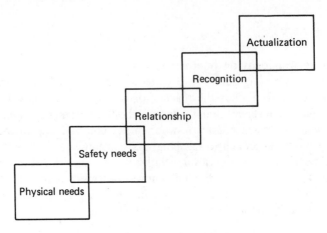

Figure 7-1.   Need satisfaction

Charts 7-1 and 7-2 have been developed to reinforce the importance of linking students' felt needs to their behavior and to the subsequent teacher response.

Now, following the model in Chart 7-1 you can demonstrate your understanding of the impact of physical needs on behavior by completing the practice chart in the Appendix (p. 271).

Teacher makes the following observation of a student in class.	Student is restless and is unable to concentrate during several morning classes.
Student report.	Teacher schedules brief, informal meeting with student and learns that breakfast is not served at home and that lunch money is sometimes not available.
Alternative solutions to be agreed upon mutually by student and teacher.	1. Refer student to social worker for family visit. 2. Refer student to principal for free-lunch 3. Discuss possible after-school jobs with student. 4. Teacher gives money to student. 5. Other.
Specific physical need that was affecting student learning.	*Food.* (It is important to note that *how* the felt need is attended to is important and, as you will notice, relates to higher-order human needs.)

Chart 7-1.   Example of physical need

DEFINITION

SAFETY NEEDS   *Feeling* safe is the next higher level of need satisfaction, the bases of which are:

1. Feeling protected from *physical* harm by the teacher, a playground supervisor, or a policeman.
2. Feeling protected from *psychosocial harm,* by virtue of:

   A. School policy protecting student rights.
   B. Adequate order and structure in work and play environment.
   C. A general feeling of security, as in trusting the teacher's judgments and decisions.

Chart 7-2 has been completed as an example. If you need practice, you may complete Chart 7-7 (p. 272), entering the ideas and issues most important to you. You may wish to form small groups to fill in the blank charts. Remember to focus on *safety needs* only, even though other interpretations may also seem appropriate.

Teacher makes the following observation of a student in class.	Student tends to stay close to adults during playground periods and after school. Previous anecdotal records state that student has difficulty forming peer relationships.
Student report.	Teacher talks to student after school and discovers that student likes games, but a certain gang of boys likes to hit him and tease him about always being with girls and adults.
Alternative solutions to be agreed upon mutually by student and teacher.	1.· Ask for names of boys and call them in. 2. Refer to principal. 3. Ask student for ideas on how to solve problem. 4. Other.
Specify safety need that was affecting student learning in the space provided.	

Chart 7-2.   Example of safety need

DEFINITION

RELATIONSHIP NEED   The next higher level is the felt need to move from focusing mostly on the self to *seeking to develop relationships with others*. The student manifests this need by relying more on each individual's behavior within the classroom, including that of the teacher, while also being aware of the group dynamics among all the members of the classroom. The key elements here are being accepted and included, feeling like a member of a group, and in some cases fulfilling the safety need by feeling safe in forming expanded relationships.

Again, you may want to fill in Chart 7-8 (p. 272) with real or hypothetical statements related to developing relationships with others. Chart 7-3 has been completed as a reference.

Teacher makes the following observation of students in class.	Students always select the same groupings when student-elected groups are formed. Several students generally not selected have tried to become included, but to no avail.
Student report.	Teacher talks to these students independently and discovers that they don't see much hope for being accepted and included as peers. They also report that there seems to be heavy competition within the class for establishing relationships with the class leaders as well as with the teacher.
Alternative solutions to be agreed upon upon mutually by students and teacher.	1. Coach the rejected students so that they will learn the social skills necessary to be accepted. 2. Open discussion with the whole class. 3. Teacher modifies his or her own behavior. 4. Students are referred to the counselor. 5. Other.
Specify relationship need that was affecting student learning in the space provided.	

Chart 7-3.   Example of relationship need

DEFINITION

RECOGNITION NEED   Being recognized by one's peers as friendly, productive, and creative are ego-satisfying manifestations of this level of
need satisfaction. At this level, recognition can be gained only through
feedback from others. Therefore, we have prepared a statement on
feedback that begins on page 277.

Now try to complete Chart 7-9 (p. 273), including both the need for
recognition and the appropriate feedback approaches. Read the statement
on feedback before proceeding with Chart 7-9. Chart 7-4 has been completed as an example.

Teacher makes the following observation of students in class.	Some students in class seem to be known as trouble makers and behave accordingly most of the time.
Student report.	Teacher talks to these students independently and discovers that the only recognition they are able to gain from other class members is for their disruptive behavior.
Alternative solutions to be agreed upon mutually by students and teacher.	1. Refer students to counselor. 2. Teacher consults with counselor about ways to reinforce positive behavior. 3. Teacher suggests to students that they had better work on their problems. 4. Parents are contacted. 5. Other.
Specific recognition need that was affecting student learning.	Students in general strive for recognition; since the students in question don't exhibit acceptable behavior, they receive no positive recognition; thus, they must resort to unacceptable behavior in order to gain recognition, even though that recognition isn't positive.

Chart 7-4.   Example of recognition need

DEFINITION

SELF-ACTUALIZATION NEED   The last or highest level that we will present here is also the most abstract. The sequence suggests that self-actualization is the highest goal in life and perhaps one that is never fully reached. Generally, individuals who have reached this level have achieved each step satisfactorily according to their own set standards. These standards vary greatly, which, once again, should remind the teacher of individual differences. Related to the individual differences among needs and standards are the individual behaviors that each person develops as a self-actualizing person. These are:
1. Requesting feedback from others.
2. Taking risks that seem necessary in order to continue to grow.
3. Making decisions based on what seems appropriate to the situation and conditions rather than going along with the majority.

This time the concepts of feedback, risk taking, and decision making are prominent. Review Chart 7-5 and then try to complete Chart 7-10 (p. 273).

Teacher makes the following observation of students in class.	Students seem to be asking more questions about the learning climate in their room.
Student report.	Teacher arranges a special class meeting that focuses on the questions students are asking. The results show that some students want to improve the interpersonal relationships among class members and some are satisfied with the present situation.
Alternative solutions to be mutually agreed upon by students and teacher.	1. A student committee is designated to define the problem and prepare alternative solutions. 2. Teacher asks for feedback from students. 3. Teacher defines the problem and suggests the solutions. 4. Teacher does not allow feedback. 5. Other.
Specific self-actualization need.	The teacher and many students see themselves as strong persons and desire feedback even though certain risks are involved.

Chart 7-5.   Example of self-actualization need

The question you are probably asking is, How do I recognize and respond to the needs of each student while also being aware of group needs and, of course, my own needs? One way is to observe how you are currently responding to the individuals with whom you work and live. But, first, we must describe two ways in which people form relationships. Our objective is for you to recognize your own use of these two styles and to use them selectively in creating a productive learning environment. The first is based on the belief that *interdependent* interpersonal relationships are most likely to become mutually rewarding and long-lasting. The second style is based on a more *dependent* approach and tends to stress compliance. These approaches are situational: Your use of one or the other will depend on the kind of relationships you are seeking in a given situation.

TWO APPROACHES TO INTERPERSONAL RELATIONSHIPS

The interdependent approach, developed by Schutz (1967), strongly suggests that relationships do not occur by chance or by need alone, but are developed through interaction with another person. Schutz believes that this interaction period comprises three phases: (1) inclusion, (2) control, and (3) affective. He suggests that when two or more persons interact, they test these stages until either the interaction discontinues or a relationship is developed. A brief summary of this approach is described by Kurpius (1971):

> During this first encounter or the inclusion phase, the persons involved must decide if the experience is worthy of continuation of the relationship. If the people involved decide that their relationship is worthy of continuation and expansion, they immediately move into the second phase, that of confronting one another in relation to the control factors in the relationship. In the control phase each is testing the other in order to understand what kind of control is being used on him, what is expected of him in the relationship, and whether or not he is able to control the other person or whether he is the more controlled. Each also learns the kinds of behaviors that will be most functional for controlling the other as well as the behaviors that are most effective in restricting or dissipating control. If during the control phase each party decides the relationship has meaning and should be continued, control factors will be tested and worked out in a satisfactory fashion at least for the immediate time. This interaction will move the relationship into Phase III, the stage of affection. This stage is typically the one in which more risk is involved, more genuineness is exchanged, more freedom and spontaneity to test and experiment with the relationship enter in, and the relationship begins taking on the potential to become a lasting one.

The second approach is described by Kelman (1964), who also views a three-step process in the development of interpersonal relationships. These steps are (1) compliance, (2) identification, and (3) internalization. Compliance is said to occur when a person accepts being influenced by another. Usually, this adjustment to the other person occurs when *a favorable impression is desired*. As is true of inclusion, compliance is the earliest level of the interpersonal interaction. The next stage, identification, is a higher level of interpersonal influence since it indicates a desire not only to establish a positive relationship with others, but also to *maintain the relationship over time*. The third stage, internalization, takes interpersonal influence to a higher level of acceptance in that the person being influenced is *now feeling comfortable with how he is being influenced*. He likes the influences he is receiving and the possible uses they may have for new learning.

These two models represent different processes for establishing interpersonal relationships. That is, the inclusion, control, and affective stages of the interdependent approach indicate a base of balanced power and influence. Each step is monitored by both parties, and there is give and take (feedback) by both parties in establishing the relationship. The dependent approach tends to be more one-directional.

As teachers, it may be difficult for us to decide which of these is more appropriate. At first, we might all say that we desire the interdependent approach. Teachers and learners alike accept the importance of, and, in fact, the necessity for interdependence between teacher and learner: We have different roles, and responsibilities must be shared.

There are times, however, when the teacher wishes to influence the learner to accept a certain point of view. For example, the teacher may want the learner to become inquiry-oriented—that is, to identify and collect information, to analyze it, and to use it appropriately. However, as you can predict, as the learners become more inquiry-oriented in learning new facts and values, they will also become more inquiry-oriented in establishing interpersonal relationships with their peers and with adults, including the teacher. When this occurs, it is important for the teacher to recognize the shift in relationship style that is involved, and be prepared to welcome the interdependent interaction that may result between student and teacher. The relationship will naturally move into the so-called control stage, giving both student and teacher a chance to explore the limits of authority and inquiry. Chances are that each will emerge, not intimidated, but more secure in the relationship and more eager to work together. This is an example of a situation in which the dependent approach evolves into an interdependent approach because of the changing needs and inputs of those involved.

Now we are ready to go back to the question of needs. As a way of demonstrating the importance of one's need to relate to another person, while recognizing the other person's need to behave differently, we have prepared a brief role-play script. Please continue by reading the script and the related instructions.

ROLE PLAY

The following script depicts one of the two approaches previously described. The dialogue is between a school principal and a beginning classroom teacher.

Teacher: I came in to see you today to talk with you briefly about your philosophy of education. I guess another reason is that I wanted to get to know you better as a person and to give you an opportunity to get to know me.

Principal: I'm glad you came in. We want to get to know our teachers better. Of course, as you know, we talked to each other at length during your initial interviews, and I think we know each other pretty well. You know, we wouldn't have hired you if I didn't think you would be an outstanding teacher. We are deeply concerned about our need to offer quality education at this school, and if you have questions, I would be glad to answer them, or you can see our curriculum supervisor.

Teacher: I was really thinking a little more along the lines of having us understand each other better as total persons, including both what we know and how we feel about the program of this school. I know right now I'm more concerned about myself and how I'm helping each of my students to be better persons, but I'm also interested in the broader program issues of this school.

Principal: You sound very motivated, which will help you as a teacher. I'm sure you already know that teaching is a very difficult task. One of the reasons we have such an outstanding school is our top-flight staff. As I said, we think you can do the job. At midyear I will hold interim evaluation sessions with each new teacher, so we can talk more then.

Teacher: Oh, I see. You prefer to wait until my evaluation sessions. Well, I guess I agree with you that it's a privilege to work here, and I'm sure I can do a good job. It was good to talk with you, and I'll be looking forward to our evaluation session.

Principal: Yes, I enjoyed our talk, also. Keep up the good work.

Instructions for Using Role-Play Script

The following steps have been developed to depict how people perceive their role and how they develop interpersonal relationships. We hope that the script you just read will provide a basis upon which you can explore the type of interpersonal working relationship *you* desire in your teaching.

Note: The following steps can be used for either preservice or in-service training; however, the language used in this text applies to preservice teachers. Please read all the steps before beginning.

1. Class members choose partners to role-play the above script.
2. Each partner now chooses a second partner, thereby forming a team of four.
3. Each team identifies two teacher and two principal roles.
4. Each teacher-principal partnership should now role-play the above script.
5. After completing the role playing, answer this question: As a teacher, which sequence would you judge has been followed in the above script?

    ___A. Interdependent approach.

    ___B. Dependent approach.
6. Maintain the same role, but this time the two teachers form partnerships and the two principals do the same. Each "teacher" should now write one example of the kind of working relationship you desire with your principal, and each "principal" should each write a script depicting the kind of relationship you as principal would desire with a new teacher. Space is provided in the Appendix, p. 271.
7. After completing the brief scripts, each team of four selects one teacher and one principal to role-play one of the scripts, which should depict the desired interpersonal working relationship between teacher and principal.
8. Score this script by answering the question asked in step 5.
9. Now select from your group one teacher and one principal to make a two-minute-or-less presentation to the total class on the interpersonal relationship *you* desire with the principal or teacher in your school.
10. Decide as a class whether you desire an *interdependent* or a *dependent* working relationship.
11. Is more discussion and practice needed? If so, write and role-play a new script depicting a teacher-parent or a teacher-student confrontation.

Here is a brief summary of the two approaches as they might apply to a teacher-principal encounter. See if your judgment of practice encounters was accurate according to these descriptions.

INTERDEPENDENT APPROACH	*DEPENDENT APPROACH*
Stage 1	
Inclusion: Teacher and principal decide if this relationship is worthy of continuation. Since both realize that they must work together, they decide that it is.	*Compliance:* Teacher accepts the influence of the principal since making a favorable impression is very imporrtant to a beginning teacher.

Stage II

Control: Teacher and principal test the kind of control being used, both understanding the importance of the relationship. Role differences are made clear. Each recognizes the need for both to work together to meet the needs of the students.

Identification: Teacher continues to accept the influence of the principal since he wants to establish and maintain a satisfactory relationship. In addition, he has been warned by another teacher not to question the philosophy or organization of the school.

Stage III

Affective: Teacher and principal have worked out the control stage, which is directly related to role responsibility rather than to power and authority, and now develop a mutually beneficial and potentially long-lasting working relationship.

Internalization: Teacher accepts the principal's influence as a necessary element in the operation of a school, and begins to incorporate the ideas and actions of the principal as his own.

IMPLEMENTING A BALANCED LEARNING ENVIRONMENT

In order to focus on how interpersonal relationships affect the learning climate, we are going to focus on two teacher leadership functions in the classroom: *task functions* and *interpersonal functions*. The task function comprises what the teacher does to attend to tasks to be accomplished and facts to be learned; the interpersonal function encompasses how the teacher fosters positive interpersonal and interdependent working relationships. The combination and balance of these two functions seem to support positive working and learning environments. For example, if during a class discussion a student said, "I am familiar with that statement in the literature," and went on to share his information, we would consider this situation to be associated with the task dimensions, which focus on academic development. If the teacher responded to that student by saying, "Thanks, John, that helps us understand the problem better," we would consider this reply to represent the interpersonal dimensions, which focus on interpersonal development.

How do we as teachers determine our influence on these two major dimensions of the classroom climate? *First,* we need to define each function. *Next,* we will describe how to assess our present leadership behavior. Last, we will define how to implement a program in a classroom to adjust the balance between the teacher's task and interpersonal functions.

The teacher must perform the task functions in order for the class to meet the objectives associated with academic development. The following list describes the common task functions that a teacher engages in to assure that the knowledge objectives are met. As a class, you may want to propose examples of each behavior for the purposes of clarification and reinforcement.

1. *Initiating action:* setting goals and objectives; providing structure, procedures, and resources with which to accomplish objectives.
Example:

2. *Information and idea seeking:* eliciting ideas from students and looking for cues that indicate that they are accomplishing tasks and learning facts more quickly.
Example:

3. *Information and idea sharing:* teaching facts, offering ideas to be tested, and relating personal experiences to information shared.
Example:

4. *Elaborating and specifying:* clearing up misunderstood information, expanding on ideas, giving examples.
Example:

5. *Summarizing:* integrating ideas and facts, including statements and ideas suggested by class members.
Example:

6. *Evaluating the discussion:* asking what was accomplished, which objectives were met, and whether the class agreed with the outcomes.
Example:

Definition of Interpersonal Function

Interpersonal teacher functions are necessary in the classroom to maintain a climate of collaboration, interdependence, and mutual satisfaction. The interpersonal functions consist of the following teacher behaviors. Once again, you may use the space provided to supply examples.

1. *Encouraging:* responding to others in a friendly, accepting, and responsive manner. Positive reinforcement for contributions, as well as the willingness to listen to and respect the ideas of others, are important.
Example:

2. *Harmonizing:* reducing tension in the class or work group by helping students to explore their differences, helping the class search for a solution to the conflict, looking at compromise as only one solution, and understanding the differences between inclusion and compliance.
Example:

3. *Expressing group feeling:* sensing and summarizing the classroom feeling toward the interpersonal relationships in the class—that is, competitive versus collaborative—sharing feelings about the present temperament or mood of the class, generally reducing group tension.
   Example:

4. *Balancing talk time:* allowing all class members to make input when appropriate, providing adequate time and opportunity for less verbal students, keeping the discussion alive and class-centered.
   Example:

Next, if you are enrolled in a university course, complete exercise 1. If you are already employed as a teacher, read all of exercise 1, but then go to exercise 2 for further instructions.

Exercise 1

We can find out where we stand now in our ability to perform both the task and interpersonal functions by engaging in a pretest with peers.

1. Select six to eight students in the class to discuss the *educational goals implicit in the material presented thus far.*
2. Select an equal number of students to function as observers.
3. Arrange chairs in two complete circles in the middle of the classroom as follows:

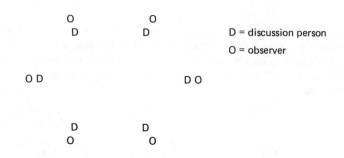

4. Each outer-circle observer is responsible for the discussion person sitting in front of him. Each time the person responds to a statement made by another person or makes an input statement, the observer should place a mark on the score sheet on page 275.

Okay, let's begin. The time will vary as topics change and as members become better able to develop the appropriate balance between task and interpersonal responses. Also, since this may be the first time you have assessed discussions in this manner, it will be helpful to obtain a score on a smaller sample of behavior so that you can begin to modify your group discussion and/or group leadership behavior as needed. Therefore, you may decide to begin with five-minute sessions at first.

Directions for Observers.   The task and interpersonal statements are listed in abbreviated form on the score sheet in the same order as on pages 258–59. After each dimension there are ten boxes, which are to be used to tally the number of times the person being observed demonstrates that particular dimension. Notice that above each box are two numbers ranging from 1 to 10 in the upper line and from 2 to 20 in the lower line. These numbers represent minutes of time and allow the observers to score the persons being observed on the basis of either one-minute or two-minute intervals. The discussion group decides on the scoring intervals, and the observers circle the number that represents the total amount of time to be scored. For example, if the first trial is for five minutes, circle the number 5 and begin the five-minute discussion session.

Let us assume you will be following the five-minute format and using one-minute intervals. As observer, your responsibilities are to:

1. Circle the number 5.
2. Place a slash mark (/) in the first (one-minute) box each time the person you are observing makes a comment. After one minute, circle the number 1 to show that one minute has passed. Next, place your tallies in the second (two-minute) box. Follow the same procedure until the five minutes are up.

After the five minutes have elapsed, you should have all of the numbers from 1 to 5 circled and as many tallies in each box as appropriate for the number and kind of responses made by the person you are observing.

How To Use the Results.   After the five minutes (or however long the session is), you should:

1. Refer to the section on feedback (page 276) to remind yourself of the purposes and criteria for giving feedback. Review the tallies and decide on the most dominant characteristics of the person you are observing. Prepare a written statement to be shared with your partner. (Allow three minutes for this.)

2. Now sit with your partner and share observations, both written and oral. (Allow three minutes.)

3. Observers and discussants reverse roles, decide on the length of time, and repeat all steps beginning with exercise 1 on page 260.

Exercise 2: Assessment of Teacher Behavior

If you are already employed and wish to determine how you manage your classroom in the area of task and interpersonal dimensions, you could:

1. Have another teacher rate you during a ten- or twenty-minute period of teaching for three or four days. At the end of this time, summarize your score and then decide if you want to adjust your teaching and leadership style.
2. Select two or three students in your class to rate you over three or four consecutive days. Again, review the findings and decide if any changes are needed.
3. Ask a teacher aide, the principal, or a parent to act as observer.
4. Ask the whole class to rate you for your overall performance in the two dimensions. In this case, use the ten boxes as a numbered rating scale from a low of 1 to a high of 10 instead of as a time scale.

Exercise 3: Student Assessment of Their Own Behavior

If you want your students to rate themselves, you could use the following steps:

1. Teach the task and interpersonal dimensions to the class. Perhaps have them prepare a bulletin board that display the dimensions.
2. Ask your students to score their own behavior while playing on a team, participating in class discussion, or working in a small group. For this purpose, they may either follow all of exercise 1 or utilize the rating scale described in Step 4 of exercise 2.

Note: For junior high and above, including teacher rating, use the scale on page 275. For some elementary age students it may be better to use a more simplified form such as the one in Figure 7-2. Select a common experience in the classroom that requires student-to-student and/or student-to-teacher interaction. Explain, for example, the dimensions of getting schoolwork accomplished (task) and of working together (interpersonal). Now select one observer for each category and set a time limit of ten to twenty minutes for each observation. Each observer will focus on the activity selected while reviewing the five statements listed under each dimension. At the completion of the observation the task observer should place a "T"

TASK DIMENSIONS

Teacher's concern
about schoolwork

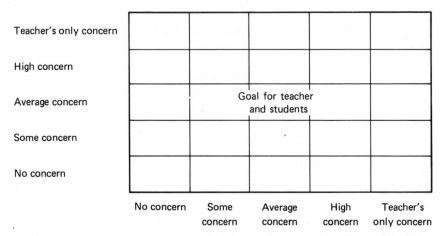

Teacher's only concern

High concern

Average concern

Some concern

No concern

| No concern | Some concern | Average concern | High concern | Teacher's only concern |

Teacher's concern about how we get along and work together

INTERPERSONAL DIMENSIONS

Figure 7-2. Simplified form for rating task and interpersonal functions

in the box describing the interpersonal dimensions. Briefly discuss the existing score and the desired score and one or two ways of moving toward the desired scores. Implement the changes and continue observations on a biweekly basis. *Continue this practice until a high concern for schoolwork and a high concern for working together are demonstrated by both teachers and students.*

DEVELOPING INTERPERSONAL RELATIONSHIPS IN A CLASSROOM THROUGH THE MICRO-LAB APPROACH

The various rating experiences just described should create some awareness, among students and the teacher alike, that certain interpersonal needs are continually operant in group situations. The classroom—a working group—is certainly no exception. Some of the personal needs that might occur to you, as a teacher or teacher trainee, are those characterized earlier as "relationship," "recognition," and "self-actualization." Here they are in a more detailed form:

1. The need for self-understanding.
2. The need to understand others.

3. The need to benefit from, and to benefit, another.
4. The need to speak more openly and spontaneously.
5. The need to experience the feeling of membership.
6. The need to accept oneself and others at any time.

(Add any others here that you feel are appropriate.)

If we accept these as general objectives to work toward in establishing an interdependent classroom, the question of procedure arises: How does one translate these objectives into a set of interpersonal experiences? We will offer here a description of the so-called micro-lab approach (Kurpius 1971), which has proved successful with many different kinds of groups working with various kinds of input. The input (or subject) of this micro-lab project is the role of *behavior* and *feelings* in defining relationships. First, consider Figure 7-3, a useful model to work toward in communicating some intrapersonal and interpersonal concepts to students.

With elementary-age students, the teacher may want to begin with a simple diagram and follow it with a series of questions on a skeletal chart. (See Figure 7-4.) The children's answers may be used to fill out the chart.

Older students could be approached through a demonstration followed by a similar, but more sophisticated, set of questions. For example:

The teacher demonstrates the internal self by standing motionless, his back to the students, and asking, "What do you know about my feelings and thoughts?" Then, the teacher demonstrates the external self by performing

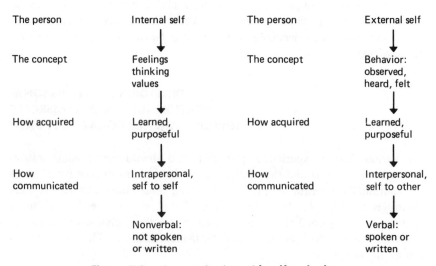

Figure 7-3. Communicating with self and others

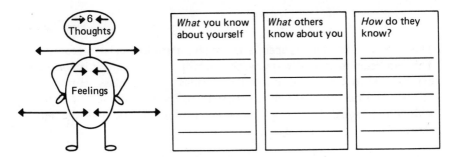

Figure 7-4.   Inquiry chart

some simple behavior and then asking the same question. Finally, the teacher performs some continued or high-order behavior that suggests a personality trait or a conflict of feelings, and then asks the question again. The teacher then asks some follow-up questions. The students' responses can be in the form of a chart or a list:

1. Why did you come to the conclusion you did in each of the three demonstrations?
2. What were some of the clues I gave you?
3. Why do you think you associate those clues with your conclusions about me?
4. What is behavior then?
5. What is positive behavior and negative behavior? Are these the same for everyone? If behavior is learned, why aren't we all alike?

The culmination of this lesson-experience ought to be a chart or set of written statements offered by the students that reflects the information in Figure 7-2. The teacher should guide and constructively edit, rather than simply provide the answers. For example, if a question is asked about non-verbal communication, respond to that person nonverbally. Perhaps use your hand to request that the student come toward you. After he or she arrives ask, "How did I tell you to come up here?" The same general procedure may be used with other nonverbal questions. That is, begin to relate the model to the class. The fact that the student recognized the hand request to come to the teacher means that the student has at some time *learned* the meaning of that signal. Also, the actual moving to the teacher indicates that the student has *purpose* in that behavior. We can only assume the purpose until the student tells us or in some other behavioral way informs us of the purpose—for instance, to obtain the correct answer, to be closer to the teacher, or to gain attention.

The next step for the teacher is to involve the class even more actively. This can begin in several ways, ways you will discover as you become more experienced in conducting micro-lab sessions in your class. However, for this first session I suggest you ask the class to focus on the self by beginning with intrapersonal (self-to-self) communication. To do this the teacher states:

> I now want you to experience some of these concepts. Let's begin with intrapersonal or self-to-self communication. (The teacher points to the model on the chalkboard.) Start by placing your head in your hands with eyes closed. Try to become relaxed, and try to block out everything and everyone in the room except yourself. Just relax and think about yourself.

After 60 to 120 seconds, most of the class will be attending to self. The class is now ready for you to explain their first exercise. Although the content of the exercise you suggest may vary greatly in future sessions, it is usually best to begin by asking each class member to focus on a positive behavior that he or she values very highly and uses often in daily life. Therefore, the teacher states:

> As you continue to relax, think of one positive behavior that you value highly and use often in your daily life.

After 60 to 120 seconds—maybe a little longer if you observe the class as unsettled and not attending to self—say:

> Now open your eyes and look about the room, and select one person whom you choose to describe this behavior to. Also, I want you to listen to your partner describe the positive behavior that he or she has chosen. Now leave your chair and go to that person.

Observe that it takes a minute or two for the students to move to that other person. Also, some persons will be selected by more than one student. In this case go to those students and explain to them that they should select another person. Don't be unduly concerned about the questions raised by the students unless a large majority don't seem to understand the activity. If this happens, interrupt the activity by saying:

> Let's stop for a brief review of what we are doing. Remember, we have identified a positive behavior that we value and use often, and we are now sharing this behavior with a person of our choice. Let's try it again.

Generally, it is best not to discuss the purpose or intent of the exercise at this time. The goal is for the pair to exchange the behavior each has identified. This first exercise is brief, so in 60 to 120 seconds request that the students return to their original chairs by saying:

> Okay, it looks as if you have exchanged your positive behaviors and are already discussing some related behaviors. Now return to your chairs, and let's talk about the experience.

After the students return to their chairs, ask for two or three of them to share the positive behavior they have identified. Use the chart (Figure 7-3) or the chalkboard to define the behavior. Also, describe to them that they have also communicated intrapersonally (self to self) and interpersonally (self to other).

You are now ready to repeat the exercise, but this time select a new topic. This could be one of several topics. The degree of abstraction will depend upon the age and experience of the group. Here are a few examples:

1. A second positive behavior.
2. A peak experience during the last week.
3. A behavior that gets the students in trouble.

After selecting the topic, ask the class to:

1. Attend to self and think about the appropriate behavior or peak experience.
2. Select another person to share the experience.

During the first exchange you will notice that students don't seem to move around the room; often, they select someone seated near them and talk rather superficially. One of the things you will notice during the second exchange is that members appear to move more freely across the room. In addition, you will be asking them to go to a different person, so they will experience decision making again.

Procedures continue to be much the same during the second exchange: The students sit and begin verbalizing their experience. During these small-group talk periods, you could walk around the room and offer to help them pinpoint and state their behaviors clearly. Since they have already defined behavior, students should have a better idea of how to identify and describe their behavior more specifically.

As soon as all pairs have exchanged behaviors, which will take another one to two minutes, ask each pair to look about the room and select another couple with whom they would like to continue to share their experience. Groups of four will now be forming. As the students mill about the room, talk to them to help them understand their task. Now that there are four students to a group, it will take a little more time for members to negotiate who will speak first or comment about the experience they are now involved in, but they usually begin the task quite rapidly. Once again, it is very important for the teacher to walk around and offer help if needed. In many cases, the students will need help to become more specific in identifying and verbalizing their behaviors. Perhaps this is the first time they have learned to focus on themselves, and some difficulty can therefore be expected, but this does not continue for long. The classroom teacher should continue to visit the groups and offer help if needed. At the close of this exercise, ask the students to return to their original seats and review briefly the total process of what happened, what the purpose of the exercise was, and what might happen at the next meeting. If time is available, you may progress to the second session.

Second Session

Begin the second session with a brief review of what happened during the first meeting, some of the purposes of that meeting, and some of the basic inputs that were made during it. If the group is responding well, you may want to attempt to move toward the feeling level of existence. If some students do not have a clear idea of the purpose of working with the feeling level, you may want to try a few more behavior exercises before moving to the feeling level. However, if when you move to the feeling level you have not previously described the difference between a behavior and a feeling, this would be a good way to open the second class period. (Perhaps compare and contrast feelings, values, ideas, and behavior through demonstrations, simple drawings, photos, or some other means.) Now continue with the micro-lab procedure by asking the students to relax themselves, to block out others in the room, and to focus on and attend to themselves. When asking the participants to focus on feelings, it is generally best to begin with positive feelings. Ask the class to think about themselves and a positive personal feeling they have had that very day. You may need to offer a few examples of positive feelings that they could have had that particular day in order to help them become more specific in identifying and describing feelings: For instance, you might say, "When I came to school this morning, several of the students greeted me in a friendly manner, and this felt good." Or, "I noticed this morning that one of the teachers was especially friendly to me, and I liked that." When you observe that the students are ready to share their experiences, ask them to choose a person with whom to share this experience as before. Following this exchange, ask each pair to select another pair and to continue to share among the four of them.

If the process is understood clearly by the participants, ask the four to seek another group of four with whom to share the experience.

As you can see, the use of micro-lab procedures is not complex and can be expanded or repeated many times. The topic that is introduced is the primary variable. Hence, the micro-lab procedure for assisting people through the different stages of communication, i.e., intrapersonal, interpersonal, verbal, and nonverbal, is merely a technique, one that can be learned very quickly. The concept that is introduced is the variable that allows the process to become a broad approach to working with classroom groups. For example, if your concept or intent was interdependence, you would work toward this goal, and in perhaps two, three, or four twenty-to-thirty-minute sessions, initial signs of interdependence could be observed in the classroom.

A common concern among older students, one in which teachers can become involved, comprises career decision making, program planning, and curriculum decisions. A possible way to approach these topics is by using micro-principles with classroom-size groups and focusing on career decision making. Again, start with a self-to-self exercise and move from one person to two, to four, to eight—to whatever size of group seems best. The assignment could be to ask each member on the one-to-one level to focus on an occupation in which they would ideally like to be employed.

A residual effect that emerges immediately is peer interaction. We are well aware of the strength of the peer group: Students do influence other students in making decisions about important issues, both emotional and intellectual. The micro-lab class meeting provides a time structure, direction, and process in which this interaction can take place.

How To Evaluate the Program

What are the effects of this approach in the classroom? One effect is that an interdependent kind of classroom relationship encourages students to become aware of one another's needs. The students become better acquainted with one another and find they are talking with each other about each other as well as about an event. Assessing the interdependence of a classroom may be possible on the basis of certain observations, such as the students' concern over who may not have a partner, or who is experiencing difficulty describing a specific behavior. Interdependence can be observed when students try to help persons in such situations. Also observable as an interdependent measure is a greater tendency for students to choose group members from outside their circle of friends. Still another factor that emerges from the micro-lab approach is the process of decision making. As the student moves from an intrapersonal to an interpersonal experience, he or she must decide, "Whom will I select?" or "Will I be selected?" The groups of two must decide whom to join in order to form the group of four, and the four must decide whom to join in order to form the group of eight. This type of activity sharpens and tends to accelerate one's decision-making abilities. Thus, we speculate that the micro-lab approach may bring about spontaneity in the thinking and decision-making processes.

SOME RESEARCH FINDINGS
ON TEACHER BEHAVIOR

The program outlined in this chapter was designed to help you continue the process of defining and developing the teacher behavior that will be most satisfying for you and your students.

Deciding which personal and professional qualities to strive for is, of course, ultimately up to you. But along the way it may help to know which teacher qualities are commonly given high ratings by students and supervisors alike. According to the research findings of Aspy (1973), highly rated teachers tend to demonstrate the following qualities:

1. They are very knowledgeable about their subject area(s).
2. They consider it important to know the relationships among class members.
3. They recognize student needs and respond to these objectively and systematically.
4. They demonstrate interest in the class and are willing to accept the learners at their present stage of development.
5. They consider student feelings to be as important as the subject matter being studied.

Given these findings, we have attempted to provide you with some training experiences that we hope will improve the interpersonal atmosphere of your classroom.

SOME FINAL WORDS OF CAUTION

Don't expect miracles in a short period of time. Interpersonal processes are developmental: They evolve rather than happening immediately. Be satisfied with cues that indicate a few gains, and don't forget the cues that signal your own personal growth.

Try to predict the "readiness level" of your students before implementing the approaches described above. If you remain open to feedback cues, you should be able to detect when your students are most ready to reexamine their own classroom behavior and that of others (including yours).

Expect to receive negative feedback from some parents. You cannot argue values with those who believe that school is only for "tasking." But you can be patient and hold to your own goals. A sudden improvement in a student's attitudes toward school should work in your favor.

Expect to receive negative feedback from some students. Since some personal needs are difficult to recognize, and cope with, the approach discussed in this chapter is obviously not a panacea. The student who resists may be signaling a strong need for privacy, one that happens to supersede other needs at the time. Try to find a way to respect that need without permanently alienating the student from the rest of the class.

APPENDIX

Specific physical need.	
Teacher makes the following observation of a student in class.	
Student report.	
Alternative solutions to be agreed upon mutually by student and teacher.	1. 2. 3. 4.

Chart 7-6.   (Fill in the spaces provided)

Specific safety need.	
Teacher makes the following observation of a student in class.	
Student report.	
Alternative solutions to be agreed upon mutually by student and teacher.	1. 2. 3. 4.

Chart 7-7.   (Fill in the spaces provided)

Specific relationship need.	
Teacher makes the following observation of a student in class.	
Student report.	
Alternative solutions to be agreed upon mutually by student and teacher.	1. 2. 3. 4.

Chart 7-8.   (Fill in the spaces provided)

Specific recognition need.	
Teacher makes the following observation of a student in class.	
Student report.	

Alternative solutions to be agreed upon mutually by student and teacher.	1.
	2.
	3.
	4.

Chart 7-9.   (Fill in the spaces provided)

Specific self-actualization need.	
Teacher makes the following observation of a student in class.	
Student report.	

Alternative solutions to be agreed upon mutually by student and teacher.	1.
	2.
	3.
	4.

Chart 7-10.   (Fill in the spaces provided)

Practice Role-Play Script
(to be used with step 6 of the role-play exercise, p. 256)

Teacher Statement: I came in to see you today to talk with you briefly about your philosophy of education. I guess another reason is that I wanted to get to know you better as a person and to give you an opportunity to get to know me.

Principal response:

Teacher response:

Principal response:

Teacher response:

GROUP PARTICIPATION OBSERVATION SHEET

TASK FUNCTIONS

TIME INTERVALS

	1	2	3	4	5	6	7	8	9	10	
	2	4	6	8	10	12	14	16	18	20	
Trials				Observed Behavior							total
1. Initiating action — 1st											
2nd											
3rd											
2. Information and idea seeking — 1st											
2nd											
3rd											
3. Information and idea sharing — 1st											
2nd											
3rd											
4. Elaborating and specifying — 1st											
2nd											
3rd											
5. Summarizing — 1st											
2nd											
3rd											
6. Evaluating the discussion — 1st											
2nd											
3rd											

INTERPERSONAL FUNCTIONS

	1	2	3	4	5	6	7	8	9	10	
	2	4	6	8	10	12	14	16	18	20	
Trial				Observed Behavior							total
1. Encouraging — 1st											
2nd											
3rd											
2. Harmonizing — 1st											
2nd											
3rd											
3. Expressing group feeling — 1st											
2nd											
3rd											
4. Balancing talk time — 1st											
2nd											
3rd											
5. Listening — 1st											
2nd											
3rd											

We stated earlier that most of our internal self (attitudes, values, feelings, and thinking) and our external self (behavior) has been learned. This learning usually occurs in relation to the amount and types of information exchanged between persons. This information can be of the cognitive (content) form, or it can be of the affective (feeling) form. It can also be verbal or nonverbal in either form.

During the human relations movement in education, this interpersonal communication became known as *feedback*. As the term implies, feedback is a communication process between two or more persons in which one person informs another person about how he or she is performing. This performance can be affective or cognitive. In any classroom, feedback is present almost all of the time. Teacher-to-students, students-to-students, and students-to-teacher are the most common forms of feedback in the classroom.

Have you ever assessed your feedback style and its consequences on the person receiving the feedback? Here are a few points to remember. Practice them yourself and perhaps teach them to your class.

Feedback, when given to another person, has three primary purposes:

1. *To identify discrepancies* between what that person assumes and what actually exists. For example, the teacher may say to a student, "Jane, I was sure you were bored in school, but now I know that you are worried about your mother's health and think constantly about her."
2. *To openly support or reinforce* behavior that is considered appropriate and is desired by another person. For example, a student says to a teacher, "Mr. Jones, you really helped me when you explained to me how to give better feedback."
3. *To modify behavior* so that actions and content are in line with the message intended. For instance, one student says to another student, "The next time our committee gives a report, it would help if we balanced the amount of talk time for each committee member. During today's report, Carol tried to share her ideas but was blocked out by some of us who have stronger voices.

Given these three purposes, there are several criteria that should be considered when we are giving feedback to another person or group of persons:

1. *Be descriptive* rather than judgmental. Describe your observations and/or reactions. Don't term the feedback "good" or "bad."
2. *Be objective* rather than subjective. Using abbreviated forms of com-

munication such as "autocratic," "friendly," or "passive" is not as useful as feeding back specific statements related to a common experience.

3. Whose needs should be met? The person giving appropriate feedback should consider both his need to give the feedback as well as the needs of the recipient of the feedback.

4. Is the feedback *accepted* by the person? Receiving feedback about behavior that appears to be difficult to change can only frustrate that person. Direct your feedback toward behaviors that the receiver can integrate into his plan of change.

5. Who *desires* the feedback? Feedback is most useful if a person solicits feedback. Imposed feedback is less helpful.

6. *When* should feedback be given. Generally, it is best to give feedback when the receiver can associate the feedback with the behavior being described. The receiver's readiness is most important.

7. *Clarify* your feedback. Check to see if the receiver understands your message. Keep discussing the statement until you are satisfied that the message is clear.

8. *Be accurate* in your feedback. As a final check, review your statement for accuracy before you offer it as feedback. Observations and perceptions can be faulty.

Practice giving feedback by following the three purposes of feedback:

1. To help others *identify* behavioral discrepancies.
2. To openly *support* and reinforce desired behaviors.
3. To *modify* incongruent behavior.

Now reinforce the application of the eight criteria for giving feedback by writing two or three feedback statements you would offer to one of your current teachers or current students.

Feedback 1. (Write the exact statement here.)

Feedback 2. (Write the exact statement here.)

Now apply each of the three purposes of feedback and each of the eight criteria to each statement. After you have assessed the statements in this manner, identify the purposes or criteria that you need to improve, and focus on these in the future.

Feedback purposes and criteria make good bulletin board projects for students to develop and present to the class.

Sometimes, teacher committees can profit from reviewing the principles of feedback.

SELECTED REFERENCES

ASPY, DAVID N. *Toward a Technology for Humanizing Education.* Champaign, Ill.: Research Press.

AVILA, DONALD L., ARTHUR W. COMBS, and WILLIAM W. PURKEY. *Helping Relationships: Basic Concepts for the Helping Professions.* Boston: Allyn and Bacon, 1971.

BLOCHER, DONALD H. *Developmental Counseling.* New York: Ronald Press, 1966.

BROWN, GEORGE I. *Human Teaching for Human Learning.* New York: Viking Press, 1971.

BUROW, JOSEPHINE M., and BILL L. KELL. *Developmental Counseling and Therapy.* Boston: Houghton Mifflin, 1970.

CLAUSEN, JOHN A., ed. *Socialization and Society.* Boston: Little, Brown, 1968.

DAHMS, ALAN M. *Emotional Intimacy: Overlooked Requirement for Survival.* Boulder, Colo.: Pruett, 1972.

EGMOND, ELMER V., ROBERT S. FOX, CHARLES JUNG, MIRIAM RITVO, and RICHARD SCHMUCK. *Diagnosing Professional Climate of Schools.* Fairfax, Va.: NTL Learning Resources Corporation, 1973.

FOX, ROBERT S., RONALD LIPPITT, and EVA SCHINDLER-RAINMAN. *Towards a Humane Society.* Fairfax, Va.: NTL Learning Resources Corporation, 1973.

FREIRE, PAULO. *Pedagogy of the Oppressed.* Trans. Myra Bergman Ramos. New York: Herder and Herder, 1972.

GAZDA, GEORGE M. *Human Relations Revelopment: A Manual for Educators.* Boston: Allyn and Bacon, 1973.

GOODLAD, JOHN I., and M. FRANCES KLEIN. *Behind the Classroom Door.* Worthington, Ohio: Charles A. Jones, 1970.

GUSKIN, ALAN E., and SAMUEL L. GUSKIN. *A Social Psychology of Education.* Reading, Mass.: Addison-Wesley, 1970.

HOLT, JOHN. *Freedom and Beyond.* New York: E. P. Dutton, 1972.

HOULE, CYRIL O. *The Design of Education.* London: Jossey-Bass, 1972.

KING, JEAN M., and HERBERT I. VON HADEN. *Innovations in Education: Their Pros and Cons.* Worthington, Ohio: Charles A. Jones, 1971.

KOLESNIK, WALTER B. *Humanism and/or Behaviorism in Education.* Boston: Allyn and Bacon, 1975.

KRATHWHOL, DAVID R., BENJAMIN S. BLOOM, and BERTRAM B. MASIA. *Taxonomy of Educational Objectives: The Classification of Educational Goals, Handbook II: Affective Domain.* New York: David McKay, 1956.

KURPIUS, DEWAYNE, J. "Developing Teacher Competencies in Interpersonal Transactions," in James E. Weigand, ed., *Developing Teacher Competencies.* Englewood Cliffs, N.J.: Prentice-Hall, 1971.

———— J. "The Micro-Lab Class Meeting" in T. F. Froehle and DeWayne J. Kurpius, eds., *Indiana Guidance Journal* (1971), pp. 65-80.

LASSEY, WILLIAM R., ed. *Leadership and Social Change.* Iowa City: University Associates, 1971.

LURIE, ELLEN. *How To Change the Schools.* New York: Random House, 1970.

MILLER, RICHARD I., ed. *Perspectives on Educational Change.* New York: Appleton-Century-Crofts, 1967.

MILLS, THEODORE M. *The Sociology of Small Groups.* Englewood Cliffs, N.J.: Prentice-Hall, 1967.

PROVUS, MALCOLM. *Teaching for Relevance.* Northbrook, Ill.: Whitehall, 1970.

ROSENBLITH, JUDY F., and WESLEY ALLINSMITH. *The Causes of Behavior: Readings in Child Development and Educational Psychology,* 2nd ed. Boston: Allyn and Bacon, 1969.

ROSENTHAL, ROBERT, and LENORE JACOBSON. *Pygmalion in the Classroom: Teacher Expectation and Pupils' Intellectual Development.* New York: Holt, Rinehart, and Winston, 1968.

SARASON, SEYMOUR B. *The Culture of the School and the Problem of Change.* Boston: Allyn and Bacon, 1971.

SCHRANK, JEFFREY. *Teaching Human Beings: 101 Subversive Activities for the Classroom.* Boston: Beacon Press, 1972.

SHEPERD, CLOVIS R. *Small Groups: Some Sociological Perspectives.* San Francisco: Chandler, 1964.

SCHUTZ, WILLIAM C. *Joy: Expanding Human Awareness.* New York: Grove Press, 1967.

WATSON, GOODWIN, ed. *Change in School Systems.* Washington, D.C.: National Training Laboratories, NEA, 1967.